The British Media Industries

The British Media Industries offers an accessible introduction to how the media in Britain operates and the impact that recent political, economic, and technological developments have had on the nature of media industries today.

Split into two parts, this book starts by exploring approaches to understanding contemporary media industries through political, economic, and technological terms. The second part delves further into issues and practices relating to individual media industries including newspapers, magazines, film, television, music, video games, and social media. The book adopts a political economy approach and is designed to engage students in an accessible way with key issues around the ownership and control of different sectors of the British media; UK and EU government regulation of the media, including content regulation and market/economic regulation; and the corporate strategies employed by leading media players, such as the BBC, Netflix, Google, and Apple.

This is an essential textbook for undergraduate students approaching British media industries for the first time and will also be relevant to students undertaking introductory courses in Media Management and Media Economics.

Vincent Campbell is Associate Professor in Media and Communication in the School of Media, Communication and Sociology at the University of Leicester, UK, where he is Deputy Head of School (Operations). His research focuses on aspects of visual communication in relation primarily to documentary and political communication.

Paul Smith is Associate Professor in Media and Communication at the Leicester Media School, De Montfort University, Leicester, UK. His research focuses on contemporary television policy, most notably the buying and selling of sports rights.

The British Media Industries

An Introduction

Vincent Campbell and Paul Smith

Routledge
Taylor & Francis Group

LONDON AND NEW YORK

Designed cover image: Vertigo3d / iStock via Getty Images

First published 2023
by Routledge
4 Park Square, Milton Park, Abingdon, Oxon OX14 4RN

and by Routledge
605 Third Avenue, New York, NY 10158

Routledge is an imprint of the Taylor & Francis Group, an informa business

British Library Cataloguing-in-Publication Data
A catalogue record for this book is available from the British Library

Library of Congress Cataloging-in-Publication Data
Names: Campbell, Vincent, 1971- editor.
Title: The British media industries : an introduction / edited by Vincent Campbell and
Paul Smith.
Description: 1 Edition. | New York : Routledge, 2023. |
Identifiers: LCCN 2022056691 (print) | LCCN 2022056692 (ebook) |
Subjects: LCSH: Internet industry--Great Britain. | Social media--Great Britain. | Mass
media--GreatBritain. | Mass media--Ownership--Great Britain. | Broadcasting--Law
and legislation--Great Britain.
Classification: LCC HD9696.8.G74 B75 2023 (print) | LCC HD9696.8.G74 (ebook) |
DDC 384.302850941--dc23/eng/20230216
LC record available at https://lccn.loc.gov/2022056691
LC ebook record available at https://lccn.loc.gov/2022056692

ISBN: 978-1-138-22691-3 (hbk)
ISBN: 978-1-138-22692-0 (pbk)
ISBN: 978-1-315-39678-1 (ebk)

DOI: 10.4324/9781315396781

Typeset in Times New Roman
by Taylor & Francis Books

MIX
Paper | Supporting
responsible forestry
FSC
www.fsc.org   FSC™ C013985

Printed in the United Kingdom
by Henry Ling Limited

Contents

Illustrations

Figure

Tables

Boxes

Acknowledgements

The authors would like to express their gratitude to everyone at Routledge for their assistance with the preparation of this book.

Vincent would also like to thank colleagues at Leicester University for their support, and friends and family for their patience through the writing of this book. In particular he would like to thank his wife Penelope and daughter Caoimhe for their inspiration and support.

Paul would like to take the opportunity to thank his colleagues (past and present) at De Montfort University, Leicester, for their support during the writing of this book. He would also like to thank his wife, Katie, and sons, Matty and Alex, who, in their different ways, have taught him more than they realise about contemporary British media industries.

Introduction

In the peak of the Covid 19 crisis, when Britain was in the midst of a series of national lockdowns, the pervasive nature of the role of the media in our lives was arguably foregrounded in a way it usually isn't. From daily televised news briefings from the government, to ever more hyperbolic public discussion of the crisis on social media platforms, to a growth in people's consumption of streaming television services and playing of video games, the media's centrality to our lives was as clear as it ever has been. Understanding those media, particularly the political and economic structures that shape how those media are organised, how they run, and how we use them, is perhaps more evidently important in the wake of Covid 19 than it has been previously. This book is a contribution to that understanding, focused on providing a sense of technological, economic, and political frameworks within which the media industries in Britain exist, and discussion of a range of specific media industry sectors to try and provide a thorough and detailed overview of the British media industries today.

What are the Media Industries?

The term industry has come to predominantly refer to a particular area of economic activity, with industries classified by the activities and/or products produced as a result of the work undertaken within that area of activity. They are such a major component of global economic activity that there are official national and international classifications of industries, such as the International Standard Industrial Classification of All Economic Activities (known as ISIC) and the United Kingdom Standard Industrial Classification of Economic Activities (known as USIC). At the broadest level, industries are grouped into primary, secondary, and tertiary sectors. Primary industries are those that directly involve natural resources, such as mining or farming. Secondary industries are those that involve manufacturing, such as making cars. Primary and secondary sectors result in particular products or tangible goods (e.g. oil, fish, cars, toasters, etc.), actual physical things that have some function or functions for which they can be used. Tertiary industries are different in that they either do not offer goods at all, instead offering services, and/or they produce what are known as 'intangible goods', that is goods that do not have a literal physical form (a digital download would be an example of this). In service industries, such as say restaurants, tourism, and education, part of what you are paying for when eating in a restaurant, choosing a university degree to study for, or buying a holiday is a particular experience provided through the services given (such as the quality of help provided by waiters, lecturers, and tour guides, respectively).

DOI: 10.4324/9781315396781-1

Historically the media industries have sat amidst the service industries, at the core of all of them being the provision of information, although in recent years, industries involving the provision of information are increasingly seen as a discrete fourth group (the 'quaternary sector'). Some media industries, of course, still produce tangible goods, such as newspapers, magazines, or DVDs, but even here the principal value of those goods is derived from their intangible contents, essentially the information they contain, rather than the raw materials from which they are made. In turn, this means that quite a lot of sense of the value (economic, cultural, etc.) of media goods rests in intangible characteristics, like notions of quality and taste, which has generated a whole set of subsidiary activities related to attempts to classify and categorise media goods in these terms, some of which have become substantial associated industries in their own rights, and in turn shape the industries they rely on. Some stem from the industries themselves, from sales charts to awards ceremonies like the BAFTAs, Oscars, and BRITs. Others demonstrate the propensity for inter-media scrutiny such as newspaper film critics, music magazines, and video game vlogging, whilst online media have made crowd-based reactions and feedback a key battlefield over value, as in 'review bombing' by disgruntled fans.

In industry classification systems, which break them down into more specific sub-sectors, media industries are collectively labelled as 'information and communication industries', then further divided into a range of smaller sectors, such as publishing (including newspapers, magazines, and various forms of software publishing like video games), broadcasting, telecommunications, and film and music production. Now, one of the interesting things about media and communication studies as an academic discipline is that historically its focus has been rather narrow in terms of the industries it has been concerned with – to the point where some scholars have argued that media studies need to be completely reoriented to account for changes in contemporary media and society, such as William Merrin in his book *Media Studies 2.0* (2014). Merrin's argument has multiple elements worthy of discussion, particularly for those just beginning their study of the media as it invites thinking about exactly what it is that you are studying, but for our purposes here it is his starting point that is of particular interest and relevance. Merrin argues essentially that media and communication studies as a discipline 'emerged in the early-mid-20th century as a response to the growing social power of newspapers, radio and cinema' (2014: p.8), and then developed over the following decades at a time when broadcast media, and most specifically television, were the dominant forms of media. His central argument is that media studies, therefore, has been heavily shaped by the social, political, and economic dominance of the structures and nature of broadcast media through the latter half of the 20th century. What he sees as the revolutionary change brought about by new digital technologies in the last few decades, in his view, need to be reflected in equally revolutionary changes in the focus of media studies.

In some regards, we would agree with Merrin that the field has tended to focus on a few specific media industries over others, and that attention to those more marginalised industries is of interest, value, and importance for understanding media industries more fully and more holistically. But it is worth thinking briefly about how and why certain media industries have come to be the focus of media studies over others, because it tells us something about why the media matter and why particular aspects of media matter as well. Strictly speaking, historically, media studies had two original starting points, emerging from other disciplines. The study of film emerged more from academic traditions of studies of literature, with an emphasis on the study of film texts (treated akin to novels, plays etc.), concerned with narratives, aesthetics, authorship, representation and so on. Studies of the film industry, the economics and politics of film production, for instance, did (and still do) occur, but the predominance of film studies was and still is focused around film texts. The other starting point for media studies came out of wider studies of communication, with links to psychology as well as to emerging communication professions and practices, such as journalism, advertising, and public relations, and the principal media industries of interest here were the press (i.e. newspapers) and broadcasting (initially radio, and then post-WWII, television). The more, what today are called social science, origins of the study of press and broadcasting combined with the more arts and humanities origins of film studies have seen media and communication studies develop into a rich and diverse field of study as the two areas have increasingly coalesced over time.

What has united interests in the press, broadcasting, and film have been notions of them being *mass* media, distinct from other kinds of information and communication industries, such as book publishing and telecommunications (such as the telephone), which historically have rarely been seen as a part of media and communication studies. Although there is more to the notion of mass media, as the discussion across the rest of this book will show, it is a foundational distinction that mass media send messages 'from a single source to many destinations simultaneously or in a similar form to an anonymous mass of people, who constitute the audience, consumer, listenership, readership, community and so on' (Long and Wall, 2009: p.3). Books may sell millions of copies but there is not the sense of such a tight time frame of consumption of a book by a coherent audience when compared to a daily newspaper, for instance. Similarly, whilst there may be many millions of telephone conversations every day, these are predominantly one-to-one conversations between individuals, compared to say a radio programme where a presenter may speak to millions of listeners. Indeed, the perceived inherent significance of the press and broadcasting industries as mass media in particular was internalised within the field to the point where a focus on these industries alone has not been felt to need explanation or justification for the most part. Textbooks about the 'British media' have routinely been focused either exclusively or mainly on the press and broadcasting (e.g. the first five editions of the seminal Curran and Seaton textbook, *Power without Responsibility*, only refer to the press and broadcasting, with the internet/new media featuring only in the most recent editions). As this book will show, this has not just been a purely academic narrowing of focus, as political, economic, and social interest and concern has often been very high with regard to the press and broadcasting particularly, in comparison to other media industries, as evidenced by the 'mainstream media' often being the focus of debates around 'fake news' today for instance. Politicians and the public daily debate and discuss the state and nature of Britain's press and broadcasting, whether it be standards in the tabloid press (see Chapter 4) or the BBC (see Chapters 7 and 8), as even the most cursory glance at social media comments on pretty much any online news story will show.

Public, political, and academic interest in the mass media has often been initially rooted in concerns about influence and impact on audiences, and society more generally. A lot of that work has been, and continues to be, essentially normative in nature – that is, offering critical evaluations of the media's contributions to all kinds of aspects of society compared to varying perceptions of what they *should* be doing. Much of that commentary is inherently pejorative in nature, in a number of different ways, but of particular interest here is how notions of production, and *industrial* production at that, has often been an explicit or implicit component of a lot of these critiques, going back at least to the 1930s and 1940s, and influential pejorative attitudes towards the 'culture industry', and how industrialisation of media production captured media and culture, and the masses who consume their outputs, in the clutches of capitalist ideology (e.g. Adorno and Horkheimer, 1947). Critiques of the value and quality of the outputs of mass popular culture have cropped up in academic and public discourses on a regular basis over the years, in influential works like Richard Hoggart's *The Uses of Literacy* (1957). To a large degree, discussion of the media industries has been framed within these kinds of normative approaches, with those in the Marxist critical political economy tradition particularly prominent (see Chapters 2 and 3). In the same theoretical tradition, normative debates in more recent decades have centred on how industrial structures compromise the capacity of media systems to serve the public interest in democratic societies (e.g. Habermas, 1992). The persistence of pejorative connotations of the notion of industry as it relates to the media – linking the perceived deficiencies and negative consequences of mass media often directly to industrial structures, processes, and principles – is at least a partial reason for the study of media industries in their own right, as a particular category within media and communication studies. This is, however, a relatively recent phenomenon within the field, and a focus of relatively few books to date (e.g. Herbert, Lotz, and Punathambekar, 2020; McDonald, 2021), especially with regard to the *British* media industries.

Structure of the Book and Some Key Trends

One of the distinctive features of the modern media landscape is that it would seem to be increasingly difficult to talk of media in purely national terms. Internet companies have global operations and global reach, film and television studios increasingly produce content via international co-productions, and even things like local newspapers are often ultimately part of multi-national conglomerates these days. To talk of specifically British media, then, might seem problematic, but there are significant ways in which national boundaries still matter, particularly in terms of how different media are perceived within particular nations, which stems from how they have developed historically, and in turn contributes to the specific economic, political, and cultural context in which the media operate in any one country. In this context, it is perhaps worth underlining the fact that our focus here is the media industries in Britain (i.e. the media accessed by audiences in Britain), and how they have developed into their current structures, which means considering not just British-based companies and organisations but the often complex and multi-faceted interactions between domestic and international organisations across media industries that operate in Britain. In this way, the book is as much about, say, Spotify and Netflix as it is about *The Times* or the BBC.

This book has two key objectives. First, it aims to consider a range of British media industries, extending our scope beyond the typical dominance of the national press and broadcasting, and incorporating a wider range of industries than has been typical to date in works of this type. Second, we intend to look at media industries as industries, and whilst we will engage with the ideological debates around developments in industry, our perspective is not the dominant critical political economy perspective, but rather one that outlines the core structures – technological, economic, political – that underpin industry developments, and how these intersect in different ways at different times with the social and cultural roles of media industries, the aspects of media that make them distinct from other kinds of industrial activity.

The book is divided into two main parts. Part I consists of three chapters, which when taken together provide a broad analytical framework for understanding the media industries. Chapter 1 focuses on the relationship between the media and technology. Chapter 2 examines the economics of the media. Chapter 3 focuses on the politics of the media industries and in particular key debates related to policy and regulation. Part II of the book then moves on to examine, in turn, a host of different sectors within the British media industries: namely, the national press, magazines, film, radio, television, music, video games, and, finally, social media. In each of these chapters we combine an historical overview of the sector with an analysis of key developments during the 21st century. These chapters demonstrate that, while the growth of online media has blurred the edges between certain sectors (e.g. traditional national newspapers offering audio-visual content via an online news web site and/or app), the British media industries are still best understood as a number of clearly discernible distinct sectors, each attempting to respond to particular challenges brought about by technological (and/or other) change/s, rather than as a single unified media industry heralded by convergence (see Chapter 1).

Each sector of the British media industries has a unique 'story to tell', but a number of general themes, or trends, are highlighted throughout the book. First, albeit in different ways, the growth of the internet, and in particular high speed (fixed line and mobile) internet access over the last decade, has had a significant impact across the British media industries. For some sectors, technological changes have undermined traditional business models (e.g. newspapers and music). For others, technological changes have facilitated major growth (e.g. videogames), or even, in one case, has enabled a whole new sector to emerge (i.e. social media). Second, largely explained by the underlying economic and political factors examined in the first part of the book, concentration of ownership is a reoccurring theme across the different sectors of the British media industries. The media industries in Britain are owned and controlled by a relatively small number of media organisations and most of these (e.g. Meta, Sky, News Corp) are not British owned. Much of Part II of this book details how British media organisations have either been acquired, or usurped, by US-based rivals (e.g. EMI in music) or, in the case of social media, have never had a significant presence. The BBC is arguably Britain's last remaining major media organisation, but even the BBC is increasingly challenged by competition from US rivals (e.g. Netflix and Sky) and a lack of political support (see Chapter 8). A third clear trend discernible across many of the different sectors examined in Part II relates to a notable shift in the type of business model commonly adopted within the British media industries. To a large degree in response to technological developments (see Chapter 1), across various sectors (e.g. music, video games, newspapers, magazines), media organisations have moved from focusing on the sale of their products to audiences (for audiences to own) to charging regular subscription fees for access to a service. Largely as a result, while it is certainly the case that there is more media content available than ever before for British audiences to enjoy, access to an increasing proportion of this content is dependent on the continued ability and/or willingness to pay. Whilst many of these trends impact on other industries, there remains something distinctive about the media industries in terms of their cultural as well as political and economic significance that will also be apparent across the book as a whole.

Part I
Understanding the Media Industries

1 Technology

Media studies is often perceived by those studying it as a very current, cutting-edge subject, addressing the latest in communication technologies and providing its students with knowledge and skills aligned with the up-to-the-minute developments in the workplace. The mass media too, in their origins at least, were received as dynamic, new innovations, often greeted with a genuine sense of awe. Comical videos of people reacting to Virtual Reality videogames (screaming, jumping, falling over, etc.) echo what are widespread but almost certainly apocryphal stories of the first film audiences in the 1890s running away from the Lumière brothers' footage of a train coming into a station, thinking they were going to get knocked down (Loiperdinger, 2004). Newness and novelty are arguably ingrained into cultural perceptions of media and communication technologies, and in recent years this has created something of a schism – both popularly but also scholarly – between the so-called 'old' and 'new' media. The relationships between 'old' and 'new' media technologies are all around us every day, and sometimes these are overtly parts of modern life generating lots of public discussion and debate, both apparently superficial, such as the loss of the headphone jack on Apple iPhones, and much more serious such as the impact of possible social media manipulation of elections by foreign powers.

Sometimes explicitly, sometimes implicitly, but always to some extent, new media technologies build on prior technologies in significant ways. You can see an example of this on many computer displays. The save icon on some pieces of software is an image of a floppy disc, a storage format of the near past, leading to a meme around this of people allegedly seeing physical floppy discs and asking why someone 3-D printed the save icon. The icon for e-mail is often an image of an envelope and so on. The technical name for these things is skeuomorphs, and they don't just occur in screen technologies – restaurants with electric table lights shaped like candles are another example (Self, 2013: p.54). In screen technologies they arguably help users, or at least certain age groups of users who recognise the earlier technologies, to navigate the various functions of the device but beyond that, like the candle-shaped electric lights, they are little more than decorative features. They are arguably symbolic of a deeper and more complicated relationship that exists between what are often seen as 'old' and 'new' media, and how 'new' media technologies habitually, at least in their early incarnations, borrow heavily from prior media technologies in terms of their form, content, and structure. Harking back to earlier forms can help a medium establish a sense of credibility and cultural value needed for the technology to catch on and become successful. This is one reason there are so many film and television adaptations of literary classics, and have been since the early days of both of those

DOI: 10.4324/9781315396781-3

media, for instance, and in turn, why so many videogames have tried to generate sales from film and TV tie-ins.

More fundamentally, some have argued that the structures created and maintained by prior technologies, and the social practices associated with them, contribute to a process called *remediation* (Bolter and Grusin, 2000). This theory argues that new technologies are heavily influenced by the structures of prior technologies, not just in terms of content, but also in terms of production, formats, and reception, to the extent that 'new' media are never entirely new. The notions of the single and album in recorded music, for instance, remain organising features of music production and consumption in the era of streaming services, even whilst the logic of that structure – stemming from the capacities of the two sizes of vinyl records (7" and 12") – has long since been technologically redundant, and has led to lots of feature articles on the 'death of the album' (e.g. Walker, 2014). So, understanding the media today, particularly the media industries today, requires thinking carefully about the complex relationships between technology and the media. It may seem, for instance, odd to spend time discussing newspapers as a prominent industry, not least because of the ever-declining audience actually reading physical newspapers (see Chapter 4), but aspects of the newspaper industry continue to structurally contribute to the media and communication industries of today in significant ways, and there are structures and processes deeper still that underpin media and communication industries that are significant for really understanding them. Nonetheless, the overt distinction between 'old' and 'new' media and their relationship to technology, and in turn to society, requires some consideration before getting to those deeper issues in later chapters.

Old and New Media

The mass media, like newspapers and linear broadcast television, the traditional objects of study for media studies, have in the last couple of decades come to be increasingly regarded as 'old' media in the wake of technologies collectively dubbed 'new' media, and the rise of new media has come to dominate much media studies scholarship of recent years (e.g. Lister et al. 2009; Flew 2014; Merrin 2014). The terms old and new are inherently problematic though as means by which to identify and classify media technologies. Chronological measures alone aren't sufficient. At the time of much early writing about 'new media' in the 1990s, for instance, things like the internet and World Wide Web were very new inventions but the World Wide Web has now been around for a generation already, so whether it is still 'new' or not is debatable. On longer historical time frames, most forms of mass media are not particularly 'old' when compared to many other technologies. Personal computers and videogame consoles are less than 50 years old, television less than a hundred years old, and cinema just over 120 years old. Newspapers are the oldest recognised mass medium, the first newspaper in Britain appearing in 1621, though they didn't start to reach mass audiences in the millions until the middle of the 19th century collectively, with individual titles only reaching the millions in the early years of the 20th century. Speaking purely chronologically, then, what is meant by 'new' media is a constantly shifting phenomenon and a common problem for media studies, particularly amongst students who often expect to be studying the very latest social media platform or app only to find academic writing behind the curve of technological development. There are two main reasons for this academic lag, one practical, one more conceptual. On a practical level, academic study of anything takes time to look at something in depth and detail, thinking about form, function, consequence, and so on. Social media comments can be written as events are happening, traditional news media journalistic accounts within hours but real insight and understanding takes longer to develop. On the conceptual level, it is often the case that it isn't actually possible to make best sense of something as it is happening, and over time what can sometimes appear to be radically new and different phenomena end up displaying characteristics and outcomes reflective of longer term, more established, and more understood structures and processes. When talking about 'new' media industries therefore, as Havens and Lotz point out:

> Although these industries are clearly growing in importance, their short histories and fluid practices tend to frustrate efforts to write about them in current and insightful ways. Newspaper and radio may seem like old, and perhaps fading media industries from the vantage point of today's media environment, but their long histories of adapting to various changes in industrial conditions are precisely what make them so useful for illustrating *concepts* of media industry operations.
>
> (2012: p.304, emphasis added)

This is not just an academic issue as media matter to societies, and even classifying a particular organisation as a media organisation is not just about semantic labels. For example, in 2016 a debate arose over whether or not Facebook is a media company or not, something its founder, Mark Zuckerberg, initially refused to acknowledge, and then only in a qualified manner as 'not a traditional media company' (in Warner, 2016). The issue emerged out of the fall-out from the 2016 US Presidential contest and the perceived role that 'fake news' distributed via social media platforms may have played in its outcome. For 'traditional' media companies, like newspapers or news broadcasters, accountability for inaccurate, spurious, and outright false claims presented as news is well established as resting with those organisations. For social media companies like Facebook and Twitter, they have emerged offering something more like the notion of telecommunications' approach to content – 'platforms' for others to send messages across, and as platforms they're not directly responsible for the messages distributed across them, in the same way that a telephone company isn't directly responsible for an abusive phone call, say. Even the very term, 'platform', to use as a label for digital media companies, is a rhetorical device that suggests a kind of passive, neutral space, like a train platform, which can be critiqued (Gillespie, 2017), but we will come back to these issues in later chapters. The key point for this chapter is that practically speaking, even amongst the creators and users of the technology themselves, there may be disagreement or incomplete understanding of what is actually going on, and conceptually, it is often the pre-existing frameworks of traditional media that, at least initially, shape expectations, judgements, usage, and reception of new media.

How new media differ, beyond how close their origins are to today, is the subject of much literature, and is both multi-faceted and contentious, but it is not a primary focus of this book (for detailed discussions see, for instance, Flew 2014; Lister et al. 2009). Three particular characteristics are worth highlighting here as they are significant for developing an understanding of contemporary media industries and the political and economic forces that shape them. These are the shift from *analogue to digital* technologies, the processes known collectively as *convergence*, and the importance of *networks* in media industries.

From Analogue to Digital

Traditional media were all in their origins, analogue in form. What that essentially means is that the information encoded in any particular medium was formed by a single, specific physical quantity of something. An analogue photograph, for instance, produces images through a complex set of chemical processes, whereby special, chemically treated photographic film is exposed to light, then given several chemical treatments before you end up with a photographic print from the original film. Music connoisseurs' preferred medium of vinyl records are created through the conversion of sound waves into vibrations of a needle carving a groove into a lacquer disk, and vinyl copies of this disk can be played back by running another needle over the groove, and the vibrations in the needle arm being converted back into sound. Now, the important point here is not the details of any specific technical process inherent to any one media technology, but rather that they were all fundamentally distinct from each other in their initial production processes – you can't take a photograph with a record player or play music with an analogue camera. Although by no means the only reason, the distinctiveness of these analogue technologies in part led to the discrete establishment of individual media production processes, formats, contents, distribution, and consumption, as well as associated skills, jobs, and professions, and to the separate industries and economic and political frameworks that continue to shape the media landscape to this day. Whilst these industries didn't develop in entire isolation from each other in all sorts of ways, the distinctive underlying technologies placed fundamental barriers on the degree and nature of relationships possible between them. When techniques emerged to enable some of these discrete technologies to be combined, often this caused significant changes to the respective, and formerly discrete, areas of activity (e.g. the transformation of film in the shift from silent to talking pictures). Otherwise, new media technologies have tended to be perceived as threats to established 'old' media industries, such as concerns over the impact of radio on newspapers in the 1920s–30s or amongst British film companies about the rise of television in the 1950s (see Chapters 4 and 6, respectively). This was partly because of the *fixity* of their analogue products – a record, a photograph, a videotape, etc. – and how these can't easily be (or sometimes at all) converted from one medium to another or compete with the capabilities of rival technologies (e.g. printed news compared to live broadcast news).

The arrival of digital technology has gradually removed some of the boundaries between media sectors by increasingly enabling any and all of the previously distinct media forms to be produced using the same fundamental technology, seeing a shift from fixity to *flux* (Lister et al. 2009: p.19). Digital technologies reduce whatever kind of signal they are recording – light, sound, text, data, etc. – into a series of numerical values expressed in binary digits. Doing this allows a signal to be converted into a series of electrical pulses of zeros and ones and reconstituted wherever (and however) you send that electrical signal. Now, that shift to digital has not necessarily been particularly noticeable to media audiences/consumers with regard to some fundamental changes in industry practices. Whether a photograph, say, is recorded on analogue or digital cameras is not something particularly discernible by the viewer, and whether or not the daily newspaper someone reads has been produced and printed using digital tools or not is also unlikely to be at the forefront of a reader's mind, even whilst such changes have had profound impacts on media production structures and professions. In other areas, such as the rise of music, game, and television streaming services, the shift to digital forms of consumption have been far more overt and subject to public debate and discussion. Regardless, it is possible to argue that:

> The passage from analogue to digital technologies is a fundamental transformation in their material basis and functioning. What appears to be an identical object is actually different, with a different material form, and different material capacities. No matter how much it looks like what we know, it *isn't* it and doesn't *act* like it.
>
> (Merrin, 2014: p.32, original emphasis)

Whilst this arguably varies significantly depending upon which media industries you're looking at, the shift to digital media as part of challenges and opportunities in contemporary media industries will be a persistent theme across this book. Just to pick one illustrative example here, digital has meant an increasing shift from what are known as *tangible* goods to *intangible* goods. A tangible good is a physical thing like a vinyl LP, for instance, whereas an intangible good is one that doesn't exist as a physical object, like a digital download of an album. Several media industries – the music industry, in particular – have been substantially challenged in the digital transition, as people moved from consuming media like music through tangible goods like records and CDs, around which the traditional music industry built its financial basis, to intangible goods like downloads and streaming. At times in the last 20 years, the death knell has been sounded more than once for the traditional music industry, rooted in the shift from analogue to digital but, interestingly, the lure of the tangible nature of the vinyl LP has seen the format somewhat resurgent in the download/streaming era (Butterfield, 2017).

Convergence

Digital technology increasingly underpinning production, distribution, and consumption practices in media industries has been one of the more overt components of the multi-faceted process known as *convergence* (Dwyer, 2010). Technological convergence is arguably embodied in the rise of the smart phone, used by almost nine in ten people in Britain by 2020 (Ofcom, 2021a); a device that enables people to look at newspaper articles, listen to radio broadcasts, watch movies, listen to music albums, play videogames, and so on. Because the development of digital media technologies appears to remove the barriers between once discrete analogue technologies, then there is often a sense of *inevitability* of those once separate sectors becoming ever closer together and intertwined. Indeed, convergence is often discussed as an inherently technological imperative – especially by policy-makers and industry leaders. But to see convergence as being driven by technology alone, or indeed at all, ignores other aspects of media industries experiencing forms of convergence that arguably reveal technological convergence as a consequence, not a cause, of these other processes.

One common response to threats of new media has been for traditional industry players to use their economic power to get involved in, or even take over, potential rival industries. Industry perspectives label this as creating *synergy* (Hardy, 2014a: p.90), that is lining up the interests of previously competing media forms to enhance production efficiencies. Companies that own film studios, television networks, publishing companies, and so on can make money from spreading content across multiple formats, though interestingly this has not always resulted in the kinds of efficiencies and enhanced profits media corporations have expected (ibid.: pp.92–3). This *industrial convergence* (Dwyer, 2010: p.9) pre-dates the rise of digital media but has continued into the digital media era. It is also referred to more critically as a process of *co-optation* (Deuze, 2009a), whereby the threats of new rivals are removed/diminished by taking those new outlets within the systems of organisation, production, and control and, crucially, within the ideological approaches of dominant media and communication industries. Indeed, some organisational pressures to digitise production thus came from the industrial convergence of cross-media ownership structures. New forms of media production and consumption emerging through new media, like citizen journalism, vlogging, podcasting, and audio/video streaming services, in turn often end up converging on operational practices used within the established major media industries, such as a reliance on revenue from advertising and promotional activities to fund their production. At the level of the major platforms, over time, differences in how new media companies (Google, Facebook, Spotify, Netflix, etc.) operate compared to traditional media companies narrow, as they become increasingly aligned with corporate, market-driven media industry principles and practices – a trend referred to as 'marketisation' (Hardy, 2014a: p.58).

An illustration of this is that, despite the language of technological convergence, and the capabilities of modern smart devices, consumers remain confronted by an array of competing devices: phones, tablets, laptops, desktops, entertainment consoles, smart TVs, and then choices within these (Xbox, PlayStation, or Nintendo; Apple or Android). Instead of a reduction of devices as a consequence of technological convergence, we have a proliferation of devices. The next likely phase of this has been dubbed the 'internet of things' where cars, fridges, toasters, etc. are all connected to the internet and digitally managed and controlled. From a technological perspective this doesn't make immediate sense. Why have all these different devices doing the same things? From the economic perspective of media industries, at least, it makes sense as it maintains consumer activity, regularly buying multiple, often only cosmetically different, devices linked to specific capabilities and exclusive content. It also enables the monetisation of user data that is generated by smart devices of lots of different kinds, in ways highly profitable to producers but also highly controversial in terms of how data might be used and by whom, such as wearable fitness devices that gather data that health insurance providers could use to alter individuals' insurance policies (Chang, 2016).

It's also a reflection of how technological convergence has brought new players into established markets as well, such as telecoms providers moving into areas of broadcast and online content provision, such that in 'the process cell phones became a serious part of mainstream media business policy, social life and public debate' (Goggin, 2011: p.2). Telecoms industries' increasing technological convergence with media industries highlights a third aspect of convergence, of particular significance in Britain, which can essentially be described as political or *regulatory convergence* (Dwyer, 2010: p.14), whereby both political attitudes and instrumental public policy relating to media and communication industries are converging amidst controversial and contested debates around questions of public accountability. In Britain, the establishment of Ofcom in the early 2000s, for instance, was an explicit consequence of regulatory convergence as the different regulatory frameworks for television, radio, telecommunications, and the internet were rolled into a single regulatory body with a single conceptual framework regarding media regulation. Whilst promoted and justified by the government of the day as a necessary and logical consequence of technological convergence, the influence of the ideology of marketisation was very prominent (as discussions in later chapters will show) with regard to how Ofcom functions as a regulator.

Networks

The third major aspect of the new media 'revolution' has been the increasing importance of networks. Networks are an intrinsic feature of pretty much everything, from the solar system to ecological food webs, from transportation networks (roads, railways) to interpersonal social networks, and, of course, communication networks from cave paintings through to the internet. For some, fundamental changes to communication networks in the last few decades, particularly but not exclusively associated with the rise of the internet, have meant that we have transitioned into a 'network society' (Castells, 2009), an indication of how some aspects of media technologies are sometimes seen as profoundly significant for society – debates around which we'll come back to later in the chapter.

Networks, in terms of their basic elements, consist of two things: nodes and links. Nodes can be anything – people, animals, computers – and the links between them can be pretty much anything too. A family tree, for instance, is a network in which the nodes are members of the family, and the links are the ways in which they are related. A railway network, alternatively, will have stations as nodes and tracks as the links. When you abstract any kind of network out into its nodes and links, you can start to see overall characteristics of that network, and different types of network display different attributes in relation to certain characteristics, crucial for thinking about the politics and economics of those networks. Two characteristics are particularly important. First, networks have varying degrees of *hierarchy*, that is the extent to which nodes are important relative to each other within the network as a whole. In a social network of a group of friends, for instance, this would likely be quite non-hierarchical, without any one person being more important than the rest. The network of the Catholic Church, on the other hand, is much more hierarchical, with the Pope the most important person in that network, with various levels of clerical ranks down to the local parish priests. Second, the degree to which the network is *centralised* or *decentralised* relates to the nature of the links between the nodes and how easy it is to move across the network. Centralised networks are ones where whatever is going across the network has to go through a particular link or set of links to get where it's going. Think of travelling somewhere by train, for instance, and to get to some destinations you might have to change trains and stations several times. The more decentralised a network, the more alternative routes across more links there are to get information from one point to another, e.g. road networks tend to be more decentralised than railways by comparison.

If we bring this back into the context of media networks, we can start to think about the nature of old media industries. Across the book, it will become clear that these tend to be both centralised and hierarchical in many media industry sectors. As indicated later, long term economic convergence has meant that even in sectors where some decentralisation might be expected, local newspapers or local radio, for instance, in terms of ownership and management at least, here too the sectors are dominated by nationwide, often global parent companies. Some of the centralisation of media industries is a consequence of deliberate policy-making, such as the initial creation of the BBC, and some of it is a consequence of aspects of media economics, like concentration of ownership, that are arguable as to whether they are emergent consequences or intended outcomes of particular structural arrangements. The underlying nature of 'old' media industries, in particular, as centralised and hierarchical networks is what is important here, as these aspects have both shaped, and been shaped by, the political and economic structures in which they have operated.

Networks have become so prominent in discussions about new media primarily because of the internet which has a different structure to traditional media and communication technologies, a consequence of a very deliberate set of choices, in a very particular context. Specifically, the objective of military researchers in the post-WWII United States was to try to find ways to ensure that US government and military command and control structures could be maintained in the event of a nuclear war. Researchers worked out that the conventional communication channels used were too highly centralised and hierarchical and would be wiped out with even a limited exchange of nuclear weapons. One observed that whilst the command-and-control communication network would be wiped out, theoretically speaking at least, small-scale, local country and western radio stations would not. There was such an abundance of these radio stations across the United States, with overlapping broadcast areas, that enough of them would theoretically survive to be able to maintain broadcasting such that a message could be communicated across the United States via surviving stations. So, the idea emerged that a command-and-control communication network needed to have a structure similar to this to survive – a structure that was intrinsically decentralised and non-hierarchical, as this would provide a highly attack resistance communication network. That principle underpinned the military and research-oriented precursors to the internet, and that intrinsic feature of its fundamental design – as a non-hierarchical, decentralised network – provides the basis, not only for the many things the internet has brought into global society, but many of the fundamental challenges to media industries as well. Traditional models of the political and economic organisation of media industries have also been highly centralised and hierarchical (whether predominantly state-based through ownership, subsidy, and regulation, or through the tendencies of the free market towards concentration of ownership, etc.) whilst the internet has introduced, or at least has appeared to introduce, forms of decentralised and non-hierarchical organisation and control sometimes labelled *network governance* (Collins, 2009). Many of the problems for the governance and management of activity online are arguably rooted in the underlying network structure of the internet that challenges conventional approaches to media and communication governance, even though it is a structure born of governmental, military, and corporate communication objectives.

Theories of Media, Technology, and Society

Much literature, and wider political and public debate, then, is concerned with the specifics of media and communication technologies – what they do, how they work, and how they change the way things are done. It's not initially controversial to state, for instance, that: 'Technology matters. It matters not just to the material condition of our lives and to our biological and physical environment – that much is obvious – but to the way we live together socially' (Mackenzie and Wajcman, 1999: pp.3–4).

Focusing on the 'the way we live together socially', though, opens up a new set of debates about the relationship between technology and society: Just how much is the way we live socially influenced, shaped, or even caused by technological change? Claims about dramatic societal impacts of particular media technologies go back at least as far as the electric telegraph for instance (Standage, 1998) and crop up with each new medium either promoted as the saviour of humanity or decried as the ruin of us all. Interestingly, a lot of the discussion around technology and society hasn't been particularly focused on media and communication technologies per se, and arguably much media and communication studies research has tended not to be particularly concerned with the technological dimension of media either. For instance:

> News, in the study of media, has been typically construed as paragraphs on a page, rather than the page itself; the headlines are examined but not the newsboys who shout them, the teletypes that clatter them out, or the code that now renders them into clickable hyperlinks.
>
> (Gillespie, Boczkowski, and Foot, 2014: p.1)

One reason for this is how, relatively early in the history of media and communication studies as a field of academic study, debates about media technology and society centred on two key figures, offering ultimately oppositional positions: the technological determinism of Marshall McLuhan versus the cultural materialism of Raymond Williams. Their positions, particularly Williams', have dominated approaches to these issues within the field, but in fact their respective positions really represent either end of a continuum of theoretical positions on the role relationships between technology and society, and awareness of that continuum is important contextual information for making sense of media industries.

Technological Determinism

The central tenet of technological determinism as an approach to understanding the relationship between technology and society is that technologies emerge and 'change, either because of scientific advance or following a logic of their own; and then they have effects on society' (Mackenzie and Wajcman, 1999: p.3). For a technological determinist, even the very notion of society itself is a consequence of the development of technology-based practices, and whilst different technologies might have greater or lesser degrees of social impact, in this perspective social change is largely driven by, and *determined* by, technological change. The emergence of cities and larger scale societies, for instance, is arguably a consequence of the development of tools for large scale farming (e.g. the plough) and the management of large groups of people living together (e.g. writing). The best-known author associated with technological determinism in relation to the media is Marshall McLuhan who is famous for the claim in his book *Understanding Media* that 'the medium is the message':

> This is merely to say that the personal and social consequences of any medium – that is, of any extension of ourselves – result from the new scale that is introduced into our affairs by each extension of ourselves, or by any new technology.
>
> (1964/2001: p.7)

In McLuhan's view, what matters about a media technology is the way it 'shapes and controls the scale and form of human association and action' (ibid.: p.9). The medium itself is the message, rather than any specific content it might contain, because it is the medium itself which transforms social interaction and behaviour. Think, for instance, of the telephone. As indicated earlier, the telephone has not been included in traditional media studies because of it not being seen as a mass medium (primarily, if not solely, for that reason), but in McLuhan's conceptualisation the telephone is an 'extension of man' through its elimination of time and space, allowing two people to talk to each other instantaneously regardless of their relative locations on Earth. He goes on to distinguish between what he calls 'hot' and 'cool' media; a hot medium being one that 'extends one single sense in "high definition"' (ibid.: p.24), and a 'cool' medium one that offers a comparatively 'low definition' level of information and requires more input from the receiver in terms of making meaning and thus being impacted by it. A photograph, for instance, contains high-definition visual information and is a 'hot' medium, whereas a cartoon contains comparatively low-definition visual information and is thus a 'cool' medium (ibid.). In a similar sense, but in terms of audio, he argues that radio is a 'hot' medium, and the telephone a 'cool' medium (ibid.: p.25). For McLuhan, media had, and continues to have, profound social consequences, and the hyperbolic style of *Understanding the Media* contains lots of statements that reflect this position, such as claiming that 'the hotting-up of the medium of writing to repeatable print intensity led to nationalism and the religious wars of the sixteenth century' (ibid.). According to this line of argument, events like the Protestant revolutions of Martin Luther and others at this time were only possible because printing allowed such critiques to be quickly and widely disseminated. Going through a whole range of technologies (both conventionally thought of as 'media' and not) in a similar vein, in a discussion of radio compared to what he regarded as the cool medium of television, McLuhan states:

> Had TV occurred on a large scale during Hitler's reign he would have vanished quickly. Had TV come first there would have been no Hitler at all... That Hitler came into political existence at all is directly owing to radio and public-address systems.
>
> (ibid.: pp.326–7)

McLuhan's logic here is that the extent to which radio extended the capacity of speech, and speech alone, to be able to reach out to millions of people over the airwaves gave figures like Hitler potential reach and influence that, in his view, was a determining feature in the rise of Hitler. Rhetorical skills of the likes of Hitler, and also of figures like wartime US President Franklin Roosevelt, known for his radio 'fireside chats', and wartime British Prime Minister Winston 'we'll fight them on the beaches' Churchill, were foregrounded via radio in a way that gave their rhetoric additional weight and influence through the concentration of audiences' focus on speech alone, compared to the 'all-involving sensory mandate of the TV image' (ibid.: p.336). Television, by contrast, focuses viewers on the image to the point of undermining the capacity of the medium for sustained, in-depth political communication, with politicians turned into 'cartoons' – a critique echoed by many commentaries on television, both political and scholarly, in the decades since McLuhan was writing.

Other considerations of technological determinism make a distinction between degrees of 'hard' and 'soft' determinism (Levinson, 1997). Hard determinism is where some form of technology has 'an inevitable, irresistible social (or other) effect'

(Levinson, 1997: p.3). Soft determinism, on the other hand, reflects the view 'that media rarely, if ever, have absolute, unavoidable social consequences' (ibid.). Levinson goes on: 'It is a system of making things possible – of the results not being able to occur without the technology – rather than the technology inevitably and unalterably creating that result' (ibid.: p.4).

Hard technological determinism is based on arguing, always retrospectively, how particular technologies inevitably determined particular outcomes, thus making the development of technologies appear teleological – that is, to claim or imply that the very reason for a technology's development was the end use to which it is put. Soft determinism, on the other hand, argues that 'the most long-lasting and significant impacts of information technology throughout history were unintended consequences of their invention' (ibid.: p.9). For example, the first text message was sent in Britain in 1992, from a computer to a mobile phone – the latter still a rather elite and uncommon object at the time. Phones capable of sending as well as receiving texts didn't appear until the following year (Arthur, 2012). Texts were initially regarded as a tool for mobile phone companies to alert customers to things like them having a voicemail or missed call information – one of the reasons for restricting the message length at only a small number of characters. At first texting was entirely free to users as phone companies hadn't thought about how they might charge for what might seem to be something very much subordinate to the primary function of a mobile phone – making phone calls. Even when charges did appear they were much cheaper than making actual calls and, crucially, functionally easier for people to use surreptitiously (in the office or classroom for instance) as well. Within a decade, 'text speak' had become firmly established as a whole new series of contractions ('l8r') and acronyms ('lol') appeared to allow complex messages to fit within the 160-character limit. The principles of texting underpinned the creation of Twitter in 2006, now one of the world's largest social media platforms. As an aside, it's worth noting how another unintended consequence of the emergence of the multi-function mobile phone, even before today's smart phones emerged, was that whereas previously telecommunications had been largely ignored by scholars of media and communication technologies 'from at least 2001 onwards, the mobile has been imagined, discussed and shaped as a form of media' (Goggin, 2011: p.2). Examples like this support the position that 'changes and developments in society interact with, and are "softly" determined by, trends in media (production, use and content)' (Deuze, 2009b: p.468).

Social Construction of Technology (SCOT)

A natural question follows from the texting example, which is to ask if it's not the specific technology alone, nor its creators, that shape how a technology impacts on society, what is it that shapes this process? The evolution of text-messaging is illustrative of one theoretical answer to this question, which is to focus on the people who come to dominate the use of any particular technology and is known as the social construction of technology. At its simplest, the theory asserts that the development, use, and impact of a technology is dependent upon the particular social groups who use the technology. If a technology ends up being taken up by very specific groups of people, for particular uses of importance to them, then a technology's subsequent development may be very heavily and noticeably shaped by those people. The example used by the originators of this theory (Bijker, Hughes, and Pinch, 1987) is the development of the bicycle in the 1880s known as the penny farthing. Early bicycles had appeared in the 18th century, amongst European aristocracy, and by the 1880s in the height of the Victorian era in Britain, objects like bicycles were still the preserve of the wealthy. At this time bicycles were direct drive, which meant there were no chains and gears, and the pedals connected directly to the front wheel, so for a bike to go faster you needed a bigger front wheel. The rider sat directly over the front wheel as well, so as designs involved ever larger front wheels to go faster, the riding position was ever more dangerous – not an issue for the wealthy young men who rode them, for whom they were status symbols. The bikes thus developed according to the desires of its primary users, who were interested in speed and danger, not practical utility. Within a few years the penny farthing's status diminished, partly due to new bicycle designs that made them safer, easier to control, and potentially faster as well, but also as social mores changed about who could and should use bikes.

The SCOT model, then, highlights how technologies are inherently embedded in social practices. Developed by one particular group for a specific set of purposes only then to be taken over, or co-opted, by particular groups of users who take the technology into unintended and unexpected directions, that aren't determined by characteristics of the technology alone but reflect how that technology serves the needs and interests of users. Examples of this abound in terms of media technologies. The mobile phone again serves as a great example. Like the penny farthing, in their early days in the 1980s phones' initial extravagant cost meant they were a luxury item, and in Britain quickly became associated with a society changing dramatically under liberal capitalist reforms under the Thatcher government. The rise of a new generation of entrepreneurs and capitalist fortune-seekers, mostly young urban professionals nicknamed Yuppies, embraced the mobile phone as both a useful tool, being always able to do business on the move, and as a status symbol of their modern, dynamic approach to work and life. They rapidly became a symbol of the era in popular culture, associated with perceived superficiality, corruption, and avaricious values of the time (as seen, for instance, in the film *The Wolf of Wall Street* (2013)).

The rise of personal computing and the internet is also often characterised in terms of particular social groups, despite the involvement of big corporations, governments, military organisations, and academics institutions. A popular history has emerged around these technologies having been largely created by communities outside of institutional structures, created by hobbyists and college drop-outs in their garages and bedrooms. Books about the rise of companies like Microsoft and Facebook have titles like *Accidental Empires* (Cringley, 1996) and *Where Wizards Stay Up Late* (Hafner and Lyon, 2003). A claimed legacy of these origins are attitudes towards notions of things like ownership, control, access, and usage of computer technologies that persist today in theories of network governance, mentioned earlier, not as a consequence of technological network structures, but reflecting the hobbyist community's culture of sharing interests, ideas, code, and so on. Devices like Kodi boxes reflect a continuation of this attitude of opposition to concepts of ownership and copyright, though the rise of NFTs (Non-Fungible Tokens) shows that such attitudes are far from universal in online spaces.

Two linked criticisms of this approach are worth mentioning here. First, there's the risk of losing the particular characteristics of technologies by focusing too heavily on the people who subsequently shape their development, arguably implying that in some senses technologies are 'neutral', and it's just how social groups come to use and shape them that matters. The infamous slogan of the National Rifle Association in the United States, 'guns don't kill people, people kill people', would be a glaring instance of this problem, patently ignoring one of the few fundamental purposes and uses of guns, and how the presence of a gun in an interpersonal conflict dramatically changes the power dynamic (Murphie and Potts, 2003: p.27). In this sense, some argue that technologies are not neutral, to be used in whatever ways people choose, but in fact are inherently *political* – that is to say that technologies either relate to (or, even arguably, generate) particular social relations of power and control – and different technologies are political in different ways (Winner, 1980). As much of this book will illustrate, a key perspective regarding the political nature of media technologies focuses on their relationship to democracy. Amongst many reasons for this perceived relationship, one is that media technologies *democratise* information – they make information available to large swathes of society, and in doing so, they have opened up the potential for ever wider proportions of society to get access to information, knowledge, and in turn the means to participate in society, including, ultimately, decision-making through the establishment of democratic states. Historically, and still today in many parts of the world, political authorities have tried to restrict and control mass media development but over time a sense of the close association between the role of mass media and the principles and practices of democracy has become ingrained in democratic societies in particular. Predominantly in democracies like Britain, then, media technologies are viewed in a value-laden sense, as very much not neutral, but rather as both enabling and embodying democratic society. Media technologies are distinctive because of their politics, whether perceived or actual, and this continues to have significant consequences for the boundaries of activity within the media industries. There have been continual attempts to separate media technologies from their political associations in that sense, such as a director of the America Federal Communication Commission in the 1980s once describing television as merely 'a toaster with pictures' (in Eggerton, 2008), whilst arguing for deregulation of the American television industry. Such assertions tend to be met with significant opposition, and thus the boundaries of how media technologies may be used are arguably shaped by their political nature.

A second criticism of the SCOT model comes from the determinist position and argues that the actual uses of any technology at any specific time are fundamentally irrelevant compared to the more essential change introduced by the new mode of human action/communication the technology offers (Murphie and Potts, 2003: p.23). So, the fact that the mobile phone was used in Britain first by Yuppies, for instance, to technological determinists doesn't change the underlying and subsequently much more widespread social change that has arguably occurred in the global spread of mobile phones, and it is that which ultimately matters. Similarly, whilst hobbyists may have significantly shaped aspects of how the personal computer and internet industries have developed, intrinsic technological attributes of computer technologies (including digital, convergence, and distributed networks) are what underpinned that hobbyist culture in the first place. The early adopters of media technologies were simply those who were first in line in the process of the technologies' impacts on society. One problem with this criticism is that it veers towards an *essentialist* position regarding technologies, the view that the consequences of any particular technology are because of essential characteristics the technology contains (Lister et al. 2009: p.13), and simply ignores the variation in the uptake, adoption, and attitudinal positions regarding technologies across countries. The 'guns don't kill people, people kill people' position of gun lobby groups in the United States isn't just a rhetorical strategy employing a conceptual fallacy to serve particular political ends, though it is that, it is also a reflection of the particular socio-cultural and politico-economic significance of guns in American history which is distinct from many other countries. To argue that this is a consequence of the technology of the gun alone, or that it's a reflection of some kind of essential political consequence of guns, is to ignore the very different position of guns in other societies. This leads us to the other end of the continuum of views that concentrates attention onto the shaping of technology by society, fundamentally inverting the technological determinist position.

The Social Shaping of Technology (SST)

The range of perspectives collectively referred to as the social shaping of technology, or SST models, argue that social contexts shape the development of a technology in the first place, with any technology's emergence, adoption, and widespread use being a consequence of a combination of a range of emergent complex social, economic, political, and cultural problems and needs. The very invention of a particular technology, in this way of thinking, is a consequence of particular social forces generating either a need to be met, or a problem to be solved. Scholars from this perspective don't focus initially on what the social consequences of a technology might be, or how a technology might change society, but rather start with exploring why a particular technology emerged when and where it did, and what processes shaped its emergence, development, adoption, and, crucially, its fundamental form. In this way, technologies aren't seen as the creative genius of isolated scientists and engineers working independently of social processes to produce technologies that change society forever, but rather as actors working within pre-existing social structures that shape the processes of invention and innovation themselves, as well as the subsequent development, adoption, and social use of technologies. Raymond Williams is the most prominent of media scholars within this perspective, arguably having shaped much media and communication theory with regard to technology (Lister et al., 2009) and offering a fundamentally oppositional approach to thinking about the social impact of broadcasting in particular, when compared to McLuhan. Of television, for instance, Williams argues that:

> The decisive and earlier transformation of industrial production, and its new social forms, which had grown out of a long history of capital accumulation and working technical improvements, created new needs but also new possibilities, and the communications systems, down to television, were their intrinsic outcome.
>
> (1974/2003: p.12)

Whilst McLuhan argued that particular political, economic, and social structures were consequences of particular technologies, Williams argues the reverse – particular technologies only appear because of particular political, economic, and social structures. Brian Winston was another prominent scholar of this position, arguing that 'there is nothing in the histories of electrical and electronic communication systems to indicate that significant major changes have not been accommodated by pre-existing social formations' (1998: p.2).

The very notion of a kind of 'technological imperative' (Murphie and Potts, 2003: p.25) – whereby technologies seem to drive society to develop ever more technologies, are seen as the primary solutions to social problems, as well as the means through which to achieve social and personal goals – might seem to reinforce a technologically deterministic understanding of the relationship between media technology and society. Thinking back to the emergence of the network structure of the internet discussed earlier, this exemplifies the point that proponents of social shaping are making. Whilst the technological network structure of the internet offers a range of affordances and consequences as a result of that structure, the structure itself emerged within a very specific socio-cultural and politico-economic context that drove its development in those particular directions. These social contexts, or what Winston calls 'supervening social necessities' (1998: p.6), are what allow for the shift from an idea or conceptualisation to a realised, existing technology. Winston goes further by pointing out that in the evolution and development of media technologies there is a further stage in the process which he refers to as 'the "law" of the suppression of radical potential' (ibid.: p.7), whereby a range of societal factors may divert, delay, redirect, and suppress perceived potentials of new technologies to disrupt existing structures – technological, economic, political, cultural, and social. One can think, for instance, of the challenges of renewable energy technologies to get a hold in a world dominated by oil – even those built around centuries-old technologies like windmills and watermills. Media history is replete with these kinds of barriers to their development, and the constant tension between the social necessities that lead to technologies being developed in the first place and the challenges to existing social structures they generate are persistent features of the debates around media, technology, and society. In similar phraseology to McLuhan, but fundamentally reversing the causal direction, for instance, Winston talks about the main factor in emergence of the telephone (alongside other technologies like the typewriter around the same time) as being 'the legal creation of the modern corporation' (ibid.: p.51). The organisational and structural needs of corporations for communication – including within emerging modern office structures, literally in the emergence of skyscrapers in the decades that followed, in accelerating global, industrial capitalism – created the context in which technologies like the telephone became required. The context of industrial capitalism and associated politico-economic processes also provided the suppression of the radical potential in the telephone, according to Winston, partly through patent law (ibid.: p.58) which stymied technological development as rival producers sought to retain control over the technology, protecting their financial interests which largely stemmed from the older, rival technology the telegraph. Possible societal challenges, through, for instance, the telephone's potential capacity for one-to-many communication, were quite quickly suppressed to the now seemingly 'obvious' one-to-one interpersonal communication tool that we associate the traditional telephone with today (ibid.: p.59–60).

Conclusion

Thinking about technology and the media, it is important not to get hung up on the specifics of technological innovations in an overly deterministic manner. Whether thinking about the early history of 'old' media technologies or the latest software tools on digital platforms, it is important to recognise that technological innovations 'are deeply social – they don't simply come from individual minds or from some "essential" property of a digital computer or a computer network' (Manovich, 2013: p.32). Analogue and digital media are, in meaningful ways, different but countering the claims of Merrin expressed earlier in the chapter, Manovich argues that:

[T]he new qualities of 'digital media' are not situated 'inside' the media objects. Rather, they all exist 'outside' – as commands and techniques of media viewers, authoring software, animation, compositing, and editing software, Wiki software, and all other software 'species'.

(ibid.)

Technological change, particularly when discussed within industries and in politics, is often constructed and presented as the inevitable march of progress for the betterment of all but dissociating technological change from its social context risks ignoring the influence that context has on a technology's inception, creation, and form, as well as its potential societal consequences. Technologies emerge not in a vacuum, but in a particular, specific set of social, cultural, economic, and political contexts, which both shape their emergence, and then in turn contribute to the contexts in which the next new technology emerges. It is the economic contexts that we turn to in the next chapter.

2 Economics

The purpose of this chapter is to demonstrate how knowledge of some key ideas and concepts from the subject of economics can assist our understanding of the media industries. For example, why do media companies always seem to be merging with, or buying, other media companies? Why is social media and 'internet search' dominated by a handful of global media corporations? Why is there so much archive or repeat programming on our screens? And why does so much media content, whether films, videogames, television programmes, or music, tend to closely replicate existing genres and successful formats? These are just some of the questions that a basic understanding of the economics of the media can help us to tackle.

With one or two exceptions (e.g. Doyle, 2013a; Cunningham, Flew, and Swift, 2015), most research on media economics and/or the media industries from within the discipline of media/communication studies has tended to adopt what is commonly referred to as the critical political economy perspective (for classic examples see Herman and Chomsky 1988; Golding and Murdock, 2005). Underpinned by neo-Marxist theory, this approach focuses largely on the issue of concentration of ownership and control within the media, which, to a greater or lesser degree, is viewed as part of the more general control of society by an elite 'ruling class'. However, whilst not wanting to underplay the importance of media ownership (discussed in this chapter and in Chapter 3), even leading figures within the critical political economy tradition now concede that the conspiratorial lens offered by Marxist theory is of only limited help when it comes to trying to understand how the media industries function on a day to day basis, including why media organisations adopt the corporate strategies that they do and with what effects (Garnham, 2011: p.42). Our approach therefore is to provide a more straightforward focus on how key ideas and concepts from mainstream economics, sometimes also referred to as neo-classical economics, offer a useful starting point for understanding how the media industries operate in contemporary Britain (and beyond). To this end, the remainder of the chapter is divided into three main parts. First, we provide some brief background on the subject of economics and the implicit value placed on competitive markets within mainstream economic theory. The second part of the chapter then details some of the most important underlying economic characteristics of media products. This leads on to the third and final part of the chapter, which analyses how these economic characteristics shape both the behaviour of individual media organisations and the structure of the media industries as a whole.

Some Economic Theory

The starting point for mainstream economics is that all societies face the so-called 'economic problem', namely, how to make best use of a society's resources (labour,

DOI: 10.4324/9781315396781-4

land, etc.), when the wants and needs of people are endless, but the resources of society are limited. Writing against the backdrop of the industrial revolution, 18th- and 19th-century thinkers, such as Adam Smith and David Ricardo, often regarded as the founding fathers of modern economics, argued that free market capitalism was the most efficient way to distribute resources and, in turn, generate wealth for both individuals and society as a whole. Famously, in *The Wealth of Nations*, first published in 1776, Smith described the market as the 'invisible hand', which brought together all the myriad of individual actions involved in the production of goods and services (i.e. supply) to satisfy the needs of society as a whole (i.e. demand) (Smith, 1999). On this basis, the promotion of an efficiently functioning free market economy can be seen as the ultimate objective of mainstream economics. However, an efficiently functioning free market economy is itself dependent on unrestricted competition between producers of goods and services. With this in mind, a whole swathe of economic theory has been dedicated to understanding the properties of what economists refer to as 'perfect competition'. For perfect competition to exist, economists have identified four key market conditions:

i   There must be many buyers and sellers, each therefore trivial relative to the industry as a whole.
ii The product for sale must be homogeneous (i.e. the same or equivalent).
iii Buyers must have perfect information about the product.
iv There must be free entry and exit for firms operating in the market.

In such conditions, market forces can be said to operate freely with no one firm (or buyer) possessing the power to dictate the market price of the product. However, in reality, such conditions rarely, if ever, exist. First, most industries are dominated by a fairly small number of big companies, a market structure known as oligopoly (e.g. supermarkets, car manufacturing, etc.). Second, the goods or services on sale are often clearly differentiated via advertising, even if they are broadly similar. Third, even in the age of the internet, buyers rarely possess complete knowledge about the quality and characteristics of products before they make their purchases, especially in the case of a 'one off' or fairly expensive item, such as a car or a holiday. And finally, the set up costs to enter most industries (e.g. staff salaries; machinery; premises; raw materials, etc.) are often substantial and represent a significant barrier to any potential new firms.

Nevertheless, the perfect competition paradigm persists within economic theory for two sometimes, but not always, interconnected reasons. First, for at least some (neo-liberal) economists, the properties of perfect competition represent a set of pro-competitive ideals which should guide government economic policy, as well as public policy more generally, including media policy (see Chapter 3). From this perspective, greater competition (as a way to improve market efficiency) is something to strive for, even if perfect competition is unlikely to ever be achieved. Second, many economists have focused on attempting to explain why actual market conditions often fail to resemble anything approaching perfect competition. It is in this vein that concepts derived from economic theory can contribute towards our understanding of the media industries. The crucial point to understand is that media products possess certain characteristics that almost inevitably lead to what economists refer to as 'market failure', rather than perfect competition.

The Economic Characteristics of Media Products

To begin with, it is worth noting that it is often far from clear exactly what constitutes a media product. For instance, an individual television programme, a subscription to a pay-TV service, an article from an online newspaper, the streaming of a pop song from an online server, or access to an entire radio station are all very different types of media product. Nevertheless, albeit very different, all of these examples (and many others) share a defining feature, namely that 'the essential quality that audiences get value from is meanings, which are not, in themselves, material objects' (Doyle, 2013a: p.14). Beyond this, media products also exhibit one or more of the following characteristics.

Dual Product Markets

Media products are often sold in what economists describe as 'a dual product market' (Picard, 1989: pp.17–19). This refers to the fact that, unlike in most other industries, media organisations will often simultaneously seek to sell two different products to two different sets of buyers: first, media firms will attempt to sell content to audiences; and, second, the audiences that have been attracted by this content are then priced and sold to advertisers (e.g. per 1,000 readers/viewers). Some sectors of the media industries gain their revenue almost exclusively from either the content market (e.g. music; video-games) or the advertising market (e.g. commercial radio; social media), but others often rely on a combination of both (e.g. newspapers; magazines).

The commercial importance of the sale of audiences to advertisers means that reliable audience measurement has long been a key component of much, if not quite all, of the media industries. After all, advertisers want to be sure that their messages are reaching the size and type (i.e. age, gender, social class, etc.) of audience claimed by media companies. For example, during the early part of the 20th century, the growth of mass circulation newspapers reliant on advertiser funding, such as the *Daily Mail*, led to the establishment of an independent body to provide authoritative newspaper sales and circulation data: the Audited Bureau of Circulation (ABC) (Williams, 2010: pp.140–1). Similarly, the British Audience Research Board (BARB) was established during the early 1980s to provide independent audience data on television viewing in Britain (currently via a representative survey panel of about 7,000 households) (BARB, 2022a). For both BARB and the ABC, the growth of digital delivery has necessitated changes to how they measure audiences. In 1996, the ABC launched the ABCe's to measure the number of unique monthly visitors to newspaper web sites, and, more recently, BARB has introduced specially designed software to capture television viewing via computers, tablets, and smart phones. To date, social media sites, such as Facebook and YouTube, have sold space to advertisers based on their own internal audience data, but the reliability of such data has been subject to serious dispute, most notably when, in late 2016, Facebook conceded that the metric it had been using to measure viewing of audio-visual material could have been inflating average viewing time by between 60 and 80 per cent. Unsurprisingly, this revelation prompted advertisers to call for the 'independent evaluation' of audiences for social media, in line with other media sectors (Jackson, 2016).

Semi-Public Goods

Media products are also, at least in part, examples of what are known in economics as 'public goods'. Public goods have two defining features: first, it is technically possible for one person to consume without reducing the amount available for someone else; and second, the impossibility of excluding anyone from consumption except at a prohibitive cost. Media products certainly possess the first of these two features. If someone watches *Stranger Things* on Netflix, it remains available to be watched by someone else, or the same person again at a later date. And, the same can be said for virtually any media product, like videogames, television programmes, web sites, and so on. Whereas, by contrast, for a private good, such as a bar of chocolate, once it is consumed it is not available for anyone else to enjoy!

Whether media products possess the second defining feature of a 'public good' (non-excludability) is more debateable. The classic example of a 'public good' often cited by economists is national defence, whereby it would be practically impossible to offer a different service to those who do and do not pay (known as the 'free rider' problem). For much of its history, broadcasting was seen to possess a similar level of 'non-excludability', but the relatively recent development of encryption-based technology has meant that access to broadcast signals can now be effectively limited to paying consumers. Beyond conventional broadcasting, however, the widespread illegal downloading/streaming of media content (e.g. music, television programmes, and movies) from various file sharing web sites suggests that the growth of the internet represents a new difficulty for media organisations attempting to restrict access to their products to paying customers. Research undertaken in 2019 on behalf of the British government's Intellectual Property Office (IPO) estimated that around 25 per cent of internet users in Britain access media content from illegal sources online. According to the IPO, over a three-month period during 2019, films, music tracks, and TV programmes were accessed illegally online by 5.7 million, 5.1 million, and 4.4 million users respectively (IPO, 2019). In response, media organisations have long argued for the robust application of copyright law, so as to ensure the creators of media content receive payment for use of their material (see Chapter 3). In this sense, the use of copyright law by media companies can be seen as an attempt to impose 'excludability' on media products, which, due to their non-perishable nature, have a tendency towards non-excludability, especially since the development of digital distribution technology (see Chapter 1). Overall then, media products are perhaps best described as 'semi-public goods' (Hesmondhalgh, 2019: p.34).

Economies of Scale

Media products have an inherent tendency towards economies of scale. Economies of scale are said to exist when long run average costs decrease as output rises. This feature is not unique to the media industries. Many large industries, especially within manufacturing, are characterised by economies of scale, but the semi-public good nature of media products makes them a particularly extreme case. As with all public goods, the initial cost of producing media products, sometimes referred to as the 'first copy costs', are fixed and make up the vast bulk of the costs incurred by a media organisation. For some premium media content this cost can be eye-wateringly high. For example, in 2016, the Netflix original drama series, *The Crown* (Season 1: 10 episodes), was estimated to have cost around £100 million to make (Martinson, 2016). In a similar vein, the average cost of a Hollywood movie is estimated to be around $60 million (*The Economist*, 2016) and a big-budget videogame, like *Red Dead Redemption 2*, reportedly cost hundreds of millions of dollars to make (MacDonald and Hern, 2018).

Whereas, by contrast, because media products are not used up during consumption, the cost of providing the product (i.e. a television drama, movie, or videogame, etc.) to one extra consumer, referred to by economists as the marginal cost, is often very low, and with the growth of digital technology can be virtually zero. This is the main reason why economies of scale within the media industries are particularly acute, even when compared to manufacturing more generally. For firms involved in, say, car or furniture production, as well as the relatively high cost of design (i.e. first-copy cost), a significant cost in production is the cost of the raw material (and labour) required for each new product. Whereas, with the media industries, as more viewers tune in, or more readers purchase a magazine, or stream music from an online service, like Spotify, the marginal cost is close to zero, and therefore the average cost (per consumer) to the media company supplying the product is reduced. As discussed more later, what this means is that media organisations have a particularly strong commercial incentive to sell to more and more consumers. Or, put another way, once the relatively high 'first-copy costs' have been covered, for media organisations each additional consumer is pure profit.

Network Effects

As outlined in Chapter 1, different types of communication network are a key feature of the media industries. In terms of economic theory, network effects are closely connected to the notion of economies of scale, but here the added value stems from a growth in demand for the product, rather than the scale of supply. Put simply, a 'network effect' is where a good or service becomes more (positive) or less (negative) valuable as more people use it. The classic example of a positive network effect often cited by economists is the provision of a telecommunications network. If just a handful of people are connected to a telephone network, then it has only limited value (i.e. there are only a small number of people to call or receive calls from). But, as extra users connect to the network, the value of the network increases for all users (i.e. because there are many more people to communicate with). To some degree, the media industries have always been subject to network effects. For example, as more people purchased television sets in Britain during the 1950s and 1960s, the value of the television network increased for both content suppliers (broadcasters) and consumers (viewers). For broadcasters, this was a straightforward case of economies of scale. As the number of potential viewers increased, so too did income for broadcasters, from either the licence fee or the sale of advertising, which, in turn, facilitated greater investment in programme production and/or increased profits. For viewers, the network effect (i.e. a demand side economy of scale) was less quantifiable, but no less significant, and took the form of the social value that stems from shared experiences and conversations made possible by the fact that so many other people were watching the same programmes, as well as the benefit of increased investment in the programming itself by broadcasters.

For the most part, however, it has been the growth of the web, and particularly social media over the last decade or so, that has underlined the importance of networks' effects for the media industries. Most obviously, the value (for the individual, if not necessarily commercially – see Chapter 12) of social media sites, such as Facebook and Twitter, is intrinsically linked to the number of users who are members of the network. More generally, increased use of the internet for the delivery of audio-visual material has also produced discernible network effects, but these are not always positive. On the positive side of the equation, social media sites like YouTube are able to make use of the inherent two-way nature of the internet to offer users more and more content uploaded by other users, as well as tailoring that content to individual user preferences. On the negative side though, the growing use of 'bandwidth hungry' audio-visual services, like Netflix and the BBC iPlayer, has 'dramatically increased' consumer demand for bandwidth, which could lead to slower broadband speeds for all users without increased investment in Britain's broadband network (Ofcom, 2015a).

High Risk Investments

Finally, in economic terms, media products are associated with particularly high levels of risk and unpredictability. This is firstly because audiences tend to use media products, like music and film/TV shows, in highly volatile and unpredictable ways, often in order to express that they are different to, or the same as, other people (Hesmondhalgh, 2019: p.31). Thus, for example, previously successful television programmes or recording artists can suddenly fall out of favour with audiences, whereas, equally, other media products, such as the BBC's *Strictly Come Dancing* programme or a videogame like *Fortnite*, can become unexpectedly successful. The combination of high production ('first copy') costs with the unpredictability of audience response means that virtually all sectors of the media industries are high risk enterprises.

A second source of commercial risk and uncertainty linked to media products stems from the inherently interdependent nature of what economists refer to as the 'vertical supply chain' (Doyle, 2013a: 20–1). Not unique to the media industries, the concept of a vertical supply chain is widely used within economics as a means to understand an industry by breaking it down into a sequence of different activities. This begins with the 'upstream' production process and works 'downstream' through different stages where the product is processed and refined, before it is then supplied to the consumer. For the media industries, the main stages in the vertical supply chain are: first, the production of the content itself; second, the packaging/aggregation of that content into a product; and, third, distribution of the product to consumers (see Figure 2.1). Whilst a number of additional stages may also exist (e.g. provision of encryption services for pay-TV), and there are also differences between sectors, the basic vertical supply chain offers a useful analytical framework for understanding the media industries. Most importantly, the vertical supply chain highlights the interdependence that exists between each stage. In simple terms, content is of little value without a means of distribution to reach consumers, but equally, a distribution infrastructure is of limited value without attractive content to attract consumers.

Historically, before the development of digital technology and the growth of the internet (i.e. when distribution was scarce), power and profit within the media industries were seen to be chiefly located in control of distribution, rather than content production (Garnham, 1987). However, as the number of delivery options for content producers has increased with technological innovation, the dominant position of distributors has arguably lessened, while at the same time the commercial power of those who produce or control popular content has increased (Christophers, 2008). Indeed, the growth of the internet has even allowed many individual consumers to become producers and distribute their own content using social media sites, like YouTube. For the most part, however, it would be an oversimplification to regard either distribution

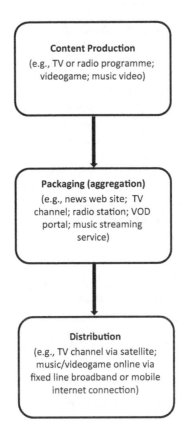

Figure 2.1 Media Industries: Vertical Supply Chain

or content as 'king' within the contemporary media industries. As is discussed more later, the challenge facing most media organisations is how best to manage the inherent uncertainties of an interdependent vertical supply chain.

The Economics of the Media and the British Media Industries

The underlying economic characteristics of media products are important because they go some way towards explaining the behaviour of individual media organisations and, in turn, general trends within the media industries. Most significantly, two interrelated aspects of the media in Britain can, at least in part, be traced back to the underlying economic characteristics of media products: i) concentration of ownership; and ii) the range and diversity of content available to media audiences.

Concentration of Media Ownership

While there is much debate over the most appropriate methodology to use when measuring the relative size of different media organisations (see Chapter 3), it is generally accepted that the British media industries are owned and controlled by a relatively small number of large organisations (i.e. concentration of ownership). For example, in their analysis of *The State of UK Media and Entertainment 2016*, the management consultants, Deloitte, pointed out that 'revenue generation is concentrated in the hands of a few companies' and that 'the top ten companies account for 68 per cent of total industry revenues' (Deloitte, 2016: pp.4–5). Similarly, the Media Reform Coalition (MRC), an organisation that campaigns in support of media pluralism, has detailed the high degree of concentration of ownership that exists within particular sectors of the British media. The MRC notes that: just three companies – DMG Media, News UK, and Reach – dominate 90 per cent of the national newspaper market; two companies – Bauer and Global Radio – own 70 per cent of Britain's local commercial radio stations; and Facebook (now renamed Meta) controls three of the main social media 'platforms and intermediaries' (Facebook, Instagram, and WhatsApp) used to access online news in Britain (MRC, 2021: p.2). Table 2.1 lists Britain's biggest media organisations (in terms of annual turnover) and offers an indication of the commercial power of a handful of large organisations, namely Sky, Virgin Media, BT, the BBC, and ITV. Perhaps most notably, Table 2.1 highlights the dominant position of Sky,

Table 2.1 Britain's Largest Media Organisations (by Annual Revenue)

	Main Media Brands	*Annual Revenues* (£billion)
Sky (owned by Comcast, US)	Sky Q; Sky television channels; Now TV; Sky Broadband; Sky Mobile	17.0 (UK, Italy and Germany)
Virgin Media O2 (jointly owned by Liberty Global, US, and Telefonica, Spain)	Virgin Media; O2 mobile	10.4
BT Consumer (part of BT Group plc)	BT TV; BT Sport; BT Broadband; EE Mobile	9.8
British Broadcasting Corporation (BBC) (publicly owned)	BBC television channels; national and local radio stations, BBC.co.uk and the BBC iPlayer	5.1
ITV plc (9.9 % owned by Liberty Global, US)	ITV television channels; ITV Hub; ITV Studios	3.5
News UK (owned by News Corp, US)	*The Sun, Sunday Sun, The Times, Sunday Times*	2.0
Channel 4 Television Corporation (publicly owned)	Channel 4, E4, Film Four; All 4	0.93
DMG Media (part of Daily Mail and General Trust plc (DMGT))	*Daily Mail, Sunday Mail;* and numerous local newspapers	0.85
Reach plc	*Daily Mirror, Sunday Mirror, Daily Record, Daily Star, OK!,* and numerous local newspapers	0.62
Global Media Group Limited	LBC, Capital, Heart, Classic FM	0.43
Financial Times (owned by Nikkei, Japan)	*Financial Times,* FT.com	0.32
Guardian Media Group plc	*The Guardian, The Observer,* the-guardian.com	0.22

Sources: Company Annual Reports and media reports.

* Figures for financial year 2020/21, or most recent available year.

Britain's leading pay-TV broadcaster, with annual revenues (£17 billion) that are almost double those of its closest rival and more than the total of the ten smaller media organisations listed taken together.

However, this point (and Table 2.1 as a whole) should be viewed with a couple of important caveats in mind related to the inherent conceptual and methodological difficulties of defining 'British media organisations' (see Introduction). First, a number of the media organisations cited here, such as BT and Virgin Media O2, generate the vast majority of their revenues from telecommunications services (fixed line and mobile), rather than through the production and circulation of media products (as defined earlier). Sky could therefore be seen to occupy an even more dominate position (in revenue terms) within the British media than Table 2.1 suggests. Second, the media organisations listed here are limited to those with publicly available information on revenues principally generated in Britain. As a result, Table 2.1 does not include a number of, mainly US-based, global media corporations, including Meta (Facebook and Instagram), Alphabet (YouTube and Google), Amazon Prime, Netflix, and Apple, who obviously constitute an increasingly important part of the British media landscape. The implications of this for British media organisations are discussed more later in this chapter, as well as throughout the rest of the book.

The concentrated pattern of ownership that characterises the media industries in Britain is largely a product of the fact that media organisations have particularly strong commercial incentives to grow in a host of different ways.

Horizontal Expansion

Horizontal expansion is where media organisations look to maximise the potential gains to be had from economies of scale by expanding their market share within their sector of the industry. For example, during the early 1990s, in an attempt to increase the long term profitability of his newspapers, Rupert Murdoch's News International (now News Corp UK) launched a British newspaper price war by cutting the price of *The Sun* by a fifth and *The Times* by a third. The result was a significant boost to the circulation of each paper, particularly *The Times*, and lasting damage to some of their rivals (Williams, 2010: p.225). Similarly, in the 2010s, it was estimated that Sky had an annual marketing budget that was bigger than ITV's entire annual programming budget (around £800 million in 2010) (Thompson, 2010). This level of expenditure on marketing no doubt played a part in enabling Sky (then BSkyB) to reach its publicly stated goal of 10 million subscribers by the end of 2010, a strategy that itself only makes full sense when the extreme economies of scale that characterise the media industries are taken into account. More recently, the same commercial logic has underpinned the expansion strategies of a number of high profile new entrants, such as Netflix and Spotify. Both have adopted a 'rush for growth' strategy characterised by huge investment and rapid expansion plans in the hope that economies of scale will lead to long term profitability. For example, between 2012 and 2017, Netflix invested around $1.8 billion on licensed, original, and co-productions in Europe as part of its international expansion strategy (i.e. beyond the United States), with a target of 'material profits' from 2017 (Madhumita, 2017).

With the same objective in mind – horizontal expansion – media organisations may also look to either take-over or merge with a competitor in the same market. This strategy is commonly known as 'horizontal integration' and, over the last few decades, it has been a defining feature of the media industries in Britain, perhaps most notably in the realm of commercial terrestrial television. Following the 1991 franchise auction, the regional structure of ITV, established when the channel was launched during the 1950s, was still clearly evident. The ITV network was divided between 15 regionally based franchises, each controlled by a separate company. However, facilitated by numerous legal and regulatory changes (see Chapter 3), the 1990s and early 2000s witnessed a whole series of mergers between the different ITV companies, which meant that, by 2003, a single company, ITV plc, had come to own and control over 90 per cent of the ITV network. Likewise, during the 2000s, the British commercial radio industry has also witnessed significant market consolidation. Most notably, since the takeover of GCap by Global Radio, in 2008, commercial radio in Britain has been dominated by just two companies, Global Radio and Bauer Radio (part of Bauer Media Group) (see Chapter 7).

British media organisations may also seek to achieve horizontal expansion by expanding their market beyond Britain. For example, over the last decade or so, British television production companies have enjoyed considerable success selling their pro- grammes and/or programme formats internationally. In 2020/21, the estimated total revenue from the international sale of British TV programmes was over £1.4 billion, with dramas like *I May Destroy You* and *It's a Sin*, as well as non-scripted formats/ shows, such as *Masterchef* and *Who Wants to be a Millionaire*, popular across the globe (PACT, 2021). In a similar vein, the last decade or so has also witnessed tradi- tional British newspapers, such as the *Daily Mail* and *The Guardian*, looking to use their online presence to expand their market beyond Britain (see Chapter 4). For both, this strategy has been an at least a partial success. In 2022, *Mail Online* and *The Guardian* were ranked respectively as the world's sixth and seventh most popular Eng- lish language news web sites (Majid, 2023).

Vertical Integration

To counter the inherent risk associated with investment in the media industries, media organisations will often look to be involved in activities at more than one stage of the vertical supply chain (see Figure 2.1). This strategy is known as vertical integration. Typically, media organisations will seek to have at least some control over both the production and distribution stages in the supply chain either by expanding their own activities, or more often, by purchasing or merging with a company involved in a complimentary activity. Using this approach, a media organisation can guarantee dis- tribution for the content it produces while also being assured a steady stream of con- tent ready to be distributed.

One of the clearest demonstrations of vertical integration in the British media industry is the pay-TV broadcaster, Sky. Sky owns and/or controls considerable assets in relation to distribution, programme aggregation, and content production. In terms of distribution, Sky owns the satellite television delivery platform developed by the broadcaster since the early 1990s, and also Sky Broadband, which was launched in 2006, following the purchase of existing broadband service, Easynet, a year earlier. Sky also wholly or partly owns a number of different television channels. Some of these were launched and developed by Sky itself, such as *Sky Sports* and *Sky Arts*, while others were acquired from rival broadcasters (horizontal integration), such as *Sky Witness*, purchased (as *Living*) from Virgin Media 2010. Finally, either through its parent company (21st Century Fox until 2018 and Comcast since then), or via long term supply deals, Sky has also had access to large amounts of highly valuable content, most notably sports rights (e.g. Premier League football), Hollywood movies, and big-budget US dramas, including an exclusive supply and co-production deal with the US broadcaster, HBO (White, 2017).

At least partly in response to Sky's move into the broadband supply market, BT, the former publicly owned telecommunications company and Britain's leading broadband supplier, launched its own television delivery platform, BT TV, and between 2012–13 invested over £2 billion acquiring the exclusive live rights to various sporting events and competitions to show on its BT Sport channels, as well as its own deal with the US network, AMC, for exclusive US dramas (Smith, Evens, and Iosifidis, 2016). Consequently, during the 2010s, a significant feature of the British media landscape was a rivalry between two vertically integrated media companies, BT and Sky, each with significant assets in media distribution and content aggregation/production.

Diagonal Integration

To reduce risks (and increase profitability), media organisations may also seek to become involved in more than one sector of the media industries, what economists refer to as 'diagonal' integration. To some extent, the growth of broadband internet access over the last decade or so has meant that established British media organisations have adopted this strategy almost by default, with, for example, traditional newspapers like the *Daily Telegraph* providing increasing amounts of audio-visual content, and magazine publishers, such as Bauer Media, providing a host of podcasts (e.g. *Grazia Beauty, Grazia Fashion*, etc.). This trend goes some way towards explaining the continued success of many of Britain's established media brands in the realm of online media. Specifically, diagonal integration has two major advantages. First, it provides an opportunity for cross-promotion. For example, with interests ranging across television, radio, publishing, and online, the BBC is arguably the most diagonally integrated media organisation in Britain and as such is able to employ its entire range of media outlets in a seemingly endless round of cross-promotion, often to the annoyance of the Corporation's commercial rivals, such as local and national newspapers (NMA, 2015).

A second advantage of diagonal integration is that it enables media organisations to offset losses in one area with profits from another. For example, within Rupert Murdoch's News Corporation, the highly expensive launch and expansion stage for BSkyB during the early 1990s was effectively subsidised by the profits accrued by the group's national newspaper publisher, News International (Horsman, 1997). During the early 2000s, however, the tables turned and it was the highly profitable Sky that subsidised the loss making of *The Times*, giving the newspaper an opportunity to develop a new commercial strategy based on a 'pay wall' and online subscriptions (see Chapter 4).

Finally, it should be stressed that, as with horizontal expansion, the incentives for diagonal (and vertical) integration are not limited to national media markets. On the contrary, by owning distribution and content assets across a number of media sectors and national markets, a media organisation can combine the advantages of each strategy on a larger scale. For the most part, however, British media organisations have tended to be victims of this strategic approach by US media organisations, rather than the perpetrators of it. Consequently, some of Britain's largest media organisations are part of US-based media corporations (see Table 2.1). Most notably, Sky, Channel 5, and News UK are wholly owned by the US-based media giants Comcast, Viacom, and News Corp, respectively. Furthermore, the last decade or so has also witnessed numerous US-based media organisations utilising online distribution to enter and/or expand into international markets, including Britain. For example, British-based television broadcasters now face competition from US owned VOD (video on demand) services, including Netflix, Disney+, and Amazon Prime. Even more starkly, social media and internet search in Britain have long been dominated by US corporations, such as Alphabet and Meta (see Chapter 11). Most of these US-based global media corporations generate annual revenues far beyond those of any of the British-based media organisations listed in Table 2.1, namely: Amazon (£297 billion), Apple (£226 billion), Alphabet (£140 billion), Meta (£66 billion), Disney (£46 billion), Netflix (£19 billion) (MRC, 2021: p.14).

High Barriers to Entry

At the same time as providing clear incentives to expand for existing media organisations (horizontal, vertical, and/or diagonal), the very high 'first copy costs' associated with media production also make it difficult for any new players to enter the industry in a significant way. In other words, the media industries tend to be characterised by what economists refer to as high barriers to entry. For example, the last national daily newspapers to be launched in Britain by industry outsiders were *Today* and *The Independent* during the late 1980s. Despite the fact that each paper was supported by an initial outlay in excess of £20 million, they both soon faced financial difficulties, which led to mergers with other media companies and in the case of *Today* eventual closure (Curran and Seaton, 2010: pp.93–4). Similarly, despite the explosion in the number of channels available to British television viewers since the launch of digital television during the late 1990s, the level of investment required to own and operate a television channel remains high enough to deter most potential new broadcasters. For example, in 2020, Channel 5, Britain's least well-resourced public service broadcaster, spent just under £100 million on original programming (Ofcom, 2021b: p.67). Consequently, few, if any, new television channels have been successfully launched in Britain without the financial support of an established media organisation. Most recently, from around 2014, the launch of a host of relatively low-cost local television channels, including Bay TV (Liverpool) and London Live, was made possible by a £25 million subsidy from the BBC.

The development of new media technology during the late 1990s provided an opportunity for a handful of new entrants to establish themselves as global media brands with relatively low start-up costs, perhaps most notably Google and Facebook. However, this period of rapid commercial growth for the internet, the so-called dot. com boom, was short-lived and ended with the dot.com bust of the early 2000s, which saw billions of pounds wiped off the values of publicly quoted internet companies as well as many dot.com business closures. Since the 2000s, the internet has resembled much more closely the rest of the media industries (see Chapter 11). Like other sectors, the internet in Britain is dominated by a relatively small number of very large international and/or national media organisations, most notably established British news and entertainment brands, like the BBC and Mail Online, and US owned internet search and social media corporations, namely Meta (Facebook and Instagram) and Alphabet (Google and YouTube). At least in part, the network effects that characterise much new media (see the discussion on p.29) mean that for a new entrant to establish a comparable online presence would require just as much, if not more, of an investment than to enter any other sector of the media industry.

The Range and Diversity of Content Available to British Media Audiences

With both the growth of the internet and the development of new digital broadcasting technology over the last couple of decades, it can be argued that British media audiences have never had so much choice over what to read, watch, and listen to (see Chapter 3). At the same time, however, the underlying economic characteristics of media products mean that media organisations often exhibit patterns of behaviour that, when taken together, can serve to limit the range and diversity of content made available to British audiences.

The 'Long Tail'

The 'semi-public good' nature of media products means that media organisations have a clear incentive to expand their market in terms of 'time', sometimes referred to as exploiting 'the long tail' (Dwyer, 2010: p.129). As a result, television broadcasters, for example, frequently seek to utilise their programmes long after they have first been broadcast. This may take the form of one or more 'catch up' repeat(s) scheduled soon after a programme is first broadcast, a whole channel broadcast one hour behind the original channel (+1 channels), or even an entire channel, such as *Gold*, dedicated to repeating archive programming. In fact, it has been estimated that nearly two thirds of the BBC's total output across its main television channels consists of repeats (Silverman, 2013). The same underlying 'semi-public good' characteristic is also exploited by Hollywood film studios, which dominate the British cinema box office revenues (see Chapter 6), through their strategy of staggering the release of blockbuster movies across a sequence of distinct release 'windows' (i.e. cinema, DVD, pay-per-view, subscription movie channel, free-to-air channel, and so on) so as to maximise the revenue that can be gained from each film release. Just as significantly, over the last decade or so many of Britain's largest media organisations have looked to utilise the 'semi-public good' character of media products by 'reversioning' much of their content for distribution via the internet (Doyle, 2010). Thus, much of the 'new' content viewed online by British audiences is content already produced for other media outlets, for example the web sites of national newspapers and the 'catch up' TV services offered by broadcasters. In the same way, despite much publicity for original series, such as *The Grand Tour* and *Orange is the New Black*, VOD services, like Netflix and Amazon Prime, still rely heavily on thousands of hours of archive and licensed programming, most notably from established TV producers, such as Viacom, Sony, and the BBC (White, 2016).

Reducing the Risk

To reduce the high levels of financial risk associated with media production, media organisations also have a tendency to produce risk averse content. As pointed out by Napoli, there is an 'oft-noted tendency for media organisations to constantly rely on established and proven genres, formulas or properties, rather than producing original or innovative content' (2009: p.167). For example, over the last decade or so, British television ratings have been dominated be annual versions of a host of talent/reality entertainment shows, such as *X-Factor, Britain's Got Talent, I'm a Celebrity Get me Out of Here* (ITV), *Strictly Come Dancing* (BBC), and *The Great British Bake Off* (BBC/C4). In a similar vein, the playlists of Britain's most listened to commercial radio stations tend to be characterised by the repetition of a small number of mainstream pop songs. One study found that each day Capital FM played over one thousand songs, but only 83 different songs, with the most popular 30 songs making up 73 per cent of their daily output (Plunkett, 2010a). Furthermore, the tendency to produce risk averse content is not restricted to British broadcasting. Within the videogames industry, for example, highly successful games, such as *Call of Duty, Halo,* and *Assassin's Creed,* spurn numerous sequels in a manner similar to that of Hollywood blockbusters as a way to almost guarantee commercial success. Or, within the music industry, collaborations have become an increasingly prominent feature of the pop charts, as major record labels seek to utilise the popular appeal of two or more star artists in an attempt to guarantee commercial success (Savage, 2020).

Impact of Advertising

The reliance of large sections of the British media industries on funding from advertising also has a discernible impact on the range and diversity of content provided. To be commercially successful, print media, free-to-air commercial broadcasters, and social media need to attract audiences of either the size and/or composition desired by advertisers. For instance, broadcasters and magazine publishers will often target young audiences, between the ages of around 18 and 30, because their relatively high levels of disposal income mean they are seen as a particularly valuable target audience by advertisers. Consequently, there exists a whole host of television channels (e.g. *MTV Hits* as well as almost all of the other music channels available) and lifestyle magazines (e.g. *Grazia* and *Closer*) targeted at young audiences. Whereas, by contrast, for audiences that advertisers find less desirable, such as the elderly, relatively few television channels and magazines are provided.

Perhaps the clearest example of the impact advertising finance on the British media is provided by the British newspaper industry, both print and online (Curran and Seaton, 2010: pp.84–91). The British newspaper industry relies heavily on advertising finance and this shapes both the type of content offered by individual newspapers and the overall structure of the industry. First, the influence of advertisers has contributed towards the polarisation of the newspaper market between (popular) newspapers that target a mass audience and (quality) newspapers that target a small, but wealthier, readership. Second, individual newspapers also include various specialised features or sections that are attractive to advertisers who can then effectively target certain groups, hence, the *Daily Mail's* daily *Femail* section and *The Guardian's Education* section. And third, Curran and Seaton (2010: p.88) go so far as to argue that reliance on advertising finance has led to the 'de-radicalisation and de-politicisation' of the British press. To illustrate this point, they cite the case of the radical left-wing newspaper the *Daily Herald,* which, when it closed in 1964, had a circulation of around 1.2 million, more than five times the circulation of *The Times.* However, its readership was mainly made up of readers with relatively low incomes and it was therefore not attractive to advertisers. Relaunched as *The Sun,* the paper was eventually sold to Rupert Murdoch in 1969, whereupon it was reoriented to offer a mix of human interest and show business news, together with a political stance that embodied everything the old *Daily Herald* had opposed.

Over the last decade or so, commercial fortunes of British newspapers have remained wedded to their ability, or not, to attract advertisers. For example, a rare story of commercial success has been the rise of the *Metro*. Launched in 1999 by Associated Newspapers (DMG), the *Metro* is a daily free newspaper distributed to commuters in various major British cities. With annual profits of around £15 million, the paper owes much of its success to the effective targeting of a relatively young (average age 37; 22 years younger than the average weekday newspaper reader overall) and affluent readership, as well as its low-cost offering of a non-political news digest (Ponsford, 2017a). The desire to attract revenue from advertisers has also led to accusations that British national and local newspapers are increasingly sacrificing traditional news values in the pursuit of stories likely to maximise online readership, commonly referred to as 'click-bait' and often taking the form of lists, or 'listicles'. One critic has even claimed that the focus on 'click-bait' at Reach (then Trinity Mirror), one of Britain's largest local news publishers, has become so intense that (a decreasing number of) journalists are required to seek permission to publish any stories that might attract less than one thousand clicks (Ponsford, 2016). Finally, it should be noted that the drive towards 'click-bait' is shared and, at least partially, driven by the growth of social media. Social media providers, like Facebook and YouTube, derive virtually all of their income from their ability to offer advertisers access to high numbers, and/or highly targeted groups, of users. However, as discussed more in the next chapter (and Chapter 11), this business model has led to growing concerns over the use of social media to spread propaganda and/or stories of uncertain provenance or accuracy, commonly known as 'fake news'. Clearly, both old and new media organisations rely heavily on funding from advertisers and this has a discernible impact on the type and range of content available to and accessed by British audiences.

Conclusion

This chapter has sought to demonstrate how a basic understanding of some key ideas and concepts from mainstream economics can enhance our understanding of the media industries. While many of the individual economic characteristics of media products outlined in this chapter (e.g. economies of scale, public good, high levels of risk and unpredictability, externalities) are certainly evident in other industries, it is the combination of each of these different characteristics within a single industry (or set of industries) that make the media industries unique. In response to the economic characteristics of media products, media organisations adopt a host of different strategies, ranging from (horizontal, vertical, and diagonal) expansion/integration to focusing on successful genres/sequels/stars. At the same time, however, it is important to see the behaviour of individual media organisations, as well as the contours of the media industries as a whole, as not solely determined by this economic context. As detailed in the previous chapter, developments in media technology also shape the nature of the media industries, and government policy and regulatory approaches are just as significant too. The latter – the politics of the media industries – is the focus of the next chapter.

3   Politics

The media industries are often the subject of widespread public discussion and debate, not least through the media itself. In recent years, for example, there has been growing concern over the conduct of social media platforms, such as Facebook, and in particular their sale of users' personal data to facilitate targeted advertising, including during the 2016 referendum on Britain's membership of the European Union (EU). For their part, the radio and television industries have been subject to public criticism on issues ranging from the relative lack of (racial, gender, class, and age) diversity represented on British television to the perceived bias of news and current affairs coverage on controversial issues, most notably Brexit. At the same time, the phone hacking scandals of the 2000s and the resulting Leveson Inquiry (2012) have done little to quell long standing public concern over the conduct of some newspaper journalists (see Chapter 4). Yet such controversial issues, and many more besides, are rarely, if ever, linked to an explicit discussion of British media policy. In other key areas of public policy, such as education or the National Health Service, it would be unthinkable to discuss, for example, school class sizes or hospital waiting lists, without mention of current government education or health policy respectively, but in public debates on the media industries the significance of government media policy (and/or its absence) is often largely neglected.

There are several interconnected reasons for the relative absence of 'media policy' from debates on the media industries. First, Britain has never had a single unified media and/or communications policy, but has rather applied different policy and regulatory approaches to different forms of media and/or communication technologies (Seymour-Ure, 1987). Second, for print media, an underlying commitment to press freedom (from government control) has meant that the British government's default position has long been non-intervention – a policy of not having a policy. And third, despite the fact that the growth of online media has led to an enormous expansion in the amount of content available to British audiences, to date at least, online content has been 'subject to little or no specific regulation' (Ofcom, 2018a: p.16).

Whatever the reasons, the absence of media policy from debates on the media industries is deeply problematic. This is because a lack of discussion about different policy options and/or regulatory possibilities creates the impression that the media industries exist in a realm beyond democratic control where politicians in Britain, or beyond, have little influence. The main purpose of this chapter is to highlight how, just as in other areas of public policy, like education and health, the media industries are, in reality, shaped, at least in part, by political choices, which ultimately reflect value judgements about the type of society we want to live in. In this sense, the media industries

DOI: 10.4324/9781315396781-5

are as much a product of our political values and choices as their underlying techno-logical and economic characteristics.

Broadly speaking, controversies about the media industries in Britain are connected to two fundamental areas of debate (Curran and Seaton, 2010: p.393). One is con-cerned with media law and the regulation of media content. Here, the main split is between libertarians, who emphasise the intrinsic value of freedom of expression, and interventionists, who want society to be protected from certain types of media content, such as violent and sexually explicit material. The second area of debate focuses on the organisation of the media industries. In line with mainstream economic theory (see Chapter 2), one side in this debate advocates free market competition, whereas the other side contends that in order to achieve certain democratic, social-cultural, and/or economic objectives, public intervention (e.g. public ownership, subsidies, laws, and/or regulations) is required. This chapter addresses each of these areas of debate in turn.

Media Law and the Regulation of Media Content

Stemming from the writings of Enlightenment and 19th-century liberal thinkers, including John Milton and John Stuart Mill, respectively, freedom of expression, and, in turn, a 'free media' is a fundamental principle of Western liberal democracies, such as Britain (Hutchison, 1999). The right to freely circulate a range of ideas, no matter how marginal or unwelcome, to citizens who are equally free to consume and contest these ideas is at the heart of democratic theory. From this perspective, freedom of expression (for individuals and media organisations) facilitates public scrutiny of those who hold power within society (e.g. governments, big business, university vice-chan-cellors, etc.) and enables citizens to make informed choices at elections. Freedom of expression also guarantees opportunities for individuals to express their (cultural and/ or political) ideas, beliefs, and views about the world (i.e. their identity). On this basis, any moves to revoke or restrict the right to freedom of expression are likely to be seen as authoritarian and as endangering the health of liberal democratic society (McQuail, 2010; Freedman, 2008).

As an abstract principle, freedom of expression, and by extension media freedom, enjoys widespread support within contemporary Britain. Few, if any, politicians, for example, would contest the general notion that media freedom is a good thing for both the individual and society as a whole. Yet, in Britain, and other liberal democracies, freedom of expression is not, and has never been, absolute (i.e. unrestricted). Numerous legal restrictions are routinely imposed on freedom of expression and/or media freedom on the grounds that some controls are necessary in order to prevent harm to individual or society. The rationale for this 'interventionist' approach was perhaps most famously articulated in the US in 1919 when the Supreme Court argued that the right to free speech, as set out in the First Amendment to the US constitution, 'would not protect a man in falsely shouting fire in a theatre and causing panic'. On this basis, the Court ruled that restrictions on free speech were justified, if a 'clear and present danger' was likely to result from the exercise of free speech (Larson, 2015). All of which inevitably raises a fundamental dilemma, namely deciding exactly what form(s) of communica-tion, if any, constitute a 'clear and present danger' (to individuals and/or society) and need to be restricted. This issue has long been, and remains, at the heart of political debates over freedom of expression and media freedom in Britain, as well as other liberal democracies.

The laws and regulations that govern media freedom in Britain today are the product of an historical (and ongoing) political balancing act between the principle of freedom of expression on the one hand and restrictions deemed necessary to protect individuals and/ or society on the other. More specifically, media content in Britain is regulated in two main ways. First, all media outlets are required to abide by the same general laws that set limits on any individual's exercise of freedom of expression in the public domain, sometimes referred to collectively as the 'law of the land'. Second, certain forms of media content, but not all (see p.44), are also controlled via additional specific laws and/or regulations.

The Law of the Land

The most significant law that governs freedom of expression in contemporary Britain is the Human Rights Act (1998). The Human Rights Act, which effectively incorporated the (1953) European Convention of Human Rights into British law, came into force in October 2000 and for the first time marked the formal existence of a right to 'freedom of expression' in British law. Article 10 of the 1998 Human Rights Act declares: 'Everyone has the right to freedom of expression. This right shall include freedom to hold opinions and to receive and impart information and ideas without interference by public authority and regardless of frontiers' (Human Rights Act, 1998, Article 10 (1)).

At the same time, however, in line with the 'balancing act' outlined earlier, the Human Rights Act also allows considerable leeway for laws and regulations to be introduced (or retained) that may serve to limit freedom of expression in order to prevent harm to individuals and/or society more generally. Some of the most significant general restrictions on media freedom include:

- Defamation: the communication of a statement which diminishes the reputation of an individual or organisation, e.g. an allegation of dishonesty, hypocrisy, or adultery. If a defamatory allegation is made in a 'permanent' form (e.g. published in a newspaper or on a social media site) the defamed person can sue the writer and publisher for libel in the civil courts. Unless the allegation can be proved true, or there is another successful legal defence (e.g. 'honest opinion'), the court will declare it to be libellous, which means the defamed person or organisation will be awarded financial damages, to be paid by the writer and/or publisher, for loss of reputation. When faced with the threat or potential threat of libel action, media organisations may well opt to err on the side of caution and refrain from publication, rather than risk the financial cost of a legal challenge.
- Obscene Publications: under the terms of the Obscene Publications Act (1959; 1964) it is an offence to publish (or knowingly distribute) material that will 'deprave and corrupt' its audience. When it was originally introduced, the Act served to effectively remove the risk of prosecution from any works for which any claim for literary merit could be made, as famously demonstrated in the 1960 trial of D. H. Lawrence's *Lady Chatterley's Lover*. More recently, the legislation has been interpreted fairly liberally and there have been few prosecutions. For example, pornography is not automatically deemed illegal under the terms of the Act, but is instead subject to specific forms of media regulation (e.g. Ofcom's *Broadcasting Code*, see p.45), or other general legislation (e.g. 'extreme pornography' (usually violent) is outlawed by Section 63 of the Criminal Justice and Immigration Act 2008).

- Official Secrets: hastily introduced amidst fears of German espionage in the years preceding WWI, Section 2 of the original (1911) Official Secrets Act made it illegal for anyone to knowingly receive and to further disclose, without proper authority, information classified as officially secret, whatever the nature of the information. The Act was the subject of considerable controversy during the 1980s when a number of high profile cases against civil servants highlighted the detrimental impact of the Act on media freedom. As a result, in 1989, the Act was reformed so as to remove the possibility of prosecution for the leaking of routine political information, but to make it easier to prosecute for revelations about intelligence work, defence, and foreign affairs. Since then, the Act has rarely been used.
- Terrorism: introduced in the aftermath of the London bombs on July 7, 2005, the Terrorism Act (2006) makes it an offence to publish a statement with the intention of directly or indirectly encouraging members of the public 'to commit, prepare or incite acts of terrorism'. The 2006 Terrorism Act also introduced offences of disseminating terrorist publications, covering all forms of electronic communication, including the internet. There are regularly 'successful prosecutions' under this legislation (CPS, 2022).
- Race Hatred: the first anti-incitement laws were passed in Britain in 1965 and have been revised on various occasions since. Under the current law – the 1986 Public Order Act (as amended by the 2006 Racial and Religious Act) – it is an offence to publish (or broadcast) threatening or abusive or insulting material either with an intention to provoke racial hatred or in circumstances where such hatred is likely to be stirred up by the publication.
- Copyright: the law against breach of copyright protects creative work that has been reduced to material form from being used by others without permission. The Copyright, Designs and Patents Act (1988), as amended following the incorporation of various European Union Directives into UK law, provides copyright owners (e.g. authors, musicians, etc.) with protection from the substantive copying of their works (without previous agreement or payment) for a typical period of 70 years.
- Privacy: Article 8 of the Human Rights Act (1998) declares that 'everybody has the right to respect for his private and family life, his home and his correspondence' (Article 8 (1)). Almost inevitably, this right has come into conflict with the right to 'freedom of expression' guaranteed by Article 10, most notably in the case of media organisations revealing aspects from the private lives of celebrities. In 2004 and 2018, respectively, the courts ruled in favour of the 'supermodel' Naomi Campbell (against the *Daily Mirror*) and Cliff Richard (against the BBC), which has led some critics to accuse judges of seeking to introduce a privacy law into Britain 'by the back door'.

While it is not our intention here to consider these areas of law in any great detail (for this see Rowbottom, 2018; Robertson and Nicol, 2007), two key points are worth emphasising in relation to the growth of online media in Britain. First, all of the general laws outlined in the previous list are applicable to online media and, if required, the law has been amended to ensure this is the case. For example, the Defamation Act was amended in 2013 to cover online communication and has subsequently been applied in a number of high profile cases, perhaps most notably, in 2017, when the outspoken right-wing political commentator, Katie Hopkins, was ordered to pay Jack

Monroe, a food writer and campaigner, £24,000 in damages, plus over £100,000 in court costs, following a public row on Twitter (Kennedy, 2017). Second, at the same time, it should be stressed that simply including online media within the existing legal framework that governs freedom of expression does not prevent subsequent widespread abuse of the law. For instance, a BBC survey on online piracy revealed that more than a third of football fans say they regularly watch matches live online via illegal streams (BBC, 2017). It is important, therefore, not to conflate the act of making something illegal with the prevention, or even effective limiting, of that behaviour. In the same way that laws on speeding do not prevent many, or even most, drivers from habitually exceeding the speed limit, so laws designed to prevent harmful communication do not necessarily prevent widespread breeches of the law online (see Chapter 11).

Media Content Regulation

The regulation of media content in Britain varies enormously between different sectors, ranging from the extensive regulation of traditional linear broadcasting to the absence of any specific regulation at all for most online media. While the underlying characteristics of different media technologies are clearly important in explaining such inconsistencies, they also reveal related political judgements over the balance between media freedom and the relative potential for different media to cause harm (to individuals and/or society). Perhaps most obviously, the absence of any statutory regulation for newspapers since the mid-19th century (beyond the laws of the land) flows from an underlying commitment to the principle of press freedom within British politics. The historical development of the press in Britain is often conceptualised, albeit over simplistically, as a struggle for freedom from the state and its attempts to exercise control through measures such as licensing and taxation – the so-called 'liberal narrative' of press history, which equates the arrival of press freedom with the removal of the final 'taxes on knowledge' in 1861 (Curran and Seaton, 2010: p.3). Consequently, while the conduct of the press, and particularly the popular press, has long been a source of public and political concern, successive British governments have shown little appetite to introduce specific laws to regulate newspaper content. Instead, the newspaper industry has been encouraged to regulate itself via various 'codes of conduct' overseen by industry led organisations, namely the General/Press Council (1953–1991) and the Press Complaints Commission (1992–2014). The extensive failings of this self-regulatory approach were laid bare by the phone hacking scandals of the early 2000s and the subsequent Leveson Inquiry (2012), but there remains limited political support for statutory regulation of the press. On the contrary, the widespread rejection of Leveson's call for the 'statutory underpinning' of press regulation by both politicians and the newspaper industry highlighted the continued sacrosanct status of press freedom in Britain (see Chapter 4).

Audio-visual media, such as broadcasting, film, and latterly videogames, have conventionally been deemed to require additional regulation because (rightly or wrongly) they are seen as inherently possessing a greater potential to influence and/or offend their audiences. For example, from the very beginnings of cinema during the early 20th century, moral and social reformers expressed concern about links between the new medium and juvenile delinquency (Williams, 2010: p.71). Partly as a result, since the early 1900s local councils have had the power to licence cinemas in their areas and may attach conditions to such licences. Most significantly, local councils normally require that all films shown carry a classification certificate issued by the British Board of Film Classification (BBFC) (e.g. 18, 15, 12, etc.). Consequently, the BBFC, which was established by the film industry in 1912 to provide guidance to local councils, has long been, in effect, the official censor of British cinema. Cinema films are therefore subject to special pre-censorship arrangements: 'a classification system operated by the BBFC that is in theory voluntary, but in practice insisted upon by local councils' (Robertson and Nicol, 2007: p.818). Following public outcry over the availability of so-called video nasties during the 1980s, the 1984 Video Recordings Act (updated by the 2010 Video Recording Act) effectively extended the BBFC's remit to include videos and DVDs. More recently, the growing sophistication of computer graphics has led to the implementation of a similar regime to oversee the publishing and sale of videogames, with games given a Pan European Game Information (PEGI) rating (i.e. 3, 7, 12, 16, 18) by the Video Standards Council. Failure to receive a BBFC or PEGI classification amounts to a ban on the sale of the product anywhere in Britain.

The domestic nature of broadcasting, sometimes even described as a 'guest in the home', has provided the rationale for the extensive regulation of broadcasting throughout its history (Ellis, 2007: pp.204–6). In Britain today, almost every area of broadcasting is subject to legal and regulatory oversight, chiefly via the 2003 Communication Act and Ofcom's (2020a) Broadcasting Code. The former sets out broad objectives for broadcasting services, known as 'high level standards', to ensure, for example, 'audiences are appropriately protected from harmful and offensive material', while the latter details a comprehensive set of rules that all licensed broadcasters are required to follow. Any breech of the Code may result in a fine, or even the revoking of the licence to broadcast. Ofcom's Broadcasting Code covers ten different areas: i) protecting the under-18s; ii) harm and offence; iii) crime, disorder, hatred, and abuse; iv) religion; v) due impartiality and due accuracy; vi) elections and referendums; vii) fairness; viii) privacy; ix) commercial references in television programming; and, finally, x) commercial communications on radio (Ofcom, 2020a). The Code can be traced back to the 1950s, following the introduction of commercial television (see Chapter 8), and has been regularly updated to reflect changes in public attitudes (e.g. on bad language), as well as new developments in technology and the broadcasting industry. Most significantly, since the 1990s, the Code has evolved to cover around 2,000, multi-channel television services, often targeted at diverse, niche, and/or multi-lingual audiences, as well as, in 2018, for the first time, an online linear television service – Amazon Prime, for its coverage of the US Tennis Open. Since 2010, the jurisdiction of the Code has also been extended to incorporate video on demand (VOD) services, such as Netflix, Amazon Prime, and All4. Finally, as part of more general changes to the regulation of the BBC, since 2017, licence fee funded BBC services (linear television and online) have also been subject to Ofcom's Broadcasting Code.

This does not mean to say, however, that all broadcasting services are regulated to the same degree. A distinction is made between services that are generally disseminated and those which are actively sought out, sometimes referred to as 'push' and 'pull' technologies respectively. Thus, whilst linear broadcast services (push technology) (BBC1, ITV, Channel 4, etc.) are fully subject to the Code, less restrictive regulations apply to subscription/pay-per-view services, as well as VOD services (pull technologies). For example, the 'watershed' regulation, whereby 'material unsuitable for children should not, in general, be shown before 2100 or after 0530' (Ofcom, 2020a, para.1.4), is a defining feature of traditional free-to-air linear broadcasting services, but for subscription services the watershed is 20:00 and there is no watershed for pay-per-view and/or VOD services, provided that 'mandatory daytime protection is in place', usually in the form of a PIN code protection. Furthermore, VOD services are also exempt from a number of areas of the Code, including the need for due impartiality and accuracy in news (Ofcom, 2018a: p.15).

While Ofcom's Broadcasting Code has been extended to cover some VOD services, most online media are not subject to any specific regulation, beyond the law of the land. Video-sharing services (e.g. YouTube), social media platforms (e.g. Facebook, Twitter, and Instagram), and search engines (e.g. Google), which direct users to online content, are not subject to any specific media regulation in Britain. However, over the last decade or so, as online media has grown in popularity, this lack of regulation has become increasingly controversial. Leading politicians have repeatedly called for social media providers to tackle the availability of harmful content on their platforms (e.g. material promoting terrorism, hate crime, self-harming, and/or suicide, etc.), or face legal intervention (see, for example, BBC, 2019). With little meaningful response from online media platforms, in 2018, the British government pledged to legislate for the introduction of a statutory 'code of practice' for social media, to cover 'the full range of online harms, including both harmful and illegal content' (DCMS, 2018). Although still to be enacted (i.e. formally made law), the subsequent (2021) Online Safety Bill proposes to impose a 'duty of care' on 'content sharing platforms and search services' to keep users safe from a range of 'harmful content' (e.g. explicit content, disinformation, etc.). The intention is for Ofcom to issue codes of practice outlining 'the systems and processes' that online services need to adopt for dealing with illegal and/or (potentially) harmful content (House of Commons, 2022a). Rather than attempting to directly regulate, or even remove, particular online content itself, Ofcom will then be responsible for overseeing the compliance of online services with its respective code(s). Under the terms of the Bill, Ofcom will have the power to issue fines of up to £18 million, or 10 per cent of a company's global annual turnover, whichever was higher, for non-compliance (DCMS and Home Office, 2020: p.73).

The regulation of online media in Britain is in a state of flux. There is broad consensus on the need to hold online media companies legally accountable for the content available on their sites. However, there remains much to debate over how to best regulate online media content without undermining freedom of expression and/or media freedom (see Chapter 11).

The Organisation of the Media Industries

Within media/communication studies, debate on how the media is (and should be) organised is often characterised as polarised between supporters of either classical political economy or critical political economy (Williams, 2003: pp.73–95). Underpinned by mainstream economic theory (see Chapter 2), the classical approach advocates free market competition as the guiding principle that ensures consumer demand (for news, entertainment, etc.) is met by a host of different media companies offering a range of different products. By contrast, critical political economy is built on the general critique of capitalism offered in the writings of Karl Marx. Writing around the middle of the 19th century, Marx viewed capitalism as creating vast disparities in wealth and opportunities within society. According to Marx, one of the defining features of the growth of capitalism was the ownership of the means of production (e.g.

factories, land, machinery, etc.) by a relatively small group of people (the 'ruling class'). This class would then use their economic power to further their own interests at the expense of the much larger working class (the proletariat). The economic power of the ruling class would extend to the ownership and control of the media industries, which, in turn, would be used to promote pro-capitalist views – the ideology of the ruling class – and to deride or exclude alternative or oppositional views or ideas (Williams, 2003: p.95). At the heart of critical political economy, therefore, is the belief that in a capitalist country, like Britain, the media reflect and serve the interests of those who have most to gain from the free market economy, chiefly big business.

However, despite their contrasting ideological roots, classical and critical schools of thought share very similar aspirations for the media industries. For proponents of classical/mainstream economics, the ideal to be strived for is 'perfect competition', where there are many buyers and sellers in an industry, who each possess minimal 'market power' (see Chapter 2). From the critical perspective, the work of the German sociologist, Jurgen Habermas, has proved particularly influential (Habermas, 1992). Habermas conceptualised the media as a (potential) 'public sphere' that is open and accessible to all groups and interests within society. For critical theorists, the 'public sphere' ideal provides essential criteria against which the performance of the actual media can be assessed (see Golding and Murdock, 2005). In this sense, classical and critical perspectives share an underlying commitment to 'media pluralism', which as a concept encompasses both diversity of ownership (i.e. the existence of a variety of separate media outlets) and diversity of output (i.e. varied media content) (Doyle, 2002). The key difference that remains between the rival schools of thought is over how to best achieve media pluralism, i.e. whether via the operation of the free market (classical) or through public intervention (critical). But, even here the divide is not always clear-cut. Within mainstream economics, it is widely acknowledged that most, if not all, industries are defined by 'market failures', rather than perfect competition (see Chapter 2). From this perspective, public intervention is often deemed necessary to either address particular concerns caused by 'market failures' (e.g. pollution), or promote competition, namely through competition law (see p.53). Equally, all but the most ardent proponents of critical political economy would acknowledge that commercial competition within the media industries often, if not always, provide audiences with increased choice and improved services (see, for example, Collins and Murroni, 1996).

Whether stemming from a classical or critical perspective on the political economy of the media, the key dilemma at the heart of the debate on the organisation of the media industries in Britain is therefore whether public intervention is required to promote/preserve media pluralism, or not (and, if so, what form should that public intervention take). To a greater or lesser degree, the media industries in Britain today have been shaped by ongoing debate on this issue. Most significantly, public intervention has had a significant impact in a number of key areas across various sectors of the British media industries, namely public service broadcasting, the promotion/protection of the British media industries and the regulation of media ownership.

Public Service Broadcasting

One of the defining features of the British media industries has long been (and remains) contrasting approaches to the organisation of traditional print media (newspapers and magazines) and broadcast media (radio and television). Since around the mid-19th century, British governments have left print media to free market competition, with the exception of some relatively minor restrictions on concentration of ownership (see pp.51–52). Alongside the absence of any specific regulation of content, unbridled commercial competition is an integral part of the liberal theory of press freedom that continues to guide the approach of most, if not all, British politicians to the newspaper industry. By contrast, from its very inception during the 1920s, broadcasting in Britain, first radio and later television, has been characterised by public intervention. Initially, this was at least in part due to the technological limitations of broadcasting, namely how 'spectrum scarcity' prevented the transmission of more than one, or a handful, of radio, or television, stations/channels without interference. 'Spectrum scarcity' necessitated (and continues to necessitate) the public licensing of (terrestrial) broadcasting services. However, alongside 'spectrum scarcity', fundamental concerns over the potential political and cultural impact of broadcasting also led the British government to support the organisation of broadcasting as a 'public service' (Williams, 2010: p.87; see Chapter 7). Public service broadcasting (sometimes also referred to as public service media in order to incorporate new online services) is a notoriously difficult concept to define, not least because its meaning has evolved over time (Scannell, 1990), but at its core it refers to a system of broadcasting that is publicly regulated and 'operated in a non-profit way in order to meet the various public communication needs of all citizens' (McQuail, 2010: pp.568–9). In Britain, during the 1920s, public service broadcasting began with the formation and licensing of the British Broadcasting Corporation (BBC). Established by the issuing of a Royal Charter, which has, together with a Licence to broadcast, been renewed at regular intervals of around a decade ever since, the BBC is publicly owned, but operates independently from government, and is (almost totally) funded via a licence fee paid by users. Since the 1920s, the BBC has been the cornerstone of British broadcasting, offering a range of radio, television, and latterly online services, which, in the words of the Corporation's first director-general, John (later Lord) Reith, 'inform, educate and entertain' British audiences (Higgins, 2014). Specifically, the BBC's current Royal Charter (2017) sets out five 'public purposes' to guide the provision of BBC services: i) to provide impartial news and information to help people understand and engage with the world around them; ii) to support learning for people of all ages; iii) to show the most creative, highest quality and distinctive output and services; iv) to reflect, represent and serve the diverse communities of all of the United Kingdom's nations and regions; and v) to reflect the United Kingdom, its culture and values to the world (DCMS, 2016).

The BBC's monopoly over British broadcasting ended during the 1950s with the introduction of a privately owned television service, Independent Television (ITV), which was funded via advertising and organised as a collection of regionally licensed services. In 1982, the BBC (1 and 2) and ITV were joined by Channel 4 (and S4C in Wales), a publicly owned, but commercially funded (via advertising), publisher-broadcaster, with a special 'minorities remit' to offer programming that caters for groups and interests not served by the established broadcasters. Finally, in 1997, Channel 5, a privately owned and advertiser funded channel, was launched with some, albeit relatively limited, public service requirements, chiefly in relation to the provision of children's programming. Albeit to varying degrees, public service obligations continue to be a legal requirement for each of these television broadcasters. Under the terms of the 2003 Communications Act, ITV and Channel 5 are required to provide 'high quality and diverse programming', whereas, reflecting its slightly different public service traditions, Channel 4 is required to provide a 'broad range' of high quality and diverse programming, but with a special emphasis on innovation, experiment, and creativity, on appealing to diverse cultural tastes, on programmers of an educational nature and on programmers that exhibit a distinctive character (Communications Act, 2003: s.265).

Whether public service broadcasters, and particularly the BBC, successfully achieve their goals in practice has always been, and continues to be, the subject of much public and political debate. Perhaps most notably, every decade or so, the BBC's Charter renewal process has provided the focal point for scrutiny of the Corporation's performance and debate on the future of public service broadcasting. For much of the postwar period, this debate was led by wide-ranging independent Parliamentary reviews (Beveridge, 1951; Pilkington, 1962; Annan, 1977; Peacock, 1986), but more recently British governments have tended to favour commissioning expert reports on particular issues or concerns (e.g. the Clementi report (2016) on the governance of the BBC). Most significantly, over the last couple of decades, criticism of public service broadcasting/ers has intensified (see Chapter 8). Much of the criticism has stemmed from proponents of a more free market approach to broadcasting (i.e. classical political economy), who argue that new technologies (e.g. digital and online) have ended 'spectrum scarcity' and removed the need for most, if not all, public intervention related to broadcasting, including the funding of the BBC via a compulsory licence fee, public ownership of Channel 4, and most of the programming restrictions imposed on privately owned public service broadcasters, ITV and Channel 5 (Booth, 2016). In response, supporters of public service broadcasting have stressed the continued contribution of the Corporation to 'our democratic and cultural welfare', ranging from impartial journalism to 'British story-telling, music, comedy, arts and children's programmes' (Barnett and Seaton, 2010: p.327). However, the impartiality of the BBC has increasingly been questioned by some who (from the critical political economy perspective) contend that BBC news coverage has always, and, with reference to the Iraq War (2003) and financial crisis (2008), continues to overwhelmingly reflect 'the ideas and interests of elite groups, and marginalis[e] alternative and oppositional perspectives' (Mills, 2016: p.6). There is little sign of an end to political debate over the BBC and public service broadcasting, but what is beyond dispute is that public service broadcasting has been and, for the time being at least, remains by far the most significant area of public intervention in the British media industries.

Promoting/Protecting British Media Industries

Albeit to nothing like the same degree as with public service broadcasting, a desire to promote British content and media production has also led to public intervention in various sectors of the media industries. Perhaps most significantly, from as early as the 1920s, fear of domination by Hollywood and the decline of British film production led to the introduction of quotas to support the British film industry. By the mid-1930s, 20 per cent of films exhibited in British cinemas were legally required to be 'British' films (Williams, 2010: p.76). During the 1950s, quotas were supplemented by direct financial support for the British film industry through the introduction of the Eady levy, which effectively required exhibitors to pay a levy on the price of each cinema ticket to British film producers. As part of their wider pro-free market agenda, the Conservative governments of the 1980s removed both quotas and financial support for film production, although public intervention continued to play an important role sustaining the British film industry via Channel 4. Financial support for the British film industry returned during the 1990s and 2000s as part of the Labour government's 'creative industries' agenda (Garnham, 2005). Together with other 'creative industries', such as fashion, the Labour government viewed the media industries as an increasingly important growth sector of the economy and a key source of future employment growth and export earnings. Against this background, in 2000, the UK Film Council was established to support the British film industry, most notably by the allocation of funds from the National Lottery to British film producers. As part of wider public spending cuts, in 2011, the UK Film Council was abolished, but National Lottery funds, now administered by the British Film Institute (BFI), continue to provide support for British film production. In 2016/17, the BFI allocated £60 million to British film-makers and over the last decade it has supported the production of British films, such as *The Girl with all the Gifts* (2016), *Brooklyn* (2015), and *The King's Speech* (2011) (BFI, 2018a: p.177). The 'creative industries' agenda also led, in 2007, to the introduction of a tax relief scheme designed to encourage film production in Britain. Under this scheme, by 2018, film production companies were able to claim a rebate of up to 25 per cent on up to 80 per cent of their expenditure for the production of British films. In 2016/17, this amounted to £415 million of public funding to support the British film industry (BFI, 2018a: p.177). During the 2010s, similar tax relief schemes were also introduced to support production in other areas of the media industries, namely 'high-end television' and 'animation' (2013), children's television (2015), and videogames (2014) (BFI, 2018b).

However, British government attempts to promote the British media industries have faced two significant problems. First, from the introduction of film quotas in the 1920s to contemporary tax relief schemes, how exactly to define a 'British film', or other 'British' media production, has been a complex and imprecise process. For example, to qualify for film tax relief requires a film to pass a 'Cultural test' and/or test/qualify as an official production, as well as fulfil a host of other criteria. According to at least some critics, such tests are not intended to assess the cultural (British) identity of a film, but rather to allow British film production facilities to compete with other countries for investment from Hollywood. As such, tax relief schemes intended to support British film (and/or other areas of media) production have been criticised for doing little more than benefitting already large, mostly US-based, media corporations at the expense of public revenue (Hesmondhalgh, 2019: pp.194–5). Following on from this line of argument, a second criticism of public intervention to support the British media industries is that while such initiatives may have some marginal value, they have done little to stem the domination of most sectors of the British media industries by a handful of mostly US-based media corporations.

Media Ownership Regulation

The case for media ownership regulation usually stems from fears over the possible negative impact of concentration of media ownership on the health of democracy. The chief concern is that concentration of ownership allows a handful of powerful media owners to limit the scope of public debate and/or even directly influence the result of a general election/referendum. British newspaper history provides plenty of examples of owners who have looked to exercise political influence in this way, ranging from the press barons of the 1930s, such as Lord Beaverbrook and Lord Northcliffe, to Rupert

Murdoch during the 1980s, 1990s, and 2000s. Murdoch has openly admitted that he instructed editors of his leading British tabloids, *The Sun* and the *News of the World*, on 'major issues', such as Europe, or over which party they should back in a general election (House of Lords, 2008: p.33). Furthermore, in the lead up to the 2003 invasion of Iraq, like their owner, with 'extraordinary unity of thought' every one of Murdoch's 175 papers worldwide supported the invasion: opinion opposed to the war was ridiculed and opinion columns were dominated by supporters of military action (Temple, 2008: p.137).

Whether biased news coverage in British newspapers can actually determine the result of a British general election/referendum has long been the topic of much academic debate (Kuhn, 2007: pp.213–25). Rather than the precise details of this debate, however, what is most important is the general perception held by many, if not all, British politicians that newspapers and particular popular tabloids, like *The Sun* and the *Daily Mail*, have the potential power to shape the political news agenda and thus influence voters. As a result, during the 1990s and early 2000s, Rupert Murdoch's newspaper ownership gave him considerable influence over British politics. Freedman (2008: p.106) details how Tony Blair's (new) Labour attempted to reassure Murdoch that they would not threaten his British media interests in return for favourable, or at least less hostile, coverage for the Labour party in Murdoch's newspapers. In a similar vein, following the 2010 general election, in his first year as Prime Minister, David Cameron met Murdoch, or his senior executives, on 27 separate occasions; and, he and three other government ministers had a total of 86 individual encounters with senior staff from News International – this at a time when the government was considering whether to permit Murdoch to further his British media interests by taking ownership of the part of Sky that he did not already own (Gaber, 2012: p.638).

As well as a threat to 'political pluralism', concentration of ownership in the media industries is also a potential threat to 'cultural pluralism', i.e. the need for a variety of cultures, reflecting the diversity within society, to find expression in the media (Doyle, 2002: p.12). For example, recent mergers between some of the UK's largest commercial radio companies (see Chapter 7) have led to increased reliance on relatively limited playlists (for music radio) and the replacement of locally produced and targeted programming with nationally networked content (Waterson, 2019a). However, in terms of 'cultural pluralism', the relationship between pluralism (of sources) and diversity (of content) is not always straightforward. Large (public or privately owned) media organisations are often best placed to provide the significant resources required to produce high quality and diverse content in areas, such as original drama (see Chapter 2). Paradoxically, therefore, some concentration of ownership may actually increase 'cultural pluralism'.

In 2014, a British government consultation document on media ownership declared that, '[s]uccessive governments have taken the view that plurality of the media is of central importance to a healthy democracy' (DCMS, 2014: p.8). In reality, however, regulations on media ownership in Britain 'have not been particularly stringent in either their substance or their application' (Kuhn, 2007: p.91). Despite a special clause in the general 1973 Fair Trading Act designed to prevent concentration of newspaper ownership, the 1980s and 1990s witnessed government approval for a host of major takeovers, including (Murdoch's) News International's purchase of *The Times* and *The Sunday Times* (1981); the purchase of *Today*, also by News International (1987); the acquisition of *The Observer* by Guardian Media Group (1993); and the acquiring of

The Independent by a consortium led by Mirror Group Newspapers (1994). In a similar vein, the 1990 Broadcasting Act (for the first time) set out specific ownership regulations to prevent the ITV network, then made up of 15 separate companies, from being dominated by a handful of the larger companies. During the 1990s and early 2000s, however, these rules were relaxed, or abolished, and following the merger of the two largest ITV companies, Granada and Carlton, in 2002, ITV became virtually a single broadcaster, ITV plc, with only STV in Scotland operating independently (Johnson and Turnock, 2005). The British government's approach to the regulation of cross media ownership has been similarly limited. The 1990 Broadcasting Act prevented national newspapers from owning more than 20 per cent of one licence within each category of national radio, terrestrial television (i.e. ITV) and 'domestic' satellite broadcasting (the 20:20 rule). However, this law was deliberately drafted so as to exclude 'non-domestic' satellite services, namely the Murdoch-owned Sky. As a result, it did not prevent Murdoch's News Corporation from expanding its British media interests from newspapers to pay-TV during the 1990s and 2000s (see Chapter 8). The 2003 Communications Act further reduced restrictions on media ownership, most notably facilitating Channel 5's takeover by Northern and Shell, the then owner of the *Daily Express* and *Daily Star*, and its subsequent (2014) sale to the US media corporation, Viacom.

In Britain today, the only specific legal restriction on concentration of media ownership is the 20:20 rule. This is supplemented by a 'public interest test', which was added to the Enterprise 2002 Act (via the 2003 Communications Act) following concerns raised about the government's deregulatory approach in the House of Lords, chiefly by Lord Puttnam (Hardy, 2014b: p.163). In the event of a significant media merger, the government can trigger a 'public interest test', to be carried out by Ofcom, and then, depending on Ofcom's advice, decide whether or not the merger should be submitted to a full investigation by the Competition and Markets Authority (see p.53), before making a final decision on whether, or in what form, the merger should be allowed to proceed.

Several key points are worth emphasising in relation to Britain's approach to media ownership regulation. The first is that the 20:20 rule is completely out of date and as such is of minimal value. The 20:20 rule was designed for (and during) an era when the media environment was dominated by traditional print newspapers and broadcasting. During the early 2000s, the British government argued that the growth of digital broadcasting and online media had increased the amount and diversity of content available to audiences to such an extent that there was less need for specific media ownership regulations designed to promote plurality (House of Lords, 2008: p.69). This view has proven simplistic and overly optimistic. For most British adults, a handful of traditional media organisations, including the BBC, ITV, and the *Daily Mail*, continue to be their most important sources for news, even if increasingly accessed online (Ofcom, 2022a: pp.18–22). At the same time, the growth of online media has also been accompanied by growing concern over the 'digital dominance' of popular online platforms, such as Facebook, and their use during elections to target particular groups of voters with tailored messages (Tambini, 2018). In 2014, the British government conceded that online media should be included in a more general update of British media ownership regulation (DCMS, 2014: p.6). However, to date at least, no update has been forthcoming. In part, this may be due to the practical difficulty of measuring media ownership in an online environment where traditional measurements, such as print newspaper circulation and television ratings, are no longer appropriate. As a partial solution, Ofcom has proposed the use of a combination of metrics, which, taken together, can be used to assess media plurality, namely i) *availability*: the number of different news sources available on each media platform and across all media; ii) *consumption*: measuring the use of different news sources across all media platforms; and iii) *impact*: using consumer research to assess the impartiality, reliability, and trustworthiness of news sources (Ofcom, 2015b). However, Ofcom's innovative approach to measuring media ownership has not removed a more significant barrier to reform, namely the lack of political desire from successive Conservative governments to tackle concentration of ownership. Ultimately, any decision (or non-decision) over the acceptable limit of media ownership in Britain is a political one about the balance between the free market and public intervention.

A second (related) key point worth emphasising about the regulation of media ownership in Britain is the inherently political nature of the 'public interest test'. As outlined on pp.51–52, whether due to a genuine commitment to free market principles, a desire to preserve British jobs in an ailing newspaper industry, or fear of the political influence of big media owners, British politicians have historically proven reluctant to intervene and prevent major media mergers. Recent examples suggest that the addition of a 'public interest test' has done little to alter this tendency. Most notably, in 2011, following a 'public interest test' the British government was 'days away' from approving News Corporation's proposed deal to take control of the part of Sky that it did not already own, only for the parallel events of the phone hacking scandal to prompt News Corporation to withdraw its bid (Hardy, 2014b: p.164). Following a 'public interest test', in 2018, the British government also approved the acquisition by Reach plc (owner of the Mirror newspapers, as well as a host of local newspapers) of the publishing assets of Northern and Shell, including the Star and Express newspapers.

Finally, it is also worth highlighting that, at least partly as a result of the limitations of Britain's media ownership regulations, general competition law is increasingly relied upon to safeguard media plurality in Britain. Stemming from the principles of mainstream economic theory, competition law is designed to promote a competitive marketplace (i.e. a high number of buyers and sellers). In Britain, the relevant laws are the 1998 Competition Act and the 2002 Enterprise Act, which focus on three key areas: abuse of a dominant position by a company; companies acting together as cartels to restrict competition in a marketplace; and mergers and acquisitions (Rodger and MacCulloch, 2009). Over the last decade or so, competition law, overseen by the Competition and Markets Authority (which replaced the Competition Commission and Office of Fair Trading in 2013), has played a prominent role within the television industry, most notably in relation to the position of Sky in the pay-TV market, as well as ruling on a host of mergers/acquisitions involving commercial broadcasters (Smith, 2013). Just as significantly, at the level of the European Union, competition law has also been the chief instrument used to tackle the market power of online-based media corporations, like Google and Apple. Since 2017, Google has been fined a total of €8.2 billion for abusing its dominant position in several different areas, including online advertising, the online market for shopping comparison sites, and the supply of the Android mobile phone operating system (Hern and Jolly, 2019). Whether the British competition authorities will prosecute anti-competitive behaviour from online media corporations with the same vigour now Britain is no longer a member of the EU is unclear. Even if it does, competition law should not be seen as a proxy for media ownership regulations designed to promote plurality. Within general competition law, the threshold of market share above which concerns are raised in relation to market dominance is typically within the range of 40–60 per cent (Hope, 2007: p.317). In all likelihood, advocates of media pluralism would (rightly) be concerned about a single company exercising control over a much smaller (or the total) share of a media market. Furthermore, while the application of competition law is often characterised by seemingly arcane debates over technical issues such as 'market definition' and what exactly constitutes abuse of a dominant position, this should not obscure the fact that the scale and scope of any public intervention to safeguard media plurality (and/or promote competition) remains a fundamentally political decision.

Conclusion

The media industries are shaped as much by political decisions (and non-decisions) as by the technological and economic characteristics set out in the previous two chapters. Whether it is the abuse of footballers online, the pay of BBC star presenters, or the influence of the *Daily Mail* on the government's policy agenda, the policy and/or regulatory response (or lack of response) from the British government is a product of political debate in the two key areas discussed in this chapter: first, the regulation of media content (freedom of speech versus protecting individuals/society); and second, the organisation of the media industries (free market versus public intervention). The sector specific detail (and history) of these debates are discussed throughout the rest of the book, but the 'big picture' to always keep in mind is that the media industries can be (and have always been) shaped by political choices underpinned by value judgements about the type of society we want to live in.

Part II
Media Industries

4   National Newspapers

National newspapers in Britain remain an extremely important part of the British media environment economically, politically, and culturally. Present in Britain since the 1620s, it's only in the last 100 years or so that what we now see as 'national' newspapers, produced in London and distributed across England, became dominant, after their circulations began to exceed those of provincial newspapers (Seymour-Ure, 1991: p.16). Whilst the historical development of the press from its origins is fascinating, and incorporates the origins of many of the national newspapers still operating today, there is only space here to highlight three key features, already significant by the time the national press became dominant in the 1920s, and which have subsequently shaped the national newspaper industry up to the present day.

First of these is a general antipathy to direct state control of the press. For the first 200 years or so of newspapers operating in Britain, the perceived potential power of the press as a challenge to authority saw statutory restrictions on printing and comprehensive licencing systems, called stamp duties, that severely limited press development to the point of risk of prison even for possessing a newspaper at times. By the early 19th century, however, political elites were embracing newspapers, often owning or subsidising newspapers aligned with their interests (such as the early years of *The Times*, founded in 1785). The systems of statutory controls on the press were not proving particularly effective, with many 'unstamped' newspapers reaching a growing working-class audience with radical political content, hence sometimes called the 'pauper press'. Political controls were increasingly seen as illegitimate within elite circles who saw that licensed, establishment newspapers were hampered economically from growing, and a campaign against these 'taxes on knowledge' eventually succeeded in getting duties removed by the latter part of the 19th century. That notion, of overt, political state intervention in the press being fundamentally wrong, has become ingrained in British society ever since, still influencing debates about the national press today such as those around the Leveson inquiry (see later in this chapter).

Second, after the removal of the stamp duties, newspapers were essentially left in a largely free market environment, and market forces began to dominate the late 19th-century press as it rapidly industrialised, and have done ever since (Curran and Seaton, 2018). Costs of production soared within a few decades, whilst cover prices began to fall dramatically, reducing per-copy sales revenue. *The Daily Telegraph*, its name a reflection of the latest technology of the day, launched in 1856 and was the first paper to sell for a single penny (Engel, 1996: pp.32–3). Although advertising had always been a feature of newspapers from their origins in the 17th century, it now started to become the principal source of revenue for many newspapers, and contributed to a gradual shift

DOI: 10.4324/9781315396781-7

towards the *popular* press for a mass audience. New newspapers in the late 19th century began to recognise, at least partly as a response to increasing reliance on advertising revenue, the commercial value of dropping or avoiding radical politics, though they often framed this as a response to presumptions of readers' interests. As one newspaper in 1888 proclaimed proudly, 'we believe the reader of the daily journals longs for other readings than mere politics' (in Engel, 1996: p.45). Audience interests in issues other than politics had always been a feature of newspapers, from accounts of witch trials in the 17th century, for instance, to the long term popularity of crime reporting (King, 2007) but it was at the turn of the 19th/20th centuries that this popular/populist approach began to dominate.

A third significant historical feature that remains prominent in the context of today's national press relates to the new owners who emerged out of the industrialisation of the press to make newspapers a powerful player in British political life. Alfred Harmsworth, later Lord Northcliffe, is the decisive individual behind the rise of the popular press, founding the *Daily Mail* in 1896, and in doing so bringing 'tabloid' journalism to Britain, and largely setting the template for journalism to this day (see Box 4.1). Alfred and his brother Harold (later Lord Rothermere) alongside William Aitken (later Lord Beaverbrook), and some others, were reaching millions of readers by the late 1910s and early 1920s. These new newspaper owners came to be dubbed 'press barons' as their significant circulations, from national (and regional) newspaper chains, gave them platforms for their strident, right-wing political views which they persistently used to criticise and challenge the elected governments of the day. Prime Minister Stanley Baldwin 1931 accused Beaverbrook and Rothermere of having 'power without responsibility' in their attempts to use their newspapers to push their political agendas. Rothermere, for instance, in the early 1930s used the *Daily Mail* to express support for the British Union of Fascists and later appeasement of Hitler's Germany. To the modern reader, tabloid newspapers offering strident support for right-wing political viewpoints should seem familiar, and in Britain this has long historical roots. Newspaper outlets for other political viewpoints existed in the run up to WWII, though, such as *The Sun*'s precursor, the left-wing *Daily Herald*, and the *Daily Mirror*, which having been sold by Rothermere moved to a more populist but left-wing stance that saw it reach around 4.5 million readers at its peak after the war (Engel, 1996: p.183). Nonetheless, concerns about national newspaper owners continue to echo down the years to the present day.

Box 4.1 Tabloid Journalism

Alfred Harmsworth coined the term 'tabloid' journalism, borrowing a medical term referring to medicines compressed or condensed into easily consumable forms (and essentially an amalgam of the words tablet and alkaloid) (Boston, 1999: pp.63–4). He was influenced by populist newspapers in the United States, and publishers like George Wisner, who said in 1835:

> News to be interesting must generally tell of wars and bloody fighting... of broken heads, broken hearts and broken bones, of accidents by fire or flood, wrongs inflicted, rights unavenged, feelings embittered, and oppressions exercised by nations, communities or individuals- especially individuals.

> (in Boston, 1999: p.66)

Tabloid journalism involves 'the use of the techniques of popular fiction – a method to reduce complexity with simple narrative devices' (Tulloch, 2000: p.138) in covering such themes. The gradual growth of a penny press in Britain in the 19th century was attracting critics, with the writer Matthew Arnold, for instance, dubbing this the 'new journalism' in 1887, 'full of ability, novelty, variety, sensation, sympathy, generous instincts; its one great fault is that it is feather-brained' (in Tulloch, 2000: p.139). Nonetheless, the appeal of such papers fit the changing times, as illustrated by T. P. O'Connor, founder of penny paper *The Star*, explaining their appeal in 1889:

> We live in an age of hurry and of multitudinous newspapers. The newspaper is not read in the secrecy and silence of the closet as is the book. It is picked up at a railway station, hurried over in a railway carriage, dropped incontinently when read. To get your ideas through the hurried eyes into the whirling brains that are employed in the reading of a newspaper there must be no mistake about your meaning: to use a somewhat familiar phrase, you must strike your reader right between the eyes.
>
> (1889/2005: p.365)

Harmsworth brought the approach to national newspapers, most successfully in the *Daily Mail*, with the first tabloid-size newspaper, with pages half the size of a broadsheet newspaper, arriving in 1903 with *The Daily Mirror*. Since then, the tabloid format of news has become pervasive, and shifted beyond newspapers into television and online news as well.

The Decline(s) of the Post-War Press

Since the end of WWII, Britain's national newspaper industry has changed markedly, and in a variety of different ways has arguably been in long term decline, though national newspapers continue to play a very significant role in Britain's political and media culture. Indeed, some aspects of the 'decline' of the national press have served to arguably heighten its political significance. Broadly speaking, the decline of the press since 1945 can be thought of as having three dimensions: the declining audience; the decline of Fleet Street; and the decline of standards.

The Declining Audience: From News-stands to Online Brands

Newspaper circulations continued to rise, even across print rationing during WWII, before national daily circulation peaked at 16.7 million in 1957 (Seymour-Ure, 1991: p.17). It has gradually declined ever since, more than halving, to around 7.6 million 60 years on (Mayhew, 2017). The leading daily in the mid-1950s was *The Daily Mirror* selling around 4.7 million copies per issue (Seymour-Ure, 1991: p.29), whilst by 2022 not one paid-for paper sold more than a million copies per issue. The decline of the national Sunday newspaper market is even more marked, going from a peak of 30.2 million per week in 1955 (Seymour-Ure, 1991: p.17) to just 5.3 million by mid-2017 (Mayhew, 2017). The leading Sunday paper in the mid-1950s was the *News of the World* selling around 7.9 million copies *on its own* at that time (Seymour-Ure, 1991:

p.31), with its replacement *The Sun on Sunday* leading the Sunday market with just over 1.2 million copies sold per issue in 2020 (Tobitt and Majid, 2022). These overall declines somewhat overshadow some variation in fortunes between the downmarket papers (or 'Red tops'), the mid-market, and the upmarket ('broadsheet' or 'quality' press). For instance, *The Sun*, a relaunch and rebrand of the old *Daily Herald* in 1969, competed directly with the market leading red-top *The Daily Mirror*, overtaking it in circulation by the late 1970s and remaining ahead ever since. In the mid-market, the *Daily Express* sold something like twice as many copies as the *Daily Mail* in 1945, but whilst the *Mail* managed to retain circulation, the *Express*' readership declined sharply in the post-war period, such that by the 1990s, the *Daily Mail* was the leading mid-market newspaper. Amongst quality newspapers there was actually a significant increase in audience from the mid-1950s to the 1990s, with the appearance of new titles (*The Independent* in 1986) and price-cutting in the 1990s that increased circulation of some titles (especially *The Times*). These are notable trends going back to the 1930s (Greenslade, 2003: p.94), possibly reflecting changes in education and literacy levels which have improved over this period (Sparks, 1999: p.58).

Since the beginning of the 21st century, declining circulations have hit all titles, and increasingly cast a shadow over the viability of the newspaper as traditionally understood, to the point where several organisations stopped publishing their circulation figures in 2020 and 2021 (Tobitt and Majid, 2022). The sale of actual physical copies of newspapers remained something news organisations cared about, at least until the Covid 19 pandemic hit, not least because of the significant costs of printing infrastructure. Around 5 per cent of claimed total circulations are made up of bulk sales, issues sold to companies like airlines and hotels, to be given free to customers, rather than individuals buying them (Ponsford, 2017a). Evidence suggests that readers of newspapers in physical print form spend more time reading them than in online or mobile formats (Thurman, 2014) making print readers, however reached, more saleable to advertisers. There is also the brand equity for newspapers being able to proclaim themselves the most widely read newspaper with the biggest circulation. Advertising revenues, perhaps surprisingly given the declining audience, actually rose for most of the second half of the 20th century (Meech, 2008: p.236), and whilst it has fluctuated in the 21st century with the rise of online advertising, it still accounted for 15.4 per cent of all ad spend in 2013, worth some £2.4 billion (Advertising Association, 2015: p.6).

Many reasons have been offered for the declining traditional newspaper audience overall. Perhaps the broadest of these have been significant lifestyle changes in the population. Just to pick one example, newspaper readership became closely tied to routines of working practices and commuting (newspapers being read on trains and trams as O'Connor said) but working practices have significantly changed with shifts towards commuting to work by car. Domestic routines like doing weekly shops at supermarkets, rather than more frequently at corner stores, have also impacted newspaper buying practices. Even for those who still use public transport, free newspapers have filled a niche once occupied by paid-for papers, particularly *Metro*. Perhaps by far the biggest contributor to declining newspaper circulations though has been the challenge of new forms of media. In the 1920s, the press lobbied effectively to limit the capacity of the early BBC radio to compete as a source of news, and otherwise saw it as a 'useful auxiliary' (Nicholas, 2000), with radio bulletins potentially prompting people to buy newspapers the next day to read more. By the time television arrived, however, the BBC had successfully asserted its independence as a rival for news, and there's little coincidence between the rise of television audiences and the decline of newspapers from the 1950s onwards, as television became dominant, with newspapers shifting ever more to vehicles of commentary and opinion as one response to this. The emergence of the internet has arguably created the most substantive multi-faceted layer of technological challenges for the traditional printed newspaper, and several approaches have been used in the response of newspapers to online platforms, built around systems of online reader payments.

Similar to perceptions of early radio, there was an initial view that putting content online openly for free might encourage people to buy physical newspapers. As audiences have built up online, and declined in print, digital advertising has become an ever more important revenue stream. Initially, online readers were not seen as valuable as print ones (Doyle, 2013b: p.14), relating partly to perceptions of the amount of time and degree of attention that online readers pay to advertising content compared to print readers (Thurman, 2014). One advantage of online readers though is so-called 'return path data', the range of underlying meta-data that is exchanged in every online action that tells organisations all sorts of information about consumers' details – for instance, precisely which articles people click on the most, what times of day, demographic details, and so on (Doyle, 2013b: p.14). As tools for providing targeted, 'algorithmic' advertising to particular groups of readers have developed, several UK-based newspapers have maintained predominantly free access to content. By early 2015, the *Daily Mail*, for instance, was reaching over 200 million people per month online, just under 14 million browsers per day (Baird, 2015), making it the English-language newspaper with the largest online audience in the world, a reach predominantly aimed at generating digital advertising revenue, necessary to generate useful returns (O'Reilly and Edwards, 2014).

At the other end of the spectrum is the use of paywalls, and wholly pay-for-access systems, centred on reader subscription services. Despite the name, this isn't really a new strategy, it's just reintroducing the notion of a reader paying for access to a newspaper's contents (Arrese, 2016) but in a context where many audiences expect, and some producers provide, content for free. The logic of paywalls is to secure a specific, consistent audience about whom the company gathers a great deal of data through subscription information, such that advertisers can be more easily attracted to the title, and thus revenues increase despite them leading to comparatively small online reach. *The Financial Times* (17 million per month in 2014, after a paywall was established in 2007) and *The Times* (5.4 million per month in 2014, after a paywall introduced in 2011), for example, are both much smaller than the *Mail*'s 200 million monthly users, but both of these outlets have proved profitable (O'Reilly and Edwards, 2014). User data indicates that for many newspapers, their online audiences are often predominantly internationally based, rather than UK based, and several papers have established online operations/editions based elsewhere in the world (like *The Guardian*'s Australian online edition) to improve that reach, given the potential for location-sensitive advertising revenue (Thurman, Hensmann, and Fletcher, 2021).

A variation on this is what is referred to as *metered* access: this is when, without paying, a reader can view a fixed number of articles in a given time period and is then invited to pay (either for individual articles or subscribe to the paper for a given period), an approach taken by *The Daily Telegraph* since 2013. Another has been to provide core content for free whilst then offering additional or premium content, including audio-visual content and live event coverage based on varying levels of subscription, like *The Guardian*'s Membership scheme (O'Reilly and Edwards, 2014). Given that online platforms place broadcast news and newspaper organisations directly in competition for audiences, newspapers have engaged in developing multi-media content production strategies in terms of content, just as broadcasters have developed text-based content production for their online output, creating issues of costs of new forms of production, pressures on journalists' workloads and required skillsets (Saltzis and Dickinson, 2008), alongside wider pressures around ever smaller production teams discussed later in the chapter.

A final model is a donor model, where readers are invited to donate money to support outlets. Much more prominent in the US, this has started to grow in the UK, to the point where *The Guardian* achieved a cash surplus in 2022, the first since 2008 (Tobitt, 2022). Aside from these strategies relating directly to readers for news content, the kinds of games, promotions, sponsorships, and side businesses newspapers began getting into in the television era have been enhanced in the online era as major areas of revenue, often run as separately paid-for services, such as *The Guardian*'s 'Soulmates' dating service (O'Reilly and Edwards, 2014), *The Sunday Times*' Wine Club, or *The Sun*'s fantasy football league 'Dream Team' (Doyle, 2013b).

The Decline of Fleet Street

The image of declining print circulation might suggest an industry in trouble, but the picture is more complicated than that, not just because of the complexities of newspaper brands moving online. In fact, national newspaper companies remained generally profitable into the 2000s (Franklin, 2008: p.13) and there are around the same number of national daily and Sunday newspaper titles today as in 1945. Symbolised by the move away from the national press' historic London home of Fleet Street, a name sometimes still used to refer to national newspapers collectively, the really consequential changes in terms of industry structures and organisation require a bit more unpacking. Fleet Street geographically links the financial centre of the City of London to the political centre of British politics in Westminster making it perfectly situated for newsgathering. Newspapers were continuously produced in Fleet Street from 1702, with the launch of the first daily newspaper, the *Daily Courant*, to 2016 when members of the London office of the Scottish newspaper *The Sunday Post* were the last to leave (Cacciottolo, 2016).

The decline of Fleet Street in the literal sense is linked to changes in relation to newspaper ownership in the post-WWII period. Almost immediately after WWII, the pre-war concerns about press ownership were reignited, particularly in the context of the predominantly Conservative press treatment of the Labour government elected in 1945. The First Royal Commission on the Press was established in the late 1940s to look at ownership, though in the end according to one critic it 'scarcely scratched the paintwork of a Press Lord's Rolls Royce' (Hennessy in Greenslade, 2003: p.48). In retrospect, with the first generation of Barons largely gone, and with several newspapers handed down to owners' sons, typically lacking their fathers' inclinations for authorial control, the first couple of decades after the war were a relatively quiet period in terms of owners (Tunstall, 1996: pp.82–3). Today, only the *Daily Mail* newspapers remain in the hands of one of the great press baron lineages (the Rothermeres).

The major problems in Fleet Street in the 1950s–60s were really linked to the newspaper workforce, and the changing market surrounding newspapers, particularly those whose political orientation were liberal or left-wing, which had always struggled commercially compared to right-wing populist titles. As mentioned, titles like the *Daily Herald* could reach millions but only amongst audiences that were distinctively unattractive to advertisers, and this situation worsened through the 1950s, with its predominantly male, working-class audience also getting older, and thus being ever less attractive to advertisers seeking new consumer markets (Greenslade, 2003: p.112). Compounding this was a lack of innovation and drive from newspaper companies themselves, which led to a spate of closures in the late 1950s and 1960s, such as the *News Chronicle*'s demise in 1960 (a liberal paper founded by the Cadbury family in 1930), generally put down to the failure of its management to properly identify and sustain a target audience (Greenslade, 2003: p.99). These closures (and some mergers) prompted a Second Royal Commission on the Press in 1962. Whilst the workforce blamed mismanagement and poor ownership for the sorry state of the industry, owners and editors blamed the increasingly important role of the trade unions, specifically print unions, in limiting the economic effectiveness of the industry, and the Commission broadly agreed (Greenslade, 2003: p.146). Despite recommendations for changes, the print unions would hold significant power over developments in the industry until the mid-1980s, even managing to close *The Times* and *The Sunday Times* for nearly a year between 1978 and 1979 in a dispute over pay and technology (Greenslade, 2003: pp.330–1).

The driver for change, and indirectly for the end of Fleet Street, came from arguably the most significant British newspaper owner since WWII (indeed, arguably the most significant media owner in Britain too), Rupert Murdoch. Murdoch entered the British newspaper industry in 1969, using money from a family newspaper company in Australia to buy the *News of the World*, and the *Daily Herald* re-launched as *The Sun*. Murdoch's approach is that of a 'media mogul' (Tunstall, 1996: p.85) rather than a traditional press baron, concerned less with owning a specific individual newspaper as a mouthpiece for his own views, and more on achieving market domination through mergers, buyouts, aggressive strategies against rivals, and achieving this across different types of media. To that end, moguls use politicians and political parties expediently, switching allegiance depending on who is currently in public favour. Predominantly right-wing and pro-free market, Murdoch's two tabloids strongly supported Margaret Thatcher's Conservatives, and Thatcher's government later supported Murdoch's highly controversial and much opposed takeover of *The Times* and *The Sunday Times* in 1984, leaving him with a share of over a third of the national newspaper market at that time. Murdoch's next step though was the real revolution that brought the end of Fleet Street. Prompted by the success of local newspaper owner Eddie Shah in legally defeating the print unions over the introduction of computer printing technology that allowed him to very cheaply launch a full colour national newspaper in 1986 (*Today*), Murdoch shifted his entire print operation of his News International papers overnight to a new site in Wapping, away from central London, using new printing and distribution systems. Violent picketing from now unemployed former print workers followed but Murdoch continued to have the backing of the Thatcher government, and his plans succeeded. The power of the print unions was essentially broken overnight, and in terms of Fleet Street itself, the nationals gradually began to move out, with editorial offices elsewhere in central London. A few operated out of floors in the Canary Wharf Tower (dubbed 'Float Street' by some), and printing and distribution centres gradually moved to outer London, or outside London altogether.

Although many at the time of Wapping dubbed this the 'death of Fleet Street' (Tunstall, 1996: p.18), the admittance of new technologies into the industry allowed a brief period of experimentation and new newspaper launches and optimism for a challenge to the established titles and their largely moribund nature. However, of several titles to launch in the wake of Wapping, only one survived in physical form into the 2010s, *The Sunday Sport*, a downmarket redtop also launched in 1986. *The Independent*, launched in 1986, and its later sister paper, *The Independent on Sunday*, went through several owners with print editions stopping in 2016, leaving online only editions, and a cut-down tabloid version called '*i*' remaining in print, having been successfully launched in 2010 (and bought by the *Daily Mail* group in late 2019). *Today* was eventually bought by Murdoch, and closed in 1995 to allow for expanded print runs of *The Times* and *The Sun* to meet increased demand in the wake of severe cover price cuts at the time. One trend for attempts to launch new newspapers, with varying success, has been in the Sunday market, some lasting very little time like the single issue of *The Planet on Sunday* in 1996, the slightly longer-lived broadsheet *The Sunday Correspondent* (1989–90), and various Sunday versions of existing daily papers, the most recent being *The Sun on Sunday*, a de facto replacement for the closure of *News of the World* in the wake of the Leveson scandal.

The most significant launch of the modern era is arguably *Metro* in 1999 by the *Daily Mail* group. It began as a metropolitan free newspaper, distributed via the transport network (given away in tube, bus, and rail stations) in London, and subsequently around many cities across the country. 'Freesheets' like this had been common in the UK at the local and regional level for some decades, their revenue coming entirely from advertising aimed at the captive market of residents getting newspapers through their letterboxes (whether they wanted them or not). *Metro*'s targeting of modern commuters, not only through distribution but in style and content, initially influenced by online news summary sites, has proved very popular with readers and subsequently therefore with advertisers too. As of 2022, it is the *only* newspaper publishing its circulation that now achieves over a million issues distributed per day (Tobitt and Majid, 2022).

Perhaps surprisingly in that context, attempts to launch more traditional paid-for newspapers continued into the 2010s with mixed success. *New Day*, an attempt at a paid-for tabloid newspaper a bit like *Metro* in style and form, was launched by Trinity Mirror (Reach since 2018) in 2016 but only lasted a few weeks after poor sales (BBC, 2016a). The strategy since then for Reach has been acquisitions rather than launches, in 2018 buying out Northern and Shell which had run the *Daily Express, Sunday Express*, and *Daily Star*, though to much less public controversy or attention than the activities of Rupert Murdoch. After the Brexit referendum in 2016, *The New European* was launched by a regional publisher as a newspaper aimed at the pro-European section of the population. Intended as a 'pop-up' publication available only for a very limited run of occasional issues, it has continued publishing as a weekly newspaper, albeit with a very small niche readership of around 20,000 going into the Covid pandemic and still surviving thereafter (Benton, 2021). A common feature linking many of these new paper launches since the 1980s has been for very small editorial teams compared to traditional newspapers. Despite long term and ongoing staffing cuts at national newspaper groups, the Telegraph Media Group, for example, still had around 500 editorial staff as of 2014 (Greenslade, 2014), whilst *Metro* had around 60 in 2017 (Ponsford, 2017a), and *New Day* had 25 in 2016 (BBC, 2016a). There were just three full time staff at *The New European* as of 2021 though its backers, and common contributors, include many big names from British media (Benton, 2021).

Declining Standards: Tabloidisation and the Regulation Problem

Arguably, the dominant theme of public, professional, and academic debates about the national press in Britain has been about standards. Falling circulations, competition from other media, price wars, reductions in production resources, and concomitant increasing demands on staff have all been seen to contribute to perceived declining standards. Against a backdrop of often interventionist proprietors interested in commercial imperatives over the public interest – or, more equitably, interested in influencing public opinion in what they think are the public interests of the country through strident political partisanship – perceptions about declining standards in the British press can generally be summed up in one word: *tabloidisation*. In a very simple sense, the evidence of this in the post-war period is pretty clear as the shift to a tabloid format is very easy to demonstrate, as shown in Table 4.1.

Table 4.1 The Post-War Shift to Tabloid Format

Title	Year Paper Became a Tabloid (italics = at launch)
The Sun	1969
Daily Mail	1971
The Sunday People	1974
Daily Express	1977
Daily Star	*1978*
Mail on Sunday	*1982*
News of the World	*1984*[1]
The Sunday Sport	*1986*
Today	*1986*[2]
Daily Sport	*1991*[3]
Sunday Express	1992
Planet on Sunday	*1996*[4]
Metro	*1999*
Daily Star Sunday	2002
The Independent	2003[5]
The Times	2004
The Independent on Sunday	2005[5]
i	*2010*
The Sun on Sunday	*2012*
New Day	*2016*[6]
The Guardian	2018[7]
The Observer	2018

([1] closed 2011; [2] closed 1995; [3]closed 2011 and relaunched online only 2011; [4] closed 1996; [5] moved to online only 2016; [6] closed 2016; [7] broadsheet until 2005, then Berliner format 2005–18),

The reluctance of the quality press to acknowledge a shift to tabloid format in the 2000s even as falling revenues demanded it, preferring the more sedate term 'compact', is an indication of how in Britain a tabloid newspaper has become a very distinctive and problematic entity (Cole, 2008: p.185). *The Guardian's* shift, in 2005, from a tabloid to a Berliner format – common in Europe but new to the UK, sized between a broadsheet and tabloid – similarly indicated the arguably tainted connotations of becoming a tabloid, though it finally succumbed in early 2018.

This shift to tabloid size is symbolic for what many have seen as a more general decline of standards, linked mainly to tabloidisation as also referring to style, tone, approach, and, crucially, *quality*. It's important to remember, though, that you could dip into almost any era of the British press and find somebody, somewhere, lamenting the appalling nature of newspapers, in terms of their sensational, salacious, invasive, and prurient nature. For instance, 'in 1932 the Bishop of Salisbury offered the very modern-sounding complaint that the "cheap press" dealt in "nothing except dirty sex affairs, murders and accidents" and was "a menace to the nation"' (O'Malley, 2013). What has increasingly distinguished the modern era from longer term historical concerns about press standards, alongside the pressures of competing for ever declining audiences, has been the confluence of three features of the legislative/regulatory environment of the press. These have arguably contributed to the direction of press form and style as well as contributed to the dominant focus of debates around press regulation in the 21st century being about standards rather than, say, ownership, or other factors. First, as indicated earlier in the chapter, since around the middle of the 19th century the notion of direct state intervention in the newspaper industry has become an institutional anathema. Even during WWII, for instance, whilst there was extensive censorship and control of information released to newspapers, the wartime government backed away from banning newspaper criticism of the war effort outright, banning only the *Daily Worker*, the paper of the British Communist Party between 1941 and 1942, and backing down after widespread parliamentary and public opposition to plans to ban *The Daily Mirror* in 1942 (Williams, 2009: p.136). So, the notion of state intervention in the fundamental operations of newspapers had become, and still remains today, a red line that no government is likely to ever try to cross.

Second, that might suggest that the press have enjoyed a real degree of solid freedom of operation, enabling them to challenge and criticise governments with impunity. However, it is a bit more complicated than that, particularly with regard to the handling of matters of national security. The press have been a component of official secrets legislation not least because government officials leaking information in the modern world have tended to do so either directly through the media, or releasing information that the media subsequently put into the public domain. The original Official Secrets Act of 1911 had a 'public interest' clause, enabling a defence that a breach of the Act could be justified if the information was in the wider public interest (e.g. evidence of government corruption say). The revised 1989 Act controversially removed the public interest clause after some damaging leaks from a civil servant about the Falklands War of 1982. A Freedom of Information law introduced in 2000 has been used by newspapers to produce genuine investigative journalism exposés, like the abuse of parliamentary expenses by MPs scandal of 2009 uncovered by the *Telegraph*, but the direction of travel in recent years has been for more legislation limiting access to state information. The emergence of sites like WikiLeaks in 2006, and the Edward Snowden case in 2013, which implicated many US allies' security agencies, including Britain's, in controversial mass surveillance activity, has led to renewed government efforts to control information flows across new media. The Investigatory Powers Act of 2016, for instance, gives wide-ranging powers for surveillance of private communications to the security agencies which raises significant concerns about the surveillance of journalists' investigations, and undermines the principle of the confidentiality of sources amongst other things, and has been widely condemned as a 'Snooper's Charter'. A review of the Official Secrets Act began in 2017, to consider whether the Act needed revision in light of the new media technologies influencing dissemination of public information, similarly has been criticised for its potential for further restricting investigative journalism further.

Whilst newspapers have continued to engage in investigative reporting in the context of public interest versus national/government security concerns, such as *The Guardian*'s involvement in the 2015 Panama Papers leak implicating large numbers of global public figures in widespread tax evasion/avoidance, this wider climate of restrictions around official information has arguably contributed to a largely quiescent press in this particular area, as shown by Defence and Security Media Advisory Notices or DSMA-Notices. DSMA-Notices are, as the name suggests, advisory rather than regulatory, so the press could breach them if they felt it was in the public interest. Sometimes mere agreements for embargoing information can be surprisingly effective, even without an official notice being issued, for instance in regard to Prince Harry engaging in active military service in Afghanistan in 2008, where all of the British news media agreed not to report his deployment until after his return from duty in exchange for access to him for subsequent stories, described by *The New York Times* as 'the secret kept by Fleet Street' (Stelter and Lyall, 2008).

The third aspect of the legislative environment that contributes to a concentration of standards relates as much to gaps in legislation as to specific laws. It wasn't until the arrival of the Human Rights Act in 1998 that rights around both press freedom and individual privacy were explicitly written into English Law (by incorporating the European Convention of Human Rights directly into English Law). These gaps sustained a large area of activity for the press which the popular, tabloid press in particular have exploited for a very long time. The absence of a specific privacy law, and reluctance for statutory intervention, has not left the press without any legal concerns in this area. The English law of defamation, for instance, puts the emphasis on the accused to prove they did not commit defamation – or libel in print/media contexts – rather than the accuser having to demonstrate how they were libelled (i.e. had their reputation damaged through untrue allegations or assertions). Not only has this enabled the rich and powerful to sue newspapers over stories about them they didn't like, the formulation of the law enabled people from all over the world to use the English courts to sue for libel regardless of the location of the accuser or accused, which led to London being regarded as the 'libel capital of the world'. Many Hollywood celebrities would often choose the UK to sue gossip magazines and newspapers over lurid stories about their private lives, for instance, though a change in the law was introduced in 2013 in an effort to stop this so-called 'libel tourism' (Nassetti, 2013).

The other main area of constraint on the press of relevance to the reporting of private citizens has been in terms of the reporting of court cases, in particular through Contempt of Court cases, whereby reporting is seen to detrimentally effect court proceedings, most typically in relation to high profile criminal cases but also in relation to other types of cases. Divorce cases were particularly big news in the late 19th and early

20th centuries, for instance, leading to eventual rulings on their reporting in the 1920s (O'Malley, 2013). Although these have on occasion proved costly to newspapers found to have committed libel (in one notorious case *The Sun* had to pay out £1 million to Elton John after fabricating a libellous story about him in the late 1980s (Engel, 1996: p.294)), neither of these aspects have particularly cowed the national press in continuing to report on public figures and high profile court cases, pretty much in whatever way they choose, with revenues more than able to absorb even large fines.

For public figures, recourse to legal action against newspapers has been and remains typically within their financial resources, but for ordinary citizens, those who featured in the press in a manner they didn't like, historically had little recourse but to appeal to the newspapers' editors or owners. But despite long standing concerns, it has proved very difficult to establish any truly effective system of self-regulation (by the press industry itself), with statutory regulation (by the state) often threatened but never realised. Over time, varying forms of self-regulation and avenues for complaint and redress for the public have been proposed. The first suggestion in the 1930s was the establishment of an independent tribunal, where complaints against the press, particularly about intrusions into privacy, would be judged, and this idea informed the First Royal Commission of the Press of 1949's decision to establish a General Council of the Press (GCP), whose very first case, perhaps presciently, concerned reporting of the Royal family (Tunstall, 1996: pp.394–5). The GCP was significantly hampered, however, as it was peopled entirely by figures within the newspaper industry, was funded by the industry, and was a voluntary organisation – only newspaper owners' goodwill in participating enabled it to function at all. The Second Royal Commission on the Press in 1962 recommended the Council's membership be opened up to non-press figures, and whilst this gave a veneer of greater independence, the funding and voluntary nature of the body continued to largely undermine its value as a check on press standards (Tunstall, 1996: p.396). A further problem was that it had no real powers of redress – even if a complainant won an adjudication against a newspaper, the most that could be expected was a measly published apology from the newspaper in question, with no incentives to give that apology the same prominence that the offending story may have garnered, and no powers to impose financial penalties either.

By the 1980s, with declining circulations, Murdoch dominating a large section of the press, and other new media moguls (like Robert Maxwell at *The Daily Mirror*) running their papers in a highly competitive manner akin to Murdoch, the push for sensationalism, scandal, and intrusion continued to accelerate and 'some tabloids went through a sort of Wild West stage' (Greenslade, 2003: p.534). The private lives of public figures, especially the Royal family, politicians, and media celebrities, had long become the meat and drink of much tabloid journalism, and newspapers were confident about using a variety of nefarious tactics in obtaining stories (rummaging through celebrities' bins, long-lens photography, using disguises to get into hospital rooms), and even in publishing large splashes on hearsay, innuendo, and rumour. By the start of the 1990s, the Conservative government – itself having been subject to a series of salacious kiss and tell stories about a number of its ministers – had had enough, and set up the Calcutt Commission in 1991, which abolished the Press Council, replacing it with a Press Complaints Commission (PCC) which would draw up a Code of Ethics, but otherwise remained a self-regulatory body funded by the industry, still with little means of requiring redress from newspapers. Almost immediately after the PCC began, however, another series of typical tabloid sex and scandal stories provoked the government to reconvene the Calcutt Commission and the second report of 1993 recommended a statutory Press Tribunal be established, with clear powers to compel newspapers to apologise and compensate successful complainants, though these recommendations were rejected by the government (Tunstall, 1996: pp.403–4).

A minor sea change occurred in the wake of the death of Princess Diana in 1997, an immensely popular public and media figure who died in a car crash being pursued by paparazzi photographers in Paris. Public outrage at press extremes saw a tightening of the PCC's code of practice, and a relative period of restraint, enhanced by the introduction of the Human Rights Act in 1998, and its privacy provisions. Given the costs and risks of taking large organisations to court, however, it remained public figures who began to take newspapers and magazines to court over privacy violations. A series of cases from the late 1990s onwards saw a precedent over the limits of press intrusion begin to emerge, criticised as a back-door route to a press privacy law (Rozenburg, 2011). One tactic developed by the rich and famous – and way beyond ordinary people to even contemplate – was, on hearing of possible salacious stories being planned by newspapers about them, to appeal to the courts to block publication of information through so-called super-injunctions (or gagging orders). Through the last decade, the extent of super-injunction use, and then much of that information creeping out on online social media anyway, has highlighted significant imbalances between the legal and regulatory frameworks surrounding different types of media, and attitudes about the privacy of public figures have often been split (Campbell, 2004).

The issue around press standards with the biggest continuing impact to the time of writing came to light in 2011, and led to the Leveson Inquiry of 2011–12, the findings and recommendations of which have dominated debates around press regulation ever since. The circumstances that led up to the Inquiry initially began in 2007 when one former Royal correspondent was jailed, and several other journalists resigned or were sacked at the *News of the World*, after it was discovered that they had used private information recovered from the mobile phones of subjects of their stories, using a private investigator who hacked into public figures' voicemail accounts. This had been pretty scandalous itself but had been largely seen as an isolated and extreme example of tabloid excesses. The then editor of the paper, Andy Coulson, resigned only to resurface a few months later as Director of Communications for the Conservative Party. In 2011 – after ongoing police investigations into those who had been hacked led to successful civil suits pursued by celebrities, and which had already led to Coulson resigning as Director of Communications for the by then Coalition government – evidence entered the public domain that the hacking of mobile phones had apparently been a systematic and widespread practice at the *News of the World*, as well as likely at other newspapers too, and not just of public figures like Royalty, politicians, and celebrities, but also ordinary members of the public. The key incident was the case of teenage murder victim Milly Dowler. Milly's disappearance in 2002 led to front page news and, it was alleged by reporters at *The Guardian* (who were investigating the extent of phone hacking by tabloid newspapers) in early July of 2011, whilst the search for the girl was still ongoing, journalists at the *News of the World* hacked her phone, in the process deleting messages which gave the impression to her distraught family and investigating police that the girl might still have been alive. It later turned out that it wasn't conclusively possible to blame the journalists for the deletion of messages which might have occurred as a result of the voicemail's automated system (Davis, 2014) but that case was the final straw in an ever-growing national scandal around press practice.

Within a few days, Rupert Murdoch and his son James (chairman of News International, the subsidiary of News Corporation responsible for the *News of the World*) announced the closure of the paper, Prime Minister David Cameron announced the establishment of a public inquiry, Andy Coulson was arrested as was News International CEO and former editor of the *News of the World* at the time of the Dowler case, Rebekah Brooks, and the Murdochs appeared before a televised session of the Culture, Media and Sport Select Committee investigating phone hacking (and where Murdoch senior received a cream pie in the face from a protestor). Details of the close personal relationships between Coulson, Brooks, Murdoch, and Cameron, as well as questions about the possible complicity between journalists and the police in high profile criminal cases, gave Lord Justice Leveson, appointed to lead the inquiry, a wide-ranging brief of issues to address. The first part of the Inquiry (2011–12) had sessions covering these areas in terms of the overall 'culture, practices and ethics of the press', whilst a second part was due to look more specifically at unlawful/improper conduct at News International, and press/police relations, after all related criminal cases were concluded.

What arguably made the difference between Leveson and earlier Commissions and Inquiries was that it wasn't just politicians or elites bringing concerns about press standards that were at the centre of the inquiry. Victims of phone hacking, and those concerned about press standards, organised themselves into a pressure group called Hacked Off. Celebrities like film star Hugh Grant gave articulate and impassioned witness testimony to the inquiry about their treatment by the press, but extra weight came from the testimonies of non-celebrities like the mother of Milly Dowler. The recommendations of the Leveson Inquiry, though distinctive, reflect the long standing problems with the regulation of press standards in Britain (Barnett and Townend, 2014), particularly in their reception and, to date, essentiality failed implementation. Leveson recommended that the PCC should be replaced with an independent self-regulatory body with a new code of conduct that had more power to fine and direct the prominence of corrections and apologies, but also that this new body should be backed by legislation to give it the independence, status, and power to effectively deal with complaints against the press. Additional to this was the idea of further incentivising membership of this regulatory body by indicating that non-members would be open to exemplary damages in cases brought to the body. Prime Minister David Cameron, like many of the national newspapers, was opposed to a regulator based on new legislation, despite widespread support for the recommendations both within and outside Parliament. After months of negotiation, a plan was proposed for any prospective press regulatory body to be scrutinised and approved by a Press Recognition Panel under a Royal Charter, thus making the body have legislative status but not directly under governmental or parliamentary control. The financial incentive component required the activation of Section 40 in the Crime and Courts Act of 2013, which would impose financial penalties on non-members who would have to pay the costs of both sides of any libel/privacy court case, whether they won or not. These solutions were warmly welcomed by Hacked Off whose members argued it offered 'the best chance in seventy years of raising the ethical base of journalism while safeguarding freedom of expression' (Cathcart, 2016: p.11). Much of the national press opposed the recommendations, arguing that either self-regulation intrinsically was more appropriate (e.g. Lloyd, 2015) and/or that improved standards would result from greater levels of journalism training (e.g. Luckhurst and Phippen, 2014). The industry essentially went its own way, establishing a new industry regulatory body, the Independent Press Standards Organisation (IPSO), seen by critics as simply more of the same kind of problematic system that existed before. In 2016,

IMPRESS (Independent Monitor for the Press) achieved Royal Charter status, but failed to attract membership from the main national newspaper organisations, not least because of questions around the financial backing from Max Mosely, a former president of the international motorsport organisation (the FIA) who lost that job following a tabloid story about his participation in an orgy. Mosely took a case to the European Court of Human Rights in 2009, trying to legally require newspapers to warn subjects of stories in advance of publication, which was unsuccessful because it was seen that the proposal amounted to a form of pre-publication censorship. For other critics of the Leveson proposals, beyond the national press themselves and their 'longstanding resistance to accountability', as one critique puts it (Thomas and Finneman, 2013: p.172), the system proposed represented a backdoor form of state regulation, significantly curtailing independent, investigative journalism, particularly around what kinds of outlets are constituted as news in an era of hyperlocal and citizen journalism (Hume, 2013).

As with previous efforts at resolving issues around press standards, the problems of implementing Leveson have seen the issue gradually overshadowed by other political issues. Amidst the post-Brexit turmoil that has led to a rapid turnover of governments, and Prime Ministers, Conservative governments, led by Theresa May (2016–19) and Boris Johnson (2019–22), have consistently tried to kill off both section 40 and Leveson part 2. The Cairncross Review of 2018, looking at issues around the maintenance of high quality journalism, was largely rejected in terms of its views on press regulation (DCMS, 2020). Dozens of civil cases regarding phone hacking continued across the 2010s with *Mirror* and *Express* owner, Reach, for instance, building a compensation fund of £70 million by the end of 2018 (Mayhew, 2019). Revelations from the scandal continued to emerge as well, such as claims that the *Sunday People* may have hacked Milly Dowler's phone (Coleman, 2020), making it the issue that just won't go away.

Conclusion

The hacking scandal highlighted how newspapers as brands, and as controversial agenda-setters for public debate, continue to be a significant component of Britain's media landscape, even as their physical sales plunge ever further in the wake of the Covid 19 pandemic. The failure to resolve the regulation issue highlights the long term institutional and ideological role the notion of a 'free' press holds in British society, even whilst concerns about ownership, commercialism, declining standards, and other kinds of communication legislation bring genuine boundaries to press freedom. Newspaper brands today, not least by competing with online alternatives on the same platforms, are increasingly adopting the strategies of online and social media sites, looking for 'click-bait' headlines, strident and emotive partisanship to generate controversy, attention, 'shares', and 'likes'. The long term paradox of a national press, or at least sections of it, remains: at the same time being widely condemned and vilified by the public deserting printed newspapers in their droves, whilst also remaining at the centre of national debate and public life. Contributing to and arguably shaping national issues and events, such as debates around immigration, general election campaigns, and the Brexit vote of 2016, the prominence of newspaper brands looks set to persist for some time to come yet, particularly given their parallel strategies of searching for international audiences and online revenues in the pursuit of becoming global news brands.

5   Magazines

When it comes to scholarly discussions of British media industries, magazines are very much a poor relation compared to the national newspaper industry (McKay, 2019: p.5) despite them arguably being 'the most successful media format ever to have existed' (Holmes and Nice, 2012: p.1). In existence as a form for more than 300 years, there are literally thousands of magazines published in Britain, from British editions of global magazine brands, like *Vogue* and *Cosmopolitan*, to niche trade titles barely reaching circulations in four figures. Some of the reasons for this rather marginalised academic focus are, in and of themselves, interesting from the perspective of thinking about different media industries, their historical developments, structures, and so on. The scholarly fixation on newspapers and broadcasting doesn't always help the student of Britain's media to get a sense of, for instance, how political, economic, social, and cultural factors combine to shape media industries in specific ways. To illustrate this, it's certainly at least partly the case that the relative marginalisation of magazines in academic discussions about the British media industries comes from peculiarities of the British magazine industry itself. Whilst in many other countries news magazines have been prominent parts of the media landscape for many decades, like *Time* in the US, *Paris Match* in France, or *Der Spiegel* in Germany, and continue to sell in the hundreds of thousands (or millions in the case of *Time*), general news magazines have not been a prominent feature of the British media landscape in the modern era. The predominance of the national press since the 1920s or so, including a distinctive strong Sunday national newspaper market, has largely precluded a market niche for general news magazines in Britain, unlike other countries where newspaper markets haven't become quite so centralised and national in character. So, when writing about media in the context of politics and democracy in Britain, magazines superficially appear to offer less obvious avenues for investigation and critical attention. Indeed, they have often been rather pejoratively dismissed as objects of serious scholarly attention in the context of discussions of journalism (Holmes and Nice, 2012: p.2). The very existence, however, of popular, general news magazines in other countries shows that it's not something essential to the nature of magazines as a media form to be largely devoid of political and news-oriented content. Moreover, even to the extent that most magazines aren't predominantly political, the politico-economic and socio-cultural significance of magazines demonstrate their continuing importance to understanding the media landscape, and the practices and forces operating within it (Campbell, 2004: p.221). There are aspects of the magazine industry that at least are partly related to the nature of the medium, but it's important to remember that industries emerge and develop in relation to each other within particular politico-economic and socio-cultural contexts, resulting

DOI: 10.4324/9781315396781-8

in distinctive characteristics within each industry sector, and the British magazine industry is no exception, as this chapter will show.

Some of the most significant work in the whole of media studies has actually focused on magazines, especially women's magazines and 'lifestyle' magazines. Such work, broadly speaking, has centred on two really important aspects of media. First, the issue of representation, how the media represents events, issues, and people, is very prominent. Much of this research is concerned with gender representation and sexuality (Ferguson, 1983; Winship, 1987; McRobbie, 1991; Gough-Yates, 2003). Second, and often linked to the issue of representation, has been an interest in media audiences, partially from a concern around effects (i.e. do particular kinds of representations of, say, women, influence how readers view women in society?) and then more broadly in terms of how audiences interact with, interpret, and negotiate media content. So, for instance, some of the key work looking at magazines and comics aimed at girls and young women examined the relationship between apparent patterns of conservative stereotypical representations of women in those titles and reader responses (Ballaster et al., 1991; Hermes, 1995). Such research tended to find that whilst patterns of representation have been, to say the very least, problematic, audiences were more interrogative and critical than many researchers expected, recognising representations as stereotypical, unrealistic, undesirable, and so on. Nonetheless, this tension between representations that even readers recognise as problematic, and magazines' continued popularity in spite of this, remains a point of debate for scholars (Holmes and Nice, 2012). The issue of gender representation in magazines has not just been a matter of scholarly interest either, on occasion becoming a focus for national political debate as well, as the 'lose the lad mags' campaign illustrates, which we'll discuss later in this chapter.

The political economy of the magazine industry is comparatively under-considered in academic work, despite occasional acknowledgement of its significance for other sectors (Holmes and Nice, 2012: p.2). Where it does get mentioned, in broad terms the dominant perception (whether explicit or implicit) is that market imperatives negatively shape patterns of representation and reception by reproducing and reinforcing the dominant ideologies of liberal capitalist society (e.g. patriarchy, heteronormativity, consumerism, etc.). At the other end of the spectrum of academic literature on the magazine industry are texts largely aimed at explaining and instructing those trying to get jobs in it, offering discussions of wider industry structures as part of discussions more focused on working principles, practices, and organisation of magazine publishing (Stam and Scott, 2014), magazine journalism (Holmes and Nice, 2012), or the industry as a whole (McKay, 2019). Yet precisely how market imperatives have created the distinctive structures in the magazine industry – and why they're distinctive from, say, the newspaper industry or broadcasting or online media, etc. – are rarely the central focus of discussion even in these kinds of texts. Consideration of the particulars of magazine industry structures help to shed light on a more nuanced and detailed evaluation of the sector, as well as generating interesting questions about fundamental issues within media industries more generally. To get into that detail, however, we need to start at the beginning with the thorny problem of defining a magazine.

Defining Magazines

The use of the word magazine to describe a printed publication in English has a specific origin, with the launch of *The Gentleman's Magazine* in 1731 (Stam and Scott,

2014: p.10). Derived from the French for warehouse or store, *magasin*, publisher Edward Cave regarded it as an appropriate description of the content of the title – a mix of material covering all sorts of issues that the 'gentleman' of the time might be interested in, from politics to poetry. It was also notable for being a publication that Samuel Johnson, author of the first definitive English dictionary, regularly wrote for. Some aspects which have come to broadly typify the distinctiveness of magazines from newspapers, it is generally agreed, originated before *The Gentleman's Magazine* first appeared. For example, *The Ladies Mercury*, appearing in 1693, is usually credited with being the first women's magazine in all but name (Holmes and Nice, 2012: p.3; Stam, 2014a: p.9). What both of these titles demonstrate that continues through to modern magazines of today are two distinctive characteristics: *miscellaneous content* focused on the interests of *specific, targeted readerships.*

In terms of miscellaneous content, from their earliest days, magazines have explored content beyond general interest news, and have tended to mix kinds of content structured around the perceived/identified interests of target audiences. Back in the 18th and 19th centuries, there weren't necessarily significant differences in publication frequencies between newspapers and magazines, aside from the emergence of daily newspapers. A focus on miscellaneous content, that might include some current affairs related material, but also include fiction, poetry, educational features, reader question and answer sections, and so on, created less pressure, in terms of audience demand, for newspaper-like publication frequency. Typically, magazines today are far more likely to be weekly or monthly than daily, but there are weekly newspapers, of course, and since the launch of *The Sunday Times Magazine* supplement in 1962, many newspapers today provide magazines, either in literal form at weekends, or in terms of content sections of daily editions. There are also magazine-style television programmes like the BBC's *One Show*, which is broadcast on consecutive week-nights, demonstrating that it is the mix of content types that is a key feature of the magazine format.

The second dimension here is the notion of a specific, targeted audience and, crucially, responding to their interests – giving them what they want. National newspapers have a degree of paternalism underpinning them – in other words, a notion of what their perceived audiences *need* rather than *want*, and those needs are linked to perceptions of a general, public interest, rather than things of interest to specific groups. That also underpins the discussion of the last chapter around newspaper standards; a shared but often implicit notion that newspapers are serving (or failing to serve) some kind of higher civic purpose for society as a whole. For much of the early period of magazine publication, when the distinction between a newspaper and a magazine would not necessarily be particularly obvious to a modern reader, there was, however a dimension to early magazines' purpose that might be characterised as being about preparing individuals for civil society (Calcutt, 2014: p.132). Titles like *The Gentleman's Magazine* or *The Lady's Magazine* (launched in 1770) provided a range of contents that served as a kind of social education for the elite classes. Calcutt points to the social value of reading *The Gentleman's Magazine*, for instance, resulting in a gentleman having 'something to say to Jane Austen's ladies, his successful appearance on the social scene being dependent on the entrée afforded not so much by aristocratic title as by this magazine title' (ibid.).

The wider general notion of social improvement and enlightenment became a significant feature of the Victorian era, perhaps typified by the *Penny Magazine*, launched in 1832 by the Society for Diffusion of Useful Knowledge (King and Plunkett, 2005).

Calcutt suggests that, in the 19th century, as the magazine market began to significantly grow 'magazines mainly enabled their readers to cultivate themselves: to perform the part expected of them in the progressive development of the individual' (2014: p.133). Yet, through the 19th century, a (what is now rather familiar) debate about the social impacts of new media forms began to emerge around the tensions between these notions of social and civic improvement and the trends being driven by audience demand. Charles Knight, for instance, publisher of the *Penny Magazine*, wrote at length refuting concerns over perceptions of cheap, mass circulation magazines as being of little quality (King and Plunkett, 2005). By the latter part of the century, it was aspects of popular magazine publishing that underpinned, both financially and in terms of editorial style, the establishment of the modern tabloid press. The success of George Newnes' *Tit-bits*, launched in 1882 and rapidly reaching hundreds of thousands of readers, and which literally comprised of bits of material taken from other publications, inspired Harmsworth's similar *Answers to Correspondents* (launched 1888), which provided the funds to launch the *Daily Mail* a few years later (Gough-Yates, 2010: p.155). Newnes is perhaps less well known than the man who became Lord Northcliffe, but is just as pivotal in the growth of the British magazine industry, and is arguably responsible for the first glossy magazine (see Box 5.1).

Box 5.1 Glossy Magazines

The earliest magazines were largely indistinguishable from newspapers in terms of their physical appearance but gradually, through the latter part of the 19th century, the intersection between technological developments and social trends led to the emergence of the 'glossy' magazine that we know today. As technologies to reproduce images, colour, and photographs emerged through the 19th century, magazines were regularly amongst the first to try to apply these technologies in periodical publication, and in turn drove these technologies' developments further. For a time, newspapers like the *Illustrated London News*, launched in 1842, dominated the market for image-based publications. The tipping point seems to have been when publishers started to see returns on investing in high quality paper for what were otherwise very niche magazines. *Racing Illustrated* and *Navy and Army Illustrated*, launched in July and December of 1895 respectively, were claimed by their publisher to be matching the circulation of well-established titles like the *Illustrated London News* within a few months of launch (Reed, 1998: p.265). When considering these titles' apparent success against failed magazine launches around the same time, 'the one really noticeable difference was in the paper quality' (ibid.: p.266). Newnes bought up *Racing Illustrated* in 1896 and relaunched it as *Country Life Illustrated*, using high quality paper and reproduction techniques across the whole magazine with editorial content and advertising treated the same, and offering what was arguably the first glossy magazine, still going today as *Country Life* (ibid.: p.267).

Today, there are clear distinctive brackets of magazine paper, such as super-calendered paper typically used for magazines with high print runs like weekly TV listing magazines, and lightweight coated paper which gives the glossy sheen to the pages of monthly magazines that will typically also have covers with a UV varnish coating, giving them that distinctive gloss look (Stam and Scott, 2014: pp.251–2). As to why readers seem to prefer glossy paper, aside from the quality of image reproduction offered, one intriguing suggestion is that our evolutionary need for water is being triggered by the sheen of glossy things that are reminiscent of the sheen of wet surfaces and bodies of water (Meert, Pandelaere, and Patrick, 2014). Whilst it might seem a trivial component compared to more obvious aspects like editorial content, or even cover design (McKay, 2019: p.215), the evolution of paper types used in the magazine industry illustrates the point made by Gillespie, Boczkowski, and Foot (2014), referred to in Chapter 1, that there has been a tendency to ignore these kinds of aspects of media production to the detriment of an in-depth understanding of media industries.

Through the 19th century, differences between newspapers and magazines began to become ever more concrete in terms of focus, essentially a distinction 'between newspaper journalism published primarily in pursuit of political interests, and magazines published in response to individual concerns, especially those of a domestic nature' (Calcutt, 2014: p.133).

Whilst much has changed both socially and culturally since the Victorian era, this notion of the use of magazines as a resource for essentially socialisation, alongside the pursuit of personal interests, remains a common underpinning of many magazines, particularly the groups of modern magazines that, since about the 1960s, have been referred to as 'lifestyle' magazines (Campbell, 2004: p.221). As Braithwaite puts it, today, the 'very nature of magazine editorial is to associate itself with *lifestyle*, or the mode of living of the sort of reader it seeks to attract' (2002: p.113, emphasis added). Similarly, whilst the decline in national newspaper readership has generated much concern about the possible consequences of an associated declining interest in political affairs (as discussed in the last chapter), that the magazine industry has, by comparison, remained robust and adaptive to change across the same time period might also be a reflection of the continuing importance of self-development, socialisation, and the importance of lifestyles to individuals, and then in turn to the importance of magazines as a locus (or even origin) of those activities.

Holmes and Nice, illustrate some of these ideas in their formulation of what they call a 'General Theory of Magazines':

1   magazines always target a precisely defined group of readers;
2   magazines base their content on the expressed and perceived needs, desires, hopes and fears of that defined group;
3   magazines develop a bond of trust with their readerships;
4   magazines foster community-like interactions between themselves and their readers, and among readers;
5   magazines can respond quickly and flexibly to changes in the readership and changes in wider society.

(2012: p.7)

Whilst one can argue that other media forms do these kinds of things as well, to varying degrees, the extent to which the magazine industry has developed over a long period of time according to these underlying criteria can be seen in the structures of the industry today.

An initial illustration of the distinctiveness of the magazine market, in this sense, is in the market for broadcasting listing magazines. In the early days of British broadcasting, newspapers were the only space through which the BBC could promote their daily programming, and newspapers briefly tried to use this to their competitive advantage by trying to charge the BBC for publishing listings. This led the BBC to set up its own vehicle for programme listings: the *Radio Times*, initially produced by Georges Newnes Ltd from 1923, before being taken entirely in-house by the 1930s (Thomson, 2013). With its listings treated under law as copyright material belonging to the BBC, *Radio Times* had a monopoly on advanced programme listings for several decades, until it was joined in 1955 by *TV Times* which covered the new ITV television channel (and later Channel 4), and with the same level of copyright control (except in the hands of the commercial terrestrial broadcasters). By 1960, these two magazines were reaching 7 million and 4 million readers weekly respectively (Stam, 2014a: p.25) with readers usually having to buy both to get listings for BBC and ITV channels. This exclusive hold on the rights to publish broadcast listings in magazine format was finally abolished in 1991, and a raft of other listings magazines were launched thereafter. In 2018, TV listings magazines accounted for the largest share of the weekly magazine market (over a third at 35.4 per cent), with *TV Choice* being the only weekly magazine to still regularly sell over a million copies per week, and the whole sector generated £138 million in revenue that year (Marketforce, 2019). The next highest selling weekly magazine was also a TV listings magazine (at just under 900,000 copies per week in 2018, and published by TI Media). *TV Choice*, launched in 1999, helped Bauer media go from a relatively small German family printing business to a billion-dollar global business, and the biggest selling magazine publisher in Britain by the end of 2018 (Bauer, 2019). So, whilst the arrival of television created all sorts of challenges for many media industries, in the magazine sector it represented a new set of *opportunities*. As Holmes and Nice put it, over time the emergence of 'new specialisms, new hobbies, new technologies, new trades, new professions' were matched by 'whole new magazine sectors to serve new cultural phenomena' (2012: p.16). It is perhaps all the more remarkable that listings magazines continue to represent such a significant proportion of the modern magazine market in an age of electronic programme guides and on-demand streaming services. Even the *Radio Times*, whilst now owned by Immediate Media (since 2011) and long past it's multi-million selling heyday, was still selling over 600,000 copies per week in 2018 making it the fifth highest selling weekly magazine in Britain (Marketforce, 2019).

Ownership: From the Local to the Global to the Local

If the history of the modern national press in Britain can be seen very broadly speaking as a history of high profile individual newspaper owners, from Northcliffe to Murdoch, the magazine industry, on a similarly broad level, is a history of constant mergers, conglomerations, and labyrinthine global corporate entities. To illustrate the historical complexities, we can look at one of the leading companies in the British magazine market at the time of writing: TI Media. Newnes' *Country Life* magazine, mentioned already in this chapter, as arguably the first glossy magazine, is published today under the TI Media banner. In the early part of the 20th century, Newnes competed alongside other publishers (of both newspapers and magazines) such as Harmsworth, Pearson, Hulton (original producer of *Farmer's Weekly* from 1934 and *Picture Post* from 1938), and Odhams (who launched the first colour weekly magazine, *Woman*, in 1937). In 1959, Odhams bought and absorbed the Newnes and Hulton companies. Meanwhile, nephew of Alfred Harmsworth, Cecil King, had built up the Mirror Group of news-papers through the 1930s, making a huge success of a relaunched *Daily Mirror*, and in 1958 was in a position to take over Amalgamated Press (another company originating with Alfred Harmsworth, and responsible, amongst other things, for historically important comic magazines like *Comic Cuts*). Renaming the group Fleetway (after the building it was housed in), just a couple of years later Fleetway and Odhams merged in 1961. The new company was repackaged as the International Publishing Corporation (IPC) in 1963, with King as the Chairman. At the time it was the largest periodical publishing company in the world. In 1970, the renamed IPC Magazines Ltd was bought out by Reed International (a conglomerate that had started as a small news-print business in Britain). In 1987, Fleetway, which had continued as a subsidiary focusing on comic-book titles mainly, was sold off, and then in 1992, Reed Interna-tional merged with Dutch publisher Elsevier to become Reed Elsevier (now branded as RELX). The IPC Magazines brand lasted until 1998, when that branch of the cor-poration became IPC Media. That lasted until 2014, when it was bought by Time Warner, and became Time Inc. UK, only to be bought out again in 2018 under the banner TI Media (itself a subsidiary of a private equity group Epiris).

Many 'British' magazines, either in origin or by general perception, today are ulti-mately part of multi-national conglomerates like TI Media. The German company Bauer, mentioned earlier, directly entered the British market with the woman's maga-zine *Bella* in 1987, and by 2008 was in a strong enough position to buy out EMAP (originally the East Midlands Allied Press – itself an amalgamation of a number of newspapers and magazine publishers) for around £1 billion. Condé Nast, an American company, launched a British edition of *Vogue* in 1916, and has had a strong presence in the British market ever since. Willian Randolph Hearst, famous American publisher of, amongst other things, *Cosmopolitan*, and inspiration for *Citizen Kane*, bought the National Magazine Company in Britain in 1910. It is still owned today by Hearst media, having been incorporated alongside magazines produced by French publishing company Hachette Filipacchi (publisher of *Elle*) into Hearst Magazines UK in 2011. Other prominent companies include the German Hubert Burda Group, that owns a number of home lifestyle magazines, and specialist magazine publishers like Future, Dennis, Redwood, and Haymarket (aside from Burda, the others here are British companies at the time of writing).

Whilst newspapers also developed into chains and corporations as well, often in the late 19th and early 20th centuries mixed in with magazines, widespread international ownership of newspapers, especially national newspapers, wasn't really a prominent feature to the point where it remains a point of contention today to have a national newspaper owned by a non-British individual (like Australian-born, US citizen Rupert Murdoch). In the British press and broadcasting, foreign ownership has been seen as problematic enough historically for regulatory limits to have been imposed. In the magazine sector, by contrast, international inroads into the British magazine market goes back a very long way with far less contention. One reason behind this is implicit in the following statement from Charles Knight, writing in 1833 about his *Penny Magazine*:

> The almost universal circulation of our 'Penny Magazine' in the United Kingdom; its republication in the United States of America; the establishment of works of similar character, (in all respects imitations,) in France, Belgium, Germany, and

Russia; and the plans already formed and announced for extending such publications to Italy, Holland, Poland and the Brazils, – these circumstances have led us to think that a popular account of all the processes necessary for its production would be of very general interest.

(in King and Plunkett, 2005: p.128)

Holmes and Nice's general theory of magazines might suggest, and the thousands of British-based magazine titles available today might support, a notion that magazines are highly specific, highly localised entities with appeal to very specific audiences. And yet, as far back as the 1830s, publishers were recognising how certain magazine formats could be easily transported to different countries and continue to be successful either as simply international distribution of the home-produced magazine, as say still happens with the American *Time* magazine or the British magazine *The Economist*, or through localised editions such as the dozens of versions of *Vogue* around the world today. Sometimes, magazines can rapidly seem to become part of national culture whilst having originated abroad. A good example of that would be *Hello!*, a photo-based weekly celebrity magazine launched in Britain in 1988, which built its brand through paying a lot of money for exclusive access to celebrities' homes, weddings, and other social events. Whether many of its readers, still amounting to nearly 250,000 per issue as of 2017, know that it's a localised version of the original Spanish title *¡Hola!*, that has been around since 1944, or just one of the dozen or so other localised editions currently available around the world, is unclear. Regardless of audience awareness or interest, it's illustrative of how the intersection of the local and the global is a key feature of the British magazine industry, and its underlying robustness in the face of challenges over time as many magazines are produced within the framework of often long standing multi-national corporations.

Magazine Sectors

British magazine companies also operate in a variety of different sub-sectors, especially in terms of specific subjects for magazine contents, but also in terms of overarching markets. The industry as a whole is largely anchored around three broad areas of targeted, specific reader communities: businesses/trades, customers of specific producers/ service providers, and socio-cultural consumer groups.

Business to Business Magazines

In terms of number and range of titles, the largest sector of magazine publishing is business to business magazines, also referred to as the trade press, with significantly more titles at around 4,500 in the UK, as of 2018, than consumer magazines at around 2,500 (McKay, 2019: p.35). These are magazines aimed directly at particular industry sectors, their companies and workers. Historically they provided spaces for communication about markets, prices, tastes, and trends beyond industries' immediate geographical locales before the days of telecommunication and broadcast media. In that sense the intrinsic value of a trade press to many, if not all, trades makes sense of this sector's existence. Even within the later landscape of telecommunications and broadcasting, the value of a trade press has persisted. A useful illustration here is the long tradition of a media industry trade press, both domestically within the UK and internationally. Some of these have a degree of wider public awareness and readership outside the media industries, titles like the Hollywood film industry magazine *Variety* for instance. Whilst some titles have gone online, or been incorporated into more prominent titles, that has mostly happened in the 2010s, and the fact that a print-based trade press in media industries still exists in physical print form today is interesting in itself. Aside from *Variety*, other prominent international media industry trade titles include *Film International* which has a London editorial office, and the international marketing title *The Drum*. *Campaign*, covering the advertising and marketing sectors, was a weekly magazine until 2017, when it became monthly, having essentially incorporated former magazines *Media Week* and *Marketing Magazine* within the *Campaign* brand in 2016. *Marketing Week*, *PrintWeek*, and *Broadcast* magazine were still publishing in the conventional format into the late 2010s. *Press Gazette*, covering more of the journalistic sides of newspaper and magazine publishing, went online-only in 2013 but remains a prominent voice within the industry. In 2003, *InPublishing* launched covering newspapers, magazines, and online publishing, whilst long running *PRWeek*, covering the public relations industry, moved to a mostly online presence with a monthly print edition from 2013, and then bi-monthly from 2016, whilst retaining the *PRWeek* brand name.

The trade press mostly carries on kind of quietly in the background of the media environment, with often very small circulations within particular trade communities. The media trade press titles don't reach more than a few thousand per issue, though reach for trade titles has never been about achieving large circulations so much as in reaching the right target audiences. On occasion, however, the potential for trade press activity and knowledge to feed into wider public debates does occur, as in the wake of the Grenfell Tower disaster in 2017, when 72 people lost their lives in a deadly fire in a block of flats in London. Housing trade title *Inside Housing* had run lots of articles over the years in the wake of an earlier deadly fire in a high-rise housing block (Lanakal House, also in London, in 2009), and when the Grenfell fire occurred, its journalists found themselves thrown into the national media spotlight for their expertise (Ruddick, 2017). More typically though, the trade press provides a rich arena for aspiring journalists and media workers to gain real-world experience in media practice, providing good routes into more high profile journalism, partly through the typically multi-title publishing companies trade titles are produced within that enable staff to move between titles, indeed often finding themselves writing for multiple titles at a time (McKay, 2019: p.37).

Customer Magazines

Another core sector of magazine publishing is often referred to as a form of 'content marketing' (McKay, 2019: p.36). It is essentially contract publishing, whereby publishers are contracted to produce specific titles for organisations, from one-offs to regularly occurring titles, aimed at reaching employees, members, and/or customers with specific marketing objectives (Dyson, 2007). Although arguably the notion of a publication aimed at specific customer groups goes back to the early days of printed periodicals a few centuries ago, there has been a much more recent substantial growth in this area. For instance, specialist publishers concentrating on the contract/custom market emerged as recently as 1983 in the UK, and between 1990 and 2002, the growth in this specialist area saw turnover nearly triple (Haeusermann, 2013: p.100). Not surprisingly, some of the big magazine publishers now have contract publishing divisions. Condé Nast, for instance, best known for titles like *Vogue*, has a contract publishing section that has produced titles for high-end companies like Ferrari and Mercedes-Benz but they have also worked with more high street retail outlets in producing what are essentially a mix of magazines and catalogues, known as 'magalogues' in the trade (Powell, 2013), for companies such as Argos (Holmes and Nice, 2012: p.42) and the now defunct Littlewoods (Plunkett, 2004). Both Argos and Littlewoods have long been famous amongst the British public for selling everyday goods primarily through catalogues – hardly the natural marketplace you would think for publishers of luxury fashion magazines. Even as catalogue companies are replaced by (or transform) into online retailers, the role of a magalogue format for e-magazines as a tool for customer persuasion remains a prominent feature of the contract sector (Holmes and Nice, 2012: p.43).

Customer magazines are the most prominent form of contract publishing that the wider public will have encountered, and they reach some of the biggest audiences of any magazines, and often have high production values reflecting significant investment in them (ibid.). They are produced across a wide range of business sectors. One notable area is magazines for transport passengers (i.e. on trains, planes, etc.) which, in turn, paved the route for the success of the free newspaper *Metro* (see Chapter 4). For example, British Airways' in-flight magazine *High Life*, established in 1967, helped to launch the concept of onboard magazines, and is provided for every flying passenger on every flight with a potential reach of 3.8 million readers globally every month (www. bamedia.co.uk/our-portfolio/in-flight/#print). As editor Andy Morris states, the magazine is 'unapologetically a British Airways magazine and our central aim is to celebrate the airline's routes and service' (in Brotherton, 2018). The value of customer magazines to the client organisations is the belief that they serve an important function in building things like brand image and brand loyalty, i.e. that you as a customer may be more likely to remember particular brand experiences and remain loyal to that brand in future consumption choices.

A study conducted for the Association of Publishing Agencies in 2005 claimed that 'no other marketing channel is as measurably effective at simultaneously building brands, driving sales and generating loyalty' (APA, 2005: p.1). The idea is that the time spent by magazine readers with customer magazines, on average around 25 minutes per reader (ibid.: p.4), works to build a relationship between the reader and the brand, in turn following through into brand identification, loyalty, and increased chances of future brand consumption. This might not sound like a very long period of time, but it's long compared to consumer attention to conventional advertisements. Many organisations feel it's a worthwhile investment delivering meaningful returns from that comparatively significant amount of audience engagement with a freely distributed magazine (third-party advertising tends, where it is used at all, at best to offset some of the cost of producing a customer magazine, and many of these titles have no third-party advertising in them). Moreover, customer magazines are regularly at the top of UK magazine circulation figures, particularly customer magazines produced by supermarkets, so titles like *Tesco Magazine* and *Good Living* (Asda's magazine) were reaching 1.9 and 1.8 million circulation figures respectively by 2017 (Ponsford, 2017b: p.9) putting them amongst the largest circulation print titles of any kind per issue in the UK. One of the factors seen as important in their effectiveness is getting a balance between promotional content – stuff saying how good the brand and its products/

services are – and editorial content (APA, 2005: p.4), concentrating not on editorial independence from the client as such, but on aspects of editorial design, writing quality, and distinctiveness. As *High Life* magazine editor Andy Morris said:

> What I think marks us out is our sense of personality—in the age of Instagram, Yelp and Tripadvisor, the only way to get people's attention is to give them a vibrant, sensory depiction of what's possible worldwide and why they specifically might find it fun. We also use big name photographers and irreverent journalists to try and keep things as bright, bold and British as possible.
>
> (in Brotherton, 2018)

Some research backs up this notion that readers respond more favourably to editorial than promotional content in customer magazines (van Reijmersdal, Neijens, and Smit, 2010). It is in this sense, of producing an engaging read, that the notion of customer magazines as a form of content marketing makes sense – marketing and advertising brands through sophisticated content production in magazine formats familiar to and popular with potential audiences. Combined with the comparative growth of customer magazines paralleling declines in newspaper publishing in recent decades, it's also an important shift in the print media labour force, especially journalists, from opportunities in outlets concentrating on independent news-focused journalism to customer-oriented content marketing, and one that has largely gone without much academic scrutiny over that time (Haeusermann, 2013).

Consumer Magazines

The category of magazine publishing which has generated the greatest amount of scholarly attention by some distance is consumer magazines. These are the kind with which you are likely to be most familiar – the ones sold over the counter directly to consumers in newsagents and supermarkets, and whose titles include some of the most familiar media brands in both UK and international media landscapes: *Vogue, GQ, Cosmopolitan, Radio Times, Hello!, Time*, and so on. Despite there being many more business to business titles, and the circulation and reach of many customer titles exceeding consumer titles these days, consumer magazines have dominated discussion and analysis of magazines in media studies scholarship.

One aspect we've not covered yet in this chapter in any detail has been circulation and readership. In the newspaper industry, the long term decline in circulation and readership since the end of WWII is one of the defining features of that industry, seen as both a cause and a consequence of many of the contentious issues surrounding them. For business to business and customer magazines the issue of circulation/reach is quite a different one to that of newspapers, as is the issue of sources of revenue. For business to business magazines, for instance, in the region of four-fifths (82 per cent) of their revenue comes from advertising (McKay, 2019: p.250) hence being able to continue to publish whilst reaching often quite small audiences – but audiences particularly valuable to other businesses as potential customers for their products/services. For customer magazines, revenue typically comes entirely, or predominantly, from the clients who have contracted companies to produce those magazines – which are normally given away for free to audiences. So, it is in the consumer magazine sector that issues of circulation and readership become particularly important to talk about, and where, broadly speaking, advertising accounts for around 38 per cent of revenue, and 62 per cent comes from sales (ibid.), though this can vary a lot within individual magazines. Indeed, the perception that magazines might be more advertising reliant that newspapers might seem justified when flicking through the pages of a lifestyle magazine like *Cosmopolitan*, where advertising seems to occupy significantly more space than editorial when compared to a newspaper. In fact, this split between advertising and sales revenue isn't that far removed from national newspapers, where popular dailies were receiving around 47 per cent of their revenue through advertising, and quality dailies around 56 per cent in 2005 (Meech, 2008: p.236). Similar to the newspaper sector, overall, circulations and readerships in the consumer magazine sector are in decline, and that has been an underlying overall trend for some time. In 2018 alone, sales dropped by 11.9 per cent on the previous year amongst titles listed by the Audit Bureau of Circulation (Marketforce, 2019). But there are substantial differences for consumer magazines that have at minimum tempered, and at times completely inverted, this notion of the British media landscape being one of fewer and fewer print media users, differences rooted in the principles in Holmes and Nice's magazine theory mentioned earlier.

One of those differences has been highlighted already in the example of broadcast listing magazines – the capacity of the magazine industry to turn challenges or competitors for audience time into opportunities to create a new magazine category. Thinking back to Chapter 1's discussion of the penny farthing bicycle as an illustration of the intersection between technology and society, we can add in the way in which the emerging magazine sector played its own role in the maintenance and expansion of cycling as an everyday activity. Holmes and Nice offer the statistic that between 1875 and 1900, no less than 31 separate cycling magazines were launched in Britain (2012: p.15). Some activities that began as marginal niches were recognised incredibly early by magazine producers and have persisted to the present day as almost ubiquitous activities that have sustained audiences over time. *Autocar* magazine, for instance, was launched in 1895 when you could count the number of cars that existed in the whole of Britain on the fingers of your hands and, perhaps less surprisingly, is still published at the time of writing. It is this flexible potential for rapid identification of new activities that has made the magazine market a particularly robust one, even in the context of overall declining sales. The closure of once highly prominent titles that defined generations' youths like the *NME* in 2018 are often particularly noteworthy, but whilst closures are common, so too are launches. In 2017 alone, for instance, over 400 new magazines were launched (Creasey, 2018).

Another feature of the magazine market is how this intersection between advertising, sales, and the identification of new interests/audiences, has become essentially the defining characteristic of consumer magazine production, such that finding 'a community of interest prepared to buy a magazine and matching their demographic profile with an advertising group is a basic skill all periodical publishers must acquire' (Stokes, 1999: p.21). Here it is clear that when launching a magazine, the consideration has to be about not only being able to identify a potential distinctive audience group, but an audience group whose attention, in turn, can then be sold to advertisers. It is here also where two points of tension begin to emerge. First, in certain magazine sectors, questions arise about how audiences are categorised into particular groups, and the extent to which those groups are *constructions* servicing the advertising industry (and its clients) rather than really servicing the needs and desires of real communities. Second, in turn, come in debates about how magazines construct and represent audience groups in terms of their contribution to wider questions around socialisation and social construction of peoples' identities and, thinking back to Chapter 3, questions about how magazines reflect, or not, value judgements about the kind of society we want to live in.

When it comes to magazines focused around interests or hobbies, like cars, cycling, or videogames, the potential tension between advertising and editorial in this context of social and political values is arguably nowhere near as evident as it is in newspapers. Close links between politicians and newspaper journalists might be questionable in terms of political journalism's watchdog function, but in a sector like cycling, say, close links between a magazine and the companies making bikes, funding professional cycling teams, and so on, might make the content more attractive to cycling enthusiasts. Moreover, whilst political leanings of newspapers are associated with the identities and characteristics of their readers (in stereotypes of *Daily Mail* or *The Guardian* readers for instance) this is far less the case for magazines focused on personal interests. When it comes to lifestyle magazines, on the other hand, the extent to which there's some kind of 'natural' intersection between a community of interest, advertisers interested in that community, and commercial clients seeking to reach that community through advertising, has been questioned for some time in terms of its societal impacts. As mentioned at the beginning of this chapter, research on women's magazines over the years has established a number of controversies around the extent to which different notions of how women and their interests are categorised. Currently, for instance, women's magazines are sub-divided by the Audit Bureau of Circulation into a number of (arguably overlapping) categories including: Women's Celebrity Weeklies (like *Hello!*), Women's Traditional Weeklies (like *Bella*), Women's Fashion/Lifestyle (like *Cosmopolitan*), Women's Home Interest (like *Your Home*), and Women's Interests (including things like wedding magazines like *You and Your Wedding*). The distinction between monthly and weekly titles reflects in part very deliberate distinctive strategies going back a century or so, with some producers concentrating on the mass market female audience in titles like *Woman's Weekly* (launched 1911) whilst others, in titles like *Vogue* (launched 1916), were very deliberately constructed to aim at a more select, but much more affluent audience (Cox and Mowatt, 2012). Whilst there have been changes in the market overall, both in terms of titles and contents, this pattern has been remarkable in its persistence over time. Amongst the shifts have been, for instance, a whole range of magazines specifically aimed at teenage girls that peaked in the 1980s and 1990s, hence the interest of researchers in now defunct teen magazines like *Jackie*, for instance (McRobbie, 1991), but which had almost entirely disappeared by the late 2010s, with only *Shout* left. Meanwhile, magazines serving older women readers, titles like *Red* (aimed at women in their 30s), or *Yours* (women in their 50s and over), have been relatively stable by comparison.

What is common across these titles categorised as being for women, again in broad terms, are constructions of British women within very specific socio-demographic characteristics. Beyond age and class, the default positions around ethnicity and sexuality continue to be a focus on white, heterosexual women, and the default positions around the various aspects of 'lifestyle' on offer concentrate on aspects such as appearance (of the body, of clothing, of the home) and aspirational efforts to improve these things through consumption – i.e. that being a happier, better person comes from consuming these products, services, and activities, as outlined in each magazine. As mentioned at the beginning of this chapter, these persistent patterns of representation and their potential impact on social attitudes around gender have been a central focus of research for some time, and Holmes and Nice broadly group such research into three normative positions regarding magazines as being either a 'baleful influence', reproducing the structural hierarchies of paternalistic society, a 'bringer of pleasure', in research which acknowledged that many women seemed to enjoy magazines regardless of the problematic representations of themselves they contained, or as a site of 'positive resistance' whereby readers are more than capable of reading texts critically as part of their wider creation and maintenance of their identities (2012: p.124).

Whilst these debates have rumbled on in magazine (and wider media) research over the decades, only on occasion have they spilled over into wider public discourses in ways that have had visible impacts on the industry sector. Men's lifestyle magazines have been around on and off for most of the history of magazines, with peaks and troughs over time, as certain types of magazines went in and out of favour (Braithwaite, 2009). After a period through the 1960s and 1970s where the term 'men's magazine' was little more than a euphemism for pornographic titles like *Penthouse* and *Mayfair*, consigned to the top shelf of newsagents (so out of sight and reach of the young), the 1980s saw a new wave of men's magazines styled after the women's high-fashion brands, with titles like *Esquire* and *GQ*. In the mid-1990s, however, another type of men's magazine emerged that became known as the 'Lad Mag'. Beginning with *Loaded* and *FHM* in 1994, lad mags offered glossy magazine consumerist content, mixed in with cruder, tabloid style editorial content, and representations of women just shy of the full-frontal nudity of the pornography titles. By the mid-2000s, weekly titles *Nuts* and *Zoo* were competing for circulations in the hundreds of thousands, and had shifted ever more towards editorial heavily interspersed with images of partially clad women, with reality TV contestants often being offered large sums of money for exclusive, candid photo-sessions, alongside a number of female models who built successful careers through appearing in lad mags (like Katie 'Jordan' Price). In 2013, a feminist 'lose the lad mags' campaign began targeting retailers, trying to get the lad mags removed from sale, on the grounds that their representations of women were fuelling sexist behaviour, were misogynistic, and potentially even in breach of the 2010 Equalities Act, constituting sexual discrimination and harassment (García-Favaro and Gill, 2016; Hegarty et al., 2018). Some retailers did stop stocking the magazines whilst others obscured their covers, in the wake of a highly public debate the campaign generated, and it helped accelerate what was already by this time a rapidly declining market. *Nuts* and *Zoo* closed in 2014, and *Loaded* in 2015, and straggling titles have continued to decline in readership. The biggest falling sub-categories of magazines in 2018 were men's lifestyle magazines, declining 25.6 per cent from 2017 (Marketforce, 2019). Whether the lad mags were pushed out of existence by this concerted campaign or were simply on their way out anyway as a rather ephemeral magazine niche isn't certain, though the relatively rapid rise and fall of a magazine niche in this way is by no means unusual.

Conclusion

Whether the magazine industry can continue to adjust to the changes of the modern media age with the same effectiveness as in the past remains to be seen, but there are some reasons to argue that it continues to be a sector with much greater flexibility to adapt to change than some other traditional media formats (McKay, 2019: p.275). As just indicated, the capacity to rapidly identify and reach new niche markets as interests and attitudes change is high in the magazine sector, such that entire niches can come and go without it necessarily having a huge impact on the industry as a whole. Another factor is the capacity for what is called *brand extension*, whereby prominent magazine brands move into other kinds of revenue generating activity, such as linking up with television companies to sponsor programmes or even entire channels like the American-originated National Geographic Channel linked to the magazine *National Geographic*. This can work in the other direction as well, with magazines launched off the back of successful television series, like *Top Gear* magazine for instance, or children's magazines titled after licenced characters like Peppa Pig. Just like those broadcast brands, magazine brands can be exported wholesale and find new markets in other countries. Running live events has become another revenue-stream for many magazine publishers, both highly publicised events like the *GQ Man of the Year* awards, and the less glamourous but particularly important in the business to business sector events like the *H & V News Awards* (that is heating and ventilation) (Stam, 2014b: p.99). As the rise of magalogues discussed earlier indicates, the shift online creates new opportunities for magazine brands to line up with product and service suppliers directly, to the point where in certain sectors a move online isn't a reflection so much of a dwindling print readership as of better revenue opportunities coming from online shopping. *Brides* magazine, for instance, was sold by Condé Nast in 2019 to a digital media company, despite both the original US magazine and the UK version being the leading titles in their respective markets. The opportunity to link the magazine brand's readers directly with the companies providing wedding services through an online platform is where the revenue growth prospects lay – and wedding planning is just one sector where that's the future for many magazine brands. Also, the rise of touch-screen mobile devices has enabled e-magazines to retain many of the characteristics of traditional magazines, allowing readers to flick through the pages of an e-magazine in a similar fashion to the print copy. Older tactics to retain and attract readers to print copies persist, like the use of cover-mounts (Holmes and Nice, 2012: p.93) giveaway gifts attached to the cover of a magazine, and particularly prominent in children's magazines for instance (though these don't necessarily help profits). Even the quality of paper stock continues to be seen as a revenue enhancer, as explained by publisher Anders Braso, speaking about *Monocle* magazine:

> The tactile nature of print is what differentiates it [...] Look, feel, smell. In any one issue of *Monocle*, we use different paper stocks, insert binding methods and finishes. While of course we are in the media business, we believe we are also in manufacturing.
>
> (in Creasey, 2018)

All in all, magazines are far from being a tired, moribund legacy media industry, instead offering a dynamic mix of long standing practices and new approaches worth significantly more attention than the sector has tended to be afforded by media scholarship.

6   Film

At the heart of the British film industry there is something of a paradox. In several regards Britain is one of the most significant countries contributing to global film culture and industry, and yet throughout its history there has been constant concern about its distinctiveness, quality, and even viability. Recent books frame the industry in often contradictory ways, such as *Who Killed British Cinema?* (Mahindru and Gems, 2017) contrasting starkly with *Stairways to Heaven: Rebuilding the British Film Industry* (Macnab, 2018) indicating an apparent tension in the state and nature of British film. An initial glance might suggest that there is much cause for an optimistic take. After all, British actors have been and continue to be amongst the biggest movie stars anywhere in the world, featuring in many of the most successful films of all time. British actors pervade the *Avengers, Star Wars, Star Trek, Mission Impossible, Harry Potter*, and many other high-grossing film franchises. Many iconic film actors are British, from Audrey Hepburn to Kate Winslet, and Michael Caine to Christian Bale. Between 2000 and 2021, British male actors were nominated for the American Academy Awards (the Oscars) for Best Actor 24 times, winning six times, most recently Anthony Hopkins for *The Father*, and for Best Supporting Actor 17 times, with four wins. Across the same period, British actresses have been nominated 27 times for Best Actress, with four wins: Olivia Colman for *The Favourite* in 2018 the most recent, and 21 times for best supporting actress with three wins. Oscars for Best Director since 2000 have gone to British directors twice from 14 nominations, and British-produced (or co-produced films) have won four times, such as *12 Years a Slave* in 2012, directed by the British director Steve McQueen. In 2010, *The King's Speech* won Best Picture, Best Director, Best Actor, and Best Original Screenplay – a quartet of British winners in a single film. Many British directors are considered amongst the best in cinema history: David Lean, the team of Powell and Pressburger, Alfred Hitchcock, John Schlesinger, Stephen Frears, Mike Leigh, Ridley Scott, Danny Boyle, Christopher Nolan, and so on. In 2020, the British film *Promising Young Woman* was nominated for Best Picture, and Best Director for Emerald Fennell, the first nomination of a British woman director, and whilst it missed out on those, Fennell did win the Best Original Screenplay, another first for a British woman film-maker.

With regard to what the British Film Institute (BFI) refer to as British 'source material' (BFI, 2021: p.13), Britain has contributed substantially to global film culture in recent years, as in the film adaptations of J. R. R. Tolkien's *Lord of the Rings* and *The Hobbit*, and J. K. Rowling's Harry Potter series. The long running James Bond series of films, originally based on the novels of Ian Fleming, are an icon of a kind of Britain represented in popular film since the 1960s to the present day. In pretty much

DOI: 10.4324/9781315396781-9

every era of the roughly 120 years of the existence of films, there are notable British producers as well, from the Korda studios of the 1930s through the Ealing Comedies of the 1950s, the social realists of the 1960s, Hammer horror and Carry-on comedies through the 1960s and 1970s, and on to prominent independent and avant-garde film-makers supported through the strength of British television finance from the 1980s onwards. Britain has also at times been one of the most favoured places for international, especially American, film production. Many blockbuster series have been filmed at least in part in Britain, like the *Star Wars, Indiana Jones*, and *Avengers* movies. According to the BFI, in 2019, the British film industry accounted for nearly a quarter (24.6 per cent) of global film revenues of around $10.3 billion (BFI, 2021: p.4).

So, one might reasonably look at this kind of apparent success and the richness of British film history, culture, and industry activity and ask why questions about the health and vitality of the industry have dominated debates for a great deal of its existence. There are continuing concerns that even where there appear to be successes, these are shaped by powerful external forces that distort how Britain is represented on screen, disrupt the potential for a stable and sustained domestic film industry, and constitute a whole range of challenges for creative workers in the sector. Understanding the position of the British film industry depends on having a sense of what have been described as its 'three main themes: that Hollywood dominates the market, that the film trade has distinctive *economic* features, and that the film trade has distinctive *cultural* characteristics' (Dickinson and Harvey, 2005: p.420, original emphasis). The tension between economic features and cultural characteristics is not unique to the film industry, indeed such tensions are an overarching feature of media industries in general as discussions across this book show. The way these have developed in the British film industry, however, is distinctive and particularly interesting because of the key difference between film and most other traditional media's development that Dickinson and Harvey put first in their list – the dominance of Hollywood. As an initial illustration of this, looking at the last decade, between 2011 and 2020, nine of the top 20 grossing films 'were UK qualifying films' (BFI, 2021: p.12). That phrase 'UK qualifying' is a key element of how films like *Star Wars Episode VII: The Force Awakens* and *Avengers: Endgame* 'qualify' as *British* films, reflecting the distinctive environment within which the British film industry operates today. This chapter looks first at the dominance of Hollywood, then at various efforts to limit that influence through economic measures, and lastly on current strategies that nominally centre on this question of the cultural nature of British film.

The Long Shadow of Hollywood

At the outset of the film industry in the 1890s, there was nothing to necessarily indicate that any one particular country would come to dominate global markets in the way that has subsequently occurred. Whilst the 'official' history of film places its origin with the French Lumière brothers' first public performances in 1895, at that time a variety of competing devices were in existence. Alongside the better-known Kinetoscope of Thomas Edison in the United States, there were several created by British inventors such as Augustin Le Prince, William Friese-Greene, Birt Acres, and Robert W. Paul (Barr, 2009: p.145; Mahindru and Gems, 2017: p.11). European film-makers led the way in the 1890s and early 1900s, particularly French companies like Pathé and Gaumont, and not only were European producers typically dominant in their home markets at this time, but they provided as much as half of all the films shown in America as well (Bakker, 2005: p.25).

WWI is often seen as a key event in the shift to the eventual global dominance of American cinema, but in fact a shift had already begun in the years running up to the war (Bakker, 2005), and in Britain in particular, the vast majority of films shown were already coming from the US by the outbreak of the war in 1914 (Street, 2009: p.185). The war undoubtedly did have an impact on European film industries, particularly in terms of limiting industry growth, innovation, and risk-taking, although data suggests that the impact on internal markets and exports wasn't as big as might have been expected (Bakker, 2005). The bigger impact seems to have been, at least partly, on public and political attitudes within European states, as audiences started to favour more domestic films over those produced by countries they'd been in conflict with – even to the point of bans of German films in France and Britain and vice versa (Bakker, 2005: p.38). Nonetheless, the lack of disruption to the American film industry's development during the war helped accelerate aspects of its progress that would enable it to come to dominate the global film landscape.

One factor has been the scale and wealth of the American film audience compared to European states' audiences in the early decades. To give a sense of this, by the mid-1920s, for instance, there were 22,000 cinemas in the US compared to 4,000 in Britain (Street, 1997: p.6). With a larger domestic audience, each film has greater opportunities to make a profit, there's more room in the market for more films to be successfully produced, and (crucially) these two factors make exporting films significantly more profitable for film producers, being that much less reliant on overseas revenue generation. With greater potential for profit comes greater potential for investment in production resources, such that film technologies, professionalisation in various aspects (camera work, lighting, set design, etc.), as well as attracting the main creative talents like directors and actors, all became things easier for the emerging American industry to start to dominate, like a centripetal force drawing resources to the US.

A second factor in the development of American dominance, and its centring on Hollywood, is the emergence of the studio system and a structure of *vertical integration* that enabled US film companies to recognise and capitalise on these circumstances. Media industries, like many others, can be thought of as having a 'vertical supply chain' that 'connects producers with consumers' (Doyle, 2013a: p.20). In the analogue era, broadly speaking, there were three parts of the film industry process that initially developed into distinctive areas of activity within its supply chain: production, distribution, and exhibition. In the beginning, these three processes were all wrapped up together, as the likes of the Lumière brothers would produce the films themselves, then cart their equipment around to various places, set up and exhibit the films as well. As the demand for films took off, specialists in each of these areas emerged, concentrating on aspects of production (film studios), distribution (both the practicalities of transporting copies of films, but more importantly the licencing and distribution deals in domestic and international markets), and exhibition (cinema chains).

The innovation of American cinema was the establishment of a system where single companies owned and controlled production, distribution, and exhibition, vertically integrating these industry processes. As such, companies could ensure control over all parts of the film process from the studio facilities, where the films were made (literal large spaces, both internal studios and external lots), the staff in front and behind the camera, the networks of licensing deals, transportation requirements to get films to cinemas, and then the cinemas themselves. Moreover, this consolidation of film production into an ever-smaller number of large companies further enabled them to coordinate collective strategies for exporting American films out to global markets, whilst at the same time lobbying for restrictions on international imports into the US market, all of which was fully in motion prior to the outbreak of WWI. Now known as the era of the Hollywood Studio system, as it was studios who came to sit at the top of the supply chain (Bakker, 2005; Street, 1997), the names of several of these former dominant companies remain today and appear at the front of many film releases, albeit they have long since been largely subsumed into larger multi-media conglomerates. For instance, the Walt Disney company acquired 20th Century Fox in 2019 which, aside from being yet another instance of not uncontroversial narrowing of media ownership, garnered a lot of publicity mainly due to Fox's rights to lucrative Marvel characters like the X-Men shifting to Disney, who already own Marvel Entertainment, the main home of the phenomenally successful Marvel Cinematic Universe.

If the aspects mentioned so far begin to give an indication of the distinctive *economic* features of the film industry, a third factor relates to the evolution and impact of American film style, contributing to continual debates about the *cultural* dimension of film as well. The earliest films were silent, so the language barriers of other media forms were not an initial problem for the global film trade, and as film narratives developed, it was European companies that initially set the trends for film form. Pretty much until the arrival of television news, factual film production was a prominent part of the film business with 'actualities', as they were originally called, amongst the most popular forms of film in the 1890s. Essentially films of recent events, these were often staged recreations, or in modern parlance the fake news of their day, nonetheless they were extremely popular leading to the development of the newsreels, first in France in 1908 (Campbell, 2004: p.143). As well as newsreels, come WWI, European governments tried to harness the propaganda potential of films as, by this point, film was the dominant form of popular entertainment and communication (Reeves, 1997: p.11). Whilst national newspapers were becoming the large-circulation political influencers that they are characterised as today, at the same time, something like 20 million tickets per week were being sold for UK cinemas by 1916 (ibid.). Of the many officially sanctioned non-fiction films made during the war, Geoffrey Malins' *The Battle of the Somme* is perhaps the most iconic, and estimates suggest it was seen by as many as 19 million Britons (ibid.: p.8). A mixture of genuine and some staged sequences from the battle (though the latter wasn't determined till decades later), the film is widely credited with reshaping war reporting, government approaches to managing wartime communications, as well as wider public and political attitudes towards conflict.

Yet whilst *The Battle of the Somme* occupies an important historical position, it was atypical of what interested the vast cinema-going audience that had grown up within just two decades of the medium's creation. As Reeves puts it:

> The heart of the cinema programme consisted of a variety of fiction films, in which drama and comedy, romance and adventure, reinforced by an increasingly important star system, persuaded ordinary people to spend some of their hard-earned cash on the 2 hours or so of entertainment which a typical programme provided.
>
> (ibid.: p.11)

Indeed, it may not have crossed your mind when reading the opening paragraph of this chapter, that the entire focus was on British contributions to *fiction* film. As it happens, Britain has been quite important in the development of non-fiction films, particularly the evolution of documentary through figures like John Grierson, and film-makers who worked with government agencies after WWI and through into WWII (Boon, 2008). In terms of the development of fiction film, though, which came to dominate audience interests and production activity even before WWI, it was the US that led the way. This wasn't necessarily because of intrinsically greater creative talents within the American film industry to make 'better' films, so much as the intersection of the advantages of the American film industry landscape to produce large numbers of high production value films that could be distributed to Europe more quickly and effectively than European films could be distributed in the US.

The traditional film history accounts position American pioneering director D. W. Griffith as one of the central forces for helping to develop what has become a dominant film style in terms of the long form narrative of the feature film, and many aspects of use of editing, camerawork (like the close-up), and so on. Arguably, however, it was as much the security of the American production environment that enabled Griffith to make hundreds of films between 1908 and 1931, and thus to begin to experiment with, and then set a successful template for, narrative fiction film style. Griffith's *The Birth of the Nation* (1915) was one of the first feature films, and demonstrates many of the tropes that later would come to typify Hollywood film style which, in turn, has come to dominate global film markets. As an historical artefact in the development of feature film narrative form it remains incredibly important but the film's prejudiced representation of African-Americans and depicting the Ku Klux Klan as heroic figures was controversial even for the time, and has been described more recently as 'the most racist movie ever made' (Scott in Brooks, 2015). It serves as a pretty stark reminder of the importance of the relationship between political economy and socio-political contexts and their consequences. More to the point for our current concerns in this chapter, at that time in Britain there was nothing of the scale, sophistication, or innovation to be able to compete with what was coming out of the US to draw British audiences away from American films (Barr, 2009: p.149). It is perhaps not a surprise then that several of what were to become some of the biggest cultural icons in the world might have been British by birth, but found their fame through American cinema, not least Charlie Chaplin who made his first film in Hollywood in 1914. Moreover, the prominence of American film from an early stage 'had an impact on British producers in terms of creating an example of the stylistics of popular cinema *and on audiences* in terms of inculcating codes of generic expectation and viewing habits' (Street, 1997: pp.5–6, emphasis added). Going either with or against those 'stylistics', the Hollywood film style has been a central theme of British film production and consumption ever since.

The Empire Strikes Back

This combination of a well organised US industrial structure, built from a large scale domestic market, and able to produce, with economies of scale and scope, films that were immensely popular with global audiences, created the framework within which the British film industry (as well as many other film industries around the world) has operated since the 1910s to today. The wider economic fallout of WWI, which led into what became the Great Depression in the late 1920s, was felt particularly strongly in Britain, which a generation earlier had been the globe's dominant superpower. In many areas of industry, Britain's once leading position was being challenged by other countries, and that wider economic context was a factor in the governmental responses to the state of the film industry in particular, as part of a move towards more protectionist policies regarding industries threatened by international competition (Hill, 2004).

By 1925, homegrown films constituted only about 5 per cent of films shown in Britain (Street, 2009: p.185) and the numbers of British films produced were declining dramatically year on year. Rather than just being a patriotic effort to support a section of British industry which, as Hollywood was showing by this time, was a potential industry that might contribute to economic growth, it also began to be seen as a potential tool of both political and economic *promotion* of countries in the international arena. Hollywood didn't just make money for the US as an effective industry, it sold the American dream through its immensely popular and spectacular movies. It is in this sense of promoting, even selling, national cultures that film has been seen for some time as what today is regarded as an example of 'soft power' (Nye, 2008). Soft power essentially refers to efforts by nations to promote their interests through cultural attractions, rather than through political, economic, or military endeavours. Whilst soft power may not be as problematic as other kinds of international power relations, nonetheless the cultural dominance of Hollywood has been controversial to say the very least, and has had a long and sustained impact on both film industries in many countries, and indeed global trade agreements as well (De Zoysa and Newman, 2002).

Whilst the language of soft power didn't exist at the time, the British Cinematograph Films Act of 1927 reflects attitudes around both the protection and support for the domestic film industry, in a fashion common to European countries across that decade, attempting to boost their own industries whilst limiting the power of Hollywood, for *both* economic and cultural reasons. It also introduced a key component of film regulation that influenced British film production to varying degrees for around 60 years or so: the introduction of *quotas*. The Act required that there should be specific proportions of films that had to be shown by exhibitors that were defined as British (as in made by a British subject or company) (Street, 2009: p.184). Quotas were a central means by which efforts were made to secure British film producers' exhibition space, i. e., cinema screens for their films to be shown on, thus giving a firmer footing for production efforts as well, and they existed in various forms up until the mid-1980s. The 1938 Cinematograph Films Act exempted European art cinema from quotas, so the target was ever more firmly Hollywood dominance, and a decade after that, post-WWII, the quota for home-produced feature films peaked at 45 per cent of films shown having to be British by 1948 (Drazin, 2017: p.122).

The quota system had an immediate impact on the production landscape in Britain, with a rapid expansion of production companies from 26 in 1927 to 59 by 1929 (ibid.), and the 'share of the domestic market increased from 4.4 per cent in 1927 to 24 per cent by 1932' as well (Street, 2009: p.186). There were two basic strategies amongst British producers in the quota era. Some concentrated on cheap, rapid production time frames to fill the quota spaces, and thus maximise the financial return, and the idea of 'quota quickies' emerged. Some companies specialised in these, like the Strand Picture Company run by Julius Hagen, often working as subsidiaries of Hollywood studios to circumvent the quota restrictions, and keeping Hollywood companies with a significant presence in aspects of British film production, distribution, and exhibition as well (Spicer, 2017; Magor and Schlesinger, 2009). The increased share of domestically produced films reflected homegrown movies' popularity with audiences, and with the arrival of sound pictures, the 'talkies', this accentuated the appeal of homegrown films, irrespective of their production/aesthetic values.

The other key strategy of many of these new companies was to make films for international markets, and there was a general feeling that talkies were a real opportunity for British film to take advantage of sound, at least partly due to Britain being the home of standard English pronunciation, and English being a globally significant language (Drazin, 2017: p.123). Britain saw rapid conversion of cinemas to exhibit talkies, the first European country to do so, arguably a consequence of quotas enabling the industry to consolidate its infrastructure (Street, 2009: p.187). An almost jingoistic belief in the appeal of 'proper' English beyond Britain, however, was not initially reflected in the response to the new films being produced, especially in America. According to one contemporary account, whilst British films were gaining an increasing audience domestically in the early 1930s, they weren't able to earn in a week what Hollywood films like Chaplin's *City Lights* were earning in a day in the US (Drazin, 2017: p.122). Attempts to produce films intended for global markets, particularly America, saw companies doing deals with the big American companies for distribution but the strategy was fraught with risk that initially did not pay off. Alexander Korda, however, managed to make it work when in 1933 he produced *The Private Life of Henry VIII*, which was a massive success in the US, making a huge profit and winning Charles Laughton the Best Actor Oscar for the title role. Sedgwick explained Korda's strategy as follows:

> Korda developed a clear three-pronged strategy of: (1) the production of *international* films - films which were rooted in time and place but in a style which was international rather than parochial; (2) the ownership and management of first rate production facilities and (3) worldwide distribution, including the American market, through United Artists.
>
> (Sedgwick, 1997: p.50, original emphasis)

Off the back of that film's success, Korda was able to obtain distribution deals with United Artists for US distribution, and financial underwriting from the private sector to contribute to film production costs, and produced a string of successful films. However, Sedgwick points to the remaining intrinsic imbalance between Korda's productions and the American producers he was largely competing with. Korda's films, despite being comparatively lavish productions in the British context, weren't able to cover the kinds of productions costs of American films through domestic box office returns. This made them far more dependent on international revenue, whilst US films could have bigger budgets, get more of that back domestically, thus making their exported film revenues much more profitable (Sedgwick, 1997: p.57).

Moreover, the shift to talkies only consolidated Britain as a key overseas market for American film, and Britain was the number one export market for US films in the 1920s and 1930s (Chibnall, 2019: p.690). That continued through and after WWII, as even whilst post-WWII cinema audiences began to fall after the arrival of television, the British market remained substantially bigger than other European markets (Stubbs, 2008: p.337). The quotas immediately started to hit Hollywood's share of the British market, and as well as making deals with domestic producers to churn out quota quickies, a third strategy developed by the Hollywood studios was setting up full subsidiaries. The first of these was established in Teddington by Warner Brothers in 1932 creating a kind of 'Hollywood-on-Thames' (Chibnall, 2019). This practice, both as a means of getting round various forms of domestic restrictions to market entry, and also a means of taking advantage of things like cheaper labour costs in other countries, became a significant feature of Hollywood film production strategies thereafter. Known as 'runaway' productions, as productions move to countries where it's cheaper to make films, these have been significant in a range of countries over the decades, but especially so in the context of the British film industry (Stubbs, 2008, 2009; Chapman, 2021).

This is not to suggest that the British film industry was wholly dominated by Hollywood behind the scenes, in spite of the quota system. The Rank Organisation, founded in 1937, within a decade had established itself as something akin to the vertically integrated companies in Hollywood (Holmes, 2005: p.27). Being the prime financier or outright owner of production studios, distribution companies, and – by the end of the 1940s – hundreds of cinemas, made Rank one of the most significant film (and media) organisations in Britain for some decades. Both either side of, and through, WWII, film was the dominant entertainment activity outside of the home, and cinema-going flourished despite the war. Rank was a key player, with involvement in many of the most recognised and celebrated British films of the 1940s. Rank's involvement with a range of studios ensured an eclectic mix of types of films. Domestically very popular Gainsborough melodramas, like *The Man in Grey* (1943) and *The Wicked Lady* (1945), were supported by Rank, alongside more critically celebrated fare like Noël Coward's *Brief Encounter* (1943) and David Lean's *In Which We Serve* (1942). Rank was also behind some of the most celebrated British film studios, such as Archer films that produced the Powell and Pressburger films like *A Matter of Life and Death* (1946), as well as Ealing Studios' famous outputs, like *Passport to Pimlico* and *Whiskey Galore* (both 1949). Whilst these films are regarded today as part of the canon of British cinema, a key problem that led to large financial losses for Rank specifically, and compromised smaller British film companies too, was that there were few instances of these films being successful in the American market, despite many explicit attempts to achieve this (Drazin, 2017: p.126). Rank would move away from full financing of films in the 1950s, and gradually moved into production of media hardware like radios, but also and most notably into production of photocopiers, hence Rank Xerox.

Rank, then, was in a position not a million miles away from the situation the *Daily Herald* found itself in as mentioned in Chapter 4; a superficially dominant position, in terms of market share and audience reach, but with a very shaky financial underpinning that wasn't sustainable in the longer term. In the immediate aftermath of WWII, the fragile global economy hit film industries as much as every other sector (Magor and Schlesinger, 2009: p.301), and contributed to a further series of measures undertaken by British governments. In 1947, on top of the quota system, the government introduced the so-called 'Dalton Duty', a tax on non-British film earnings in the UK, largely intended to contribute to policies trying to tackle balance of payment issues (where imports were exceeding exports), and which briefly led to American studios refusing to export any films into the British market (Stubbs, 2008: pp.337–8). Whilst this was relatively quickly resolved, it contributed to an actually increased involvement of the US film industry into Britain, with an ever-bigger degree of runaway production activity (Stubbs, 2008). In 1949, the National Film Finance Corporation (NFFC) was established by the government, working with taxpayer money, and with companies like Rank, to provide funds for film production (Porter, 2009: p.270), and then in 1950 the Eady Levy was introduced, initially voluntarily, and then made compulsory under the 1957 Cinematograph Films Act. Named after the civil servant tasked with administering the system, the Eady Levy required exhibitors to retain 'a proportion of the ticket price and give half of this sum to fund British film production' (Magor and Schlesinger, 2009: p.302). The levy was influenced in part by growing post-WWII global agreements on international trade, in this case the General Agreement on Tariffs and Trades (GATT) which contained provisions restricting individual countries in their ability to provide what amounted to 'state aid' subsidies for film, and which this system avoided (ibid.). Similar concerns about policies amounting to state aid would appear later in relation to film policy in the 2000s when Britain was still part of the European Union, and was a key factor in the establishment of the 'cultural test' for tax relief for films (discussed later).

Despite the continuation of quotas, and the introduction of the levy, through the 1960s British film continued to be heavily dominated by the US, even dubbed as 'Hollywood, England' by one author (Walker, 1974). Indeed, by 1967 'ninety percent of funding for "British films" came from the USA' (Magor and Schlesinger, 2009: p.302). One reason for this was that, through the many subsidiaries and other strategies used by the Hollywood companies (such as use of British studios and talent), they themselves were able to qualify for the Eady Levy and NFFC finance (Stubbs, 2008: p.342; Magor and Schlesinger, 2009: p.302; Chapman, 2021: p.177). This became increasingly attractive for Hollywood companies into the 1960s as US film audiences declined rapidly against the rise of television. International audiences became ever more important parts of Hollywood activity adding a further incentive to using the financially conducive production environment afforded by the state-supported systems in Britain (and elsewhere). Again, it's possible to look at memorable films and film-makers from this era, and not immediately see a problem per se with these structural arrangements. British structural support contributed to the rise of the so-called British New Wave, for instance. These were typically black-and-white social realist films dealing seriously with a range of social issues around class, gender, and race, in films like Tony Richardson's *A Taste of Honey* (1961), Karel Reisz's *Saturday Night and Sunday Morning* (1960), and John Schlesinger's *Billy Liar* (1963). In turn, many of these directors attracted American money for subsequent films produced in Britain, the American money leading to more lavish, and often not economical even if critically successful films, like Richardson's *Tom Jones* (1963) (Chapman, 2021). Also, as Stubbs notes: 'the decision to base a film in Britain was primarily motivated by two factors: the commercial prospects of the project and the film-making style desired by its producers' (2009: p.17).

By the 1960s, Britain as a source of talent, both in front and behind the camera, that could be exploited by Hollywood was well established, but also British 'content' was something that was increasingly appealing to international audiences, as evidenced by the James Bond series of films, that began with *Dr. No* (1962). The shift from studio lots to more location shooting, widescreen, and colour formats, all intended to compete with television in terms of production values, also favoured production away from Hollywood for certain types of films, and even where studio lots were used, those at places like Shepperton or Pinewood were cementing themselves as regular bases for Hollywood film productions whether the substantive content of productions was British or not.

Television, Thatcher, and the Cultural Test

The 1950s and 1960s were a transitional period in all sorts of ways, but one of particular note is in that transition from film to television as the dominant medium of screen entertainment. Holmes (2005) discusses the quite different approaches to television between Hollywood and the British film industry, linked in part to the differing structures of both film and television in the respective countries. A commonality was a, not untypical, suspicion in the 'old' media industry of the new medium of television, which quite quickly became an obvious threat as cinema audiences began to decline, never to return to the peaks of the 1940s. Sometimes television was a subject for films, such as in the Ealing comedy *Meet Mr. Lucifer* (1953), in which the gift of a television set leads to all sorts of problems, or *Make Mine a Million* (1959), another comedy this time poking fun at both the staid BBC of the time, and the perceived coarseness of television advertising that emerged with the arrival of ITV in the middle of the decade. The ITV franchise system had provided film companies with opportunities to get into the television business, and some did so: Associated British Picture Corporation (ABPC) won one of the franchises (ABC TV), and the cinema chain company Granada won the franchise for the North-West. Rank invested in Southern TV after the franchise auction, so film companies, particularly with distribution/exhibition interests, got into British television early on (Holmes, 2005: p.27).

The rise of television audiences and the fall of film audiences was consequential everywhere, and a knock-on consequence of the decline of US film-going was the eventual collapse of the Hollywood studio system, with concomitant impacts on British film production that had been so reliant in one way or another on US finance. In Britain, though, the relationship between film and television companies provided something of a lifeline of sorts, as the 'comfortable duopoly' of the public service BBC and the advertising-funded ITV enabled film-makers to continue working, albeit more often on projects aimed at the small screen rather than cinemas. Through the 1970s, highly popular television series, typically comedies, often resulted in feature film releases like the BBC's *Dad's Army* and ITV's *On the Buses* (both 1971). Many of the Hollywood studios' subsidiaries closed or were sold off, notably studio spaces (such as at Borehamwood, Pinewood, etc.), often to television companies. Film productions did continue through the decade and American films did continue to get made in British studios, such as *Star Wars* at Elstree in 1977, and some notable British films still appeared as well, like 1971's *Get Carter*, but the 1970s is a decade where British film was heavily overshadowed by television.

The 1980s, however, were a pivotal decade for dramatic change in the British film industry, and television remained a key feature of those changes. Channel 4 launched in 1982 with a specific remit of being a televisual publisher rather than producer, providing new opportunities for independent producers to get access to television. Through a programme strand called 'Film on Four' that would later become Film Four International, that broad brief incorporated film production as well. Giles states that 'between 1981 and 1990 Channel Four partially funded the production of some 170 films by independent companies' making it a major player in the industry at the time (1993: p.74). Budgets were tiny, however, such that the first year saw 20 films being produced for around $9.6 million, the cost of a single typical Hollywood feature film of the time (ibid.: pp.74–5). Like the New Wave of a generation earlier, Film Four films developed a distinctive set of themes around social issues, such as ethnicity, race, and class, and brought a new spate of critically acclaimed film-makers into wider public recognition. The careers of now celebrated directors, like Mike Leigh (who also worked with the BBC) with *High Hopes* (1986) and Stephen Frears with films like *My Beautiful Launderette* (1985), were heavily supported by Channel 4. Film Four films were also often antagonistically juxtaposed with the wider political climate of the 1980s, perhaps reflecting Channel 4's origins in mid-1970s' government policy compared to the profoundly different approach to screen media of the Thatcher government (just as in other industries as mentioned in other chapters). For the film industry, Thatcherite changes were the most dramatic for decades with complete removal of most of the measures of statutory support for film, the quotas and levy system most notably, and also significant reduction in state support for the NFFC, restructured and redirected to being a vehicle for private screen finance (and involving television producers as well). The long standing structures were not seen as providing much meaningful support by this time anyway, but the key point was that the very notion of state support to the film industry was brushed aside as an unnecessary measure, no longer needed (Magor and Schlesinger, 2009: p.303).

An important aside here lies in two notable changes in the ways audiences accessed film in the 1980s. Cinema attendance had continued to decline (one reason the levy on ticket revenues had become ever less effective) and bottomed out in 1984, with a little over 50 million people going to the cinema that year in total – amounting to the average person going to the cinema just once per year, compared with the at least once a week in the 1940s peak. Although multi-screen cinemas were not new, having been around at least as far back as the 1930s, in the 1980s the multiplex cinema arrived, the first of which in Britain was in Milton Keynes in 1985. Following their successful expansion in the US, the idea of the multiplex enabled multiple screenings of films to maximise audiences, particularly for the blockbuster movies, whilst pooling a lot of the facilities needed to support screens (ticketing, food, and drink) in a cost-effective manner. Another factor in recovering film audiences (doubling in Britain by the end of the 1980s from the 1984 low) was rather paradoxically linked to the emergence of home video (Walker, 2022). Concerns that video might kill off cinemas, if not film entirely, were quickly offset by the home rental market that built up around video. Releasing films on video for rental after cinema distribution, and then for sale after that, exploited the semi-public nature of media products (as mentioned in Chapter 2), as well as opened up a market for re-monetising Studios' film archives through rental/sales of 'classic' films, a strategy used effectively by companies like Disney. But video also reinforced the experiential quality of seeing films at the cinema, and like the introduction of widescreen and colour – but more effective than gimmicks like drive-in cinemas – video helped to reignite audience interests in cinema attendance. Also, video offered another distribution channel for film-makers, and whilst the 'straight-to-video' distribution approach was often seen culturally as a marker of low quality, a kind of 1980s version of quota quickies, it was a means to offset the decline of independent cinemas that were providing spaces for independent productions that the multiplexes were not offering.

Despite the returning film audience, the rise of the video market, and the investment from television companies like Channel 4, film production in Britain did not substantially rise in the years after the shift to the Thatcherite market-driven policy framework, reaching a post-WWII low point of just 30 films being produced in 1989 (Russell, 2017: p.378). Although global film markets picked up too, and Hollywood productions increased overall, other countries at this time started to get into the market for runaway productions, so Britain was competing with countries like Canada and Australia for inward investment. In the mid-1990s, the newly established National Lottery was used as a pot for film funding, amongst other causes, and that was cemented through the establishment of the UK Film Council in 2000, but at this time it was tax incentives that 'came to be regarded as a more "market-friendly" alternative to quotas and levies' as a primary means of supporting the industry (Hill, 2016: p.711). Tax-based measures became central to the Blair government's (1997–2007) approach to film, that, despite being a Labour government, retained much of the neo-liberal, pro-market logic of the 1980s. As mentioned earlier, global trade agreements in the post-WWII era had long established a tension between principles of free trade with nations' protectionist ambitions for industries of significance to them. Over the decades of various agreements, some degrees of exception were built-in with regard to cultural industries, whereby states could support particular cultural industries because of their cultural rather than economic importance. By the late 1990s, the European Union was becoming a much more substantive actor in member-states' affairs than it had been when Britain joined its predecessor in 1973, and it was already a major area of political controversy. Within the rules of the EU's single market – designed to enable as free and equitable trade between member-states as possible – actions like tax incentives for film production could not be enacted by individual member-states without a range of measures to ensure that they were only being done 'to promote culture and heritage conservation' (EC in Hill, 2016: p.712). In the early 1990s, some tax relief schemes were introduced by British governments with little real consideration of EU requirements for clear cultural rather than just economic justification, but by the early 2000s, a combination of increased EU authority and a more pro-EU British government saw the introduction of the 'cultural test' (see Box 6.1), a points-based set of criteria for qualifying for tax credits for filmmakers, that includes requirements beyond British finance, facilities, and personnel to include cultural contribution (Hill, 2016: p.712).

Box 6.1 The Cultural Test

Introduction first in 2007 for film (and later in 2014, with variations, for some kinds of television production, and for videogame production), these are criteria for receiving tax relief/credits for producing a film in Britain:

  Section A – cultural content A1: Film set in the UK or a European Economic Area (EEA) – Up to 4

A2: Lead characters British or EEA citizens or residents – Up to 4

A3: Film based on British or EEA subject matter or underlying material – 4

A4: Original dialogue recorded mainly in English or UK indigenous language or EEA language – Up to 6

Section B – cultural contribution The film demonstrates British creativity, British heritage, and/or diversity – Up to 4

Section C – cultural hubs

  C1:

a   At least 50% of the principal photography or SFX takes place in the UK – 2

b   At least 50% of the VFX takes place in the UK – 2

c   An extra 2 points can be awarded if at least 80% of principal photography or VFX or SFX takes place in the UK – 2

C2: Music Recording/Audio Post Production/Picture Post Production – 1

  Section D – cultural practitioners

D1: Director – 1

D2: Scriptwriter – 1

D3: Producer – 1
D4: Composer – 1
D5: Lead actors – 1
D6: Majority of cast – 1
D7: Key staff (lead cinematographer, lead production designer, lead costume designer, lead editor, lead sound designer, lead visual effects supervisor, lead hair and makeup supervisor) – 1
D8: Majority of crew – 1

Source: BFI, full details at: www.bfi.org.uk/apply-british-certification-tax-relief/
cultural-test-film/summary-points-cultural-test-film

The relatively brief period of small but sustained subsidy to film production administered through the UK Film Council, especially in combination with continued (if often reduced) finance from television companies like Film Four, saw the persistence of a notable format of British films, and a new generation of creative talent. Shane Meadows, with films like *This is England* (2006), continued the tradition of small budget, socially conscious films, whilst *The King's Speech*, mentioned at the beginning of this chapter, was a huge commercial success from a tiny UK Film Council budget depicting the other end of British cinema content. It is a 'heritage' film, cosily presenting a rather fantastical image of the Royal family in the run up to WWII in a tradition stretching back to Korda but also one that achieved its success just as the new Conservative-led Coalition government (2010–15) was abolishing the UK Film Council in a range of public cuts, justified on the grounds of the 'austerity' needed in the wake of the 2008–9 global financial crisis (Newsinger, 2012: p.133).

The cultural test, on the other hand, seems to have done little to meaningfully generate/ deliver a more robust or diversified representation of British culture on screen, indeed it has arguably enabled something of a return to the predominance of American finance, and American production values and priorities into film production in Britain. This is how many Marvel movies, for instance, can qualify as British films. In 2014, the wholesale acquisition of a British film studio by a US company, not seen since the 1940s, occurred when Warner Brothers purchased the Leavesden studios in 2014, ostensibly to solidify the sets for the Harry Potter series of films, which now serve as the centre piece of a Warner Brothers Studio Tour experience (Russell, 2017: p.379). Indeed, even in the wake of Covid 19, and the virtual halting of film production and cinema exhibition for large chunks of 2020 and 2021, this has done little to stem a new wave of development of screen produc-tion facilities in the UK, as the growth in use/demand for screen content for streaming services has created demand for more content production. In the late autumn of 2020, for instance, multi-million-pound deals were signed for new production studios in the UK, whilst famous existing sites like Pinewood, Shepperton, and Elstree were massively increasing in size, largely fuelled by the demands, and currently deep pockets, of the major streaming services (Sweney, 2020a; Dams, 2020), though that boom is not reaching down to struggling domestic independent film producers (Alberge, 2022).

Conclusion

The potential for distributing films digitally, via streaming services, directly into peo-ple's homes has been a technical possibility for some years, but hadn't been a prominent feature of industry strategies until Covid 19 brought long periods of empty cinemas around the world, closed by various national government lockdowns. The American Studios weighed up the risks of delayed cinema launches, mixed cinema/ online releases, or entirely online releases. Perhaps more than any of the other major media industries, cinema was heavily impacted with cinemas closed, and the economics of production, distribution, and exhibition fundamentally disrupted. Prior to Covid though, increasing pressures on traditional industry structures were becoming apparent, mainly from the emerging streaming services that were moving from essentially archive services for film and television producers to significant investors in their own productions, a notable example being Netflix-funded and streamed *Roma* (2018) which garnered multiple awards, including the Best Director Oscar for Alfonso Cuarón. *Mank* (2020) was another Netflix production nominated for multiple Oscars including all the main categories (Picture, Director, Actor, Actress) though in the end it didn't win in those categories. The challenge of streaming services, with ever faster broadband speeds and ever better 4K resolution televisions, has caused real ructions in the film industry. The likes of Martin Scorsese claim that streaming services are 'devaluing' films by turning them into 'content' (Scorsese, 2021), even as they too gravitate to the new platforms to fund and screen their work. Scorsese's *The Irishman* (2019) was a Netflix production after all. Much like the model of British television funding British film production, and television being the most likely places for audiences to see those films from the 1980s onwards, the streaming platforms offer both opportunities for finance and reaching audiences but also challenges for meeting the distinctive environment of streaming screen services compared to both traditional television and cinemas. The strengths of British television in establishing discrete streaming services at least affords a new route for exhibition for British films, with both free services like the pioneering BBC iPlayer and All 4, and the growing number of subscription services, giving a longevity to films like Henry Blake's *County Lines* (2019) they could not receive in conventional cinema exhibition. The perennial challenge of British films remains, however, to try and both not be so dependent on US film or British television, and also to provide something distinctive from the almost polarised kinds of films that have been produced over the decades. On one side are typically bleak, social commentary films like *County Lines* and, on the other, the internationally marketable heritage films like *Downton Abbey: A New Era* (2022) that depict a rose-tinted picture of the upper classes/aristocracy. Both types of film have emerged and persisted within industry structures reflecting a mix of governmental ideologies and political pressures over time, but also the still continuing influence of Hollywood.

7   Radio

Radio is an important, yet often overlooked, part of the British media industries. The significance of radio in Britain is twofold. First, historically, the establishment of Britain's foremost media institution, the British Broadcasting Corporation (BBC), together with its commitment to the principles of public service broadcasting, can be traced back to the 1920s and the early years of radio. As put by the BBC itself, 'our mission has remained the same for almost 100 years. We act in the public interest, serving all audiences through the provision of impartial, high-quality and distinctive output and services which inform, educate and entertain' (BBC, 2019: p.2). To fully understand the BBC today, as well as ongoing debate over its future and the scale and scope of public service broadcasting/media more generally, requires an understanding of the historical development of radio in Britain. A second major reason why the radio industry warrants our attention is that listening to the radio remains very popular. According to Radio Joint Audience Research (RAJAR), the official organisation responsible for measuring radio audiences in Britain (jointly owned by the BBC and the Radiocentre, on behalf of the commercial sector), 49.7 million adults, or 89 per cent of the adult (15+) population, tuned in to their selected radio stations each week in the first quarter of 2022 (RAJAR, 2022a).

Radio's ability to withstand the rise of television, as well as more recent developments in online media, has led it to be labelled a 'resilient medium' (Starkey, 2017). Such resilience owes much to the 'secondary nature' of radio listening (Crisell, 1994: pp.12–13). Unlike television, radio can be fully experienced while a listener is engaged in a wide range of other activities, whether inside the home (cleaning, cooking, etc.), or outside (driving, working, etc.). At the same time, however, it would be an oversimplification to see the development of the radio industry in Britain as merely a product of the inherent characteristics of the medium itself. On the contrary, as with other sectors of the media industries, the radio industry has been (and continues to be) shaped by the combination of a host of different technological (e.g. online distribution), economic (e.g. the strategies of commercial radio groups), and political (e.g. the funding and regulation of the BBC) factors.

The remainder of this chapter is divided into two main sections. The first part focuses on the historical development of radio in Britain, with a particular focus on the formation of the BBC and development of public service broadcasting. The second part of the chapter then moves on to examine the commercialisation and expansion of radio in Britain since the 1970s and in doing so highlights some of the key features of the contemporary radio industry, including concentration of ownership within the commercial sector, rivalry between the BBC and commercial radio broadcasters, and,

DOI: 10.4324/9781315396781-10

finally, perhaps most importantly, the impact of the growth of online delivery on radio in Britain today.

The Historical Development of Radio in Britain

From Wireless Telephony to Public Service Broadcasting

The Italian, Guglielmo Marconi, is widely regarded as 'the father of radio'. It was he who, in the early years of the 20th century, did more than anyone else to develop radio communications technology, or as it was known at the time, 'wireless telephony' (Crisell, 2002: p.15). Marconi's invention was quickly adopted by the British government for military and strategic communications in situations where wired communication proved difficult, such as between navy ships and/or the shore. Others, however, were already contemplating alternative uses for the new technology. As early as 1916, David Sarnoff, an employee of the American Marconi Company, predicted that wireless technology could be used to transmit regular entertainment and information, which would in turn stimulate sales of radio receivers. In the United States, Sarnoff's vision quickly became a reality and Marconi and other wireless manufacturers were keen to establish a regular broadcasting service in Britain too. In 1920, the Marconi Company carried out one of Britain's first major experiments in broadcasting, when the famous Australian operatic soprano, Dame Nellie Melba, broadcast a special concert sponsored by the *Daily Mail* newspaper. This event attracted mass public attention and demonstrated the enormous potential of wireless technology for broadcasting (Briggs, 1961: pp.49–50). As a result, the British government was inundated with applications from wireless manufacturers wanting to launch regular broadcast services. However, the government faced two significant problems. First, it did not relish the inevitably controversial task of having to decide which company/ies be allowed to broadcast and it was even less keen to undertake the equally controversial task of providing the broadcast service itself. Second, the government feared that 'spectrum scarcity' would almost inevitably lead to interference between the signals of rival broadcast services, as well as with official government/military communications. There were already reports from the US of a 'chaos of the airwaves' that was beginning to undermine demand for radio sets (Coase, 1950: p.20). The British government's solution was to propose that the separate rival companies joined together to form a single broadcasting company – a broadcasting cartel (Briggs, 1961: pp.105–6). After much discussion, the manufacturers agreed to the government's plan and a new co-operative broadcast company was formed – the British Broadcasting Company (the Company). The Company's affairs were to be overseen by a board of directors (two representatives from each of the main firms) and controlled on a day to day basis by a newly appointed general manager. It was funded from two separate sources: an annual licence fee paid by wireless owners and the royalties from wireless set sales (Briggs, 1961: pp.115–8). Finally, concerns over the potential influence of the broadcast service led the British government to insist that the manufacturers agree to government regulation of the content broadcast. The Company's licence to broadcast included a clause obliging it to, 'broadcast matter to the reasonable satisfaction of the Postmaster-General [the government minister responsible for broadcasting]' (Coase, 1950: p.17). In response to lobbying from the newspaper industry, which saw the growth of radio as a commercial threat, specific restrictions were also placed on the broadcasting of news and advertising, with advertising prohibited altogether and news limited to reports from an approved news agency (Briggs, 1961: pp.130–3; p.164). These restrictions were accepted with few complaints. After all, as long as wireless set sales increased, the manufacturers had only a passing interest in the content of broadcasting service itself.

Within a few months of beginning officially licensed broadcasting, the Company was in serious financial difficulty. Rather than buying the relatively expensive Company wireless sets, thousands of listeners were buying cheap kits of non-Company manufactured ready-made parts, designed for easy home construction. Most listeners were also not bothering to purchase official licences from the Post Office (Briggs, 1961: p.150). In 1925, with the Company's original two year licence soon to expire, the manufacturers made it clear that they were no longer prepared to fund the broadcast service. Faced with this situation, the government established an independent Parliamentary Committee to consider the future of broadcasting in Britain. The (Crawford) Committee's report proved to be a significant landmark in the history of British broadcasting, signalling a shift from broadcasting being seen primarily as a way to stimulate the sale of wireless sets to its conceptualisation as a public service. The most ardent proponent of this new approach, known as public service broadcasting, was the Company's general manager, John Reith. Reith believed that broadcasting was a precious national resource (Reith, 1924). He argued that a broadcaster had the 'moral obligation' to provide a national service for everybody who was prepared to listen (Briggs, 1961: pp.236–8). For Reith, it was in the very nature of the medium that it should be available to all (i.e. a public good – see Chapter 2). He proclaimed that broadcasting:

> ran as a reversal of the natural law that the more one takes, the less there is left for others, [with broadcasting] there is no limit to the amount which may be drawn off. It does not matter how many thousands there may be listening; there is always enough for others.
>
> (Reith, 1924: p.52)

Following on from this, and echoing the sentiments of 19th-century thinkers, like Matthew Arnold, Reith also argued that broadcasting had the potential to culturally enlighten Britain. For Reith, a broadcaster had the duty to 'bring into the greatest possible number of homes... all that is best in every department of human knowledge, endeavour and achievement' (Reith, 1924: p.26). However, Reith maintained that broadcasting would only be able to fulfil its public service role if certain regulatory conditions were met. First, to ensure that, 'one general policy may be maintained throughout the country and definite standards promulgated', broadcasting needed to remain a monopoly (quoted in Coase, 1950: p.49). Second, 'an assured source of funding' (i.e. a licence fee) was required to enable the broadcaster to pursue 'the best of everything', rather than cater for advertiser demands or audience whims (Negrine, 1989: p.98). And third, to ensure it operated 'as free as possible from interference both by business and government', such a broadcaster should be run by a public corporation, composed of representatives of the public with no other sectional interests at stake (Briggs, 1961: p.299).

Reith's vision for the establishment of a public service broadcaster received widespread support. Not least because, by the 1920s, public corporations acting in the public interest had become an established policy response to problems encountered in other industries too, such as gas, electricity, and water (Curran and Seaton, 2010: p.105). It was no surprise then when the Crawford Committee recommended that the Company's broadcasting service continue, but 'conducted by a public corporation acting as a Trustee for the national interest and its status and duties should correspond with those of a public service' (Crawford, 1926, para. 20(a)). Following agreement from the government, on January 1, 1927, the British Broadcasting Company became the British Broadcasting Corporation (the BBC). The BBC was formally established by the issuing of a royal charter, which detailed the Corporation's organisational structure. Just like the Company, the BBC was to be managed by a board of governors, who would be responsible in law for all the BBC's activities, and a director-general, who would be answerable to the governors. Attached to the Charter, was a ten-year licence to broadcast, which largely reiterated the regulatory conditions undertaken by the Company (Smith, 1974: pp.56–9).

The Growth of Radio and the Challenges of Public Service Broadcasting

The late 1920s and 1930s witnessed the rapid growth of radio listening in Britain. After 1928, no programmes were heard by fewer than a million listeners and some attracted 15 million (Crisell, 2002: p.22). By 1939, the BBC had an estimated 40 million listeners (of a population of 48 million) (Stourton, 2017: p.23). During this period, radio replaced the music hall as one of the most popular forms of mass entertainment and staying in to listen to the 'wireless' became a more popular evening activity than going to a public venue to be entertained by performers on a stage (Crisell, 1994: p.19). In parallel, the BBC itself emerged as a national institution. When it became a corporation, the BBC had 773 staff, by 1938 there were 5,000 (Crisell, 2002: p.30). During the 1930s, the BBC also moved to a new purpose built headquarters, Broadcasting House, Portland Place, London, and both its networks, the National Programme and the Regional Programme, were available to the vast majority of listeners.

However, the implementation of Reith's vision for public service broadcasting was not (and has never been) straightforward. Two fundamental issues became apparent during the early history of radio, which, to varying degrees, have challenged the BBC ever since. First, mostly in relation to news and current affairs, it soon became evident that there is an inherent tension between the Corporation's commitment to offer an independent public service and the fact that the BBC is ultimately dependent on the British government for its very existence and funding, albeit indirectly via a licence fee. The nature of this problem became evident before the Company had even become a Corporation. In 1926, the country was engulfed by a general strike. Due to striking newspaper workers, broadcasting became the public's only source of news. Some within the British government, including the then Chancellor of the Exchequer, Winston Churchill, argued that the government should commandeer the Company for propaganda purposes, but the Prime Minister, Stanley Baldwin, rejected any such action on the grounds that an 'independent' broadcasting company was likely to have more public credibility. Reith's response was to ensure the Company's news broadcasts broadly reflected the government's position, providing information on day to day events, but nothing that supported the unions, or would encourage the strike to spread. The result was that the Company's reporting of the strike was criticised by the unions, but was never wholly identified with the government (Briggs, 1961: pp.376–80). The strike quickly lost momentum and the BBC's conduct proved enough to convince the government of the merits of public service broadcasting. For subsequent critics of the BBC, however, the Corporation's coverage of the general strike epitomised the 'actual as opposed to the assumed meaning of impartiality' that can characterise BBC news coverage, particularly at times of national crisis (Tracey, 2000: p.43).

Following the general strike, during the 1920s and 1930s, news was a fairly marginal feature of the BBC's output. Regulations to protect the circulation of (evening and daily) newspapers meant that news bulletins were not heard before the early evening and even then relied largely on relaying information from news agencies, rather than independent BBC journalism. It was WWII (1939–45) that provided a catalyst for the rapid development of the BBC's own independent news service. Albeit never with absolute freedom from government censorship, at the outbreak of war the BBC took the policy decision to 'tell the truth', as far as the truth could be ascertained, rather than create propaganda (Stourton, 2017: p.10). Reporters, such as Wynford Vaughan-Thomas and Richard Dimbleby, provided reports from 'war zones' and radio news reports served the public's intense desire for the latest news with an immediacy newspapers could not match. During the war, radio also provided a way for political leaders and Royalty to address their people simultaneously. Most notably, Winston Churchill, Prime Minister from May 1940, made broadcasts heard by millions across Britain. By the end of the war, the status of the BBC, as well as radio more generally, 'could hardly have been higher' (Rudin, 2011: p.13).

With the growth of television from around the mid-1950s, there was a marked decline in the importance attached to radio by the British public as a source of political news. Nevertheless, some BBC radio news and current affairs programmes remain popular and continue to be focal points for debate over the Corporation's impartiality, most notably the flagship *Today* programme (launched in 1957). For example, in 2003, *Today* was at the forefront of a bitter dispute between the government and the BBC over the Corporation's coverage of Britain's involvement in the US led invasion of Iraq, which ultimately led to the resignation of both its Chairman, Gavyn Davies, and its director-general, Greg Dyke (Smith, 2008). By contrast, albeit on a more mundane level, since 2016, *Today* has frequently been criticised for being too supportive of the government and Brexit supporters (e.g. Mills, 2019). Whether such criticisms are justified or not, it is certainly the case that in the realm of radio, as with television and online, providing independent and impartial public service broadcasting remains a major challenge for the BBC.

A second fundamental issue with the implementation of public service broadcasting, which also became apparent during the early years of radio, concerned the Corporation's more general programming policy. From the outset, the BBC faced the challenge of how to provide a service that would, in Reith's words, offer 'the best of everything', but also at the same time appeal to all its listeners. During the 1920s and 1930s, Reith's approach focused more on the former than the latter. The BBC provided listeners with a wide range of classical music (Bach, Beethoven, etc.). In a similar vein, the Talks Department, established in 1927, broadcast contributions from distinguished speakers, like the playwright George Bernard Shaw, the economist John Maynard Keynes, and the writer H. G. Wells. A committed Christian, Reith also decreed that no programmes be broadcast on Sunday mornings, so as not to clash with church services. However, even Reith's BBC understood the need to 'bring the audience along' on the 'journey to the cultural uplands' (Hendy, 2013: p.59). To this end, the Corporation employed several different strategies. First, particular attention was given to the education of the ordinary listener. For instance, from 1927 to 1936, a 20-minute programme, *The Foundations of Music*, was broadcast five times a week with the express intention to spread knowledge and enjoyment of classical music (Street, 2002: p.56). Second, the BBC also offered significant amounts of lighter programming. During the early years of the BBC, 'popular music' and 'dance music' together accounted for more than 35 per cent of output and 'light orchestral' music another 12 per cent (Briggs, 1961: p.357). Third, intrinsically linked to the previous point, the BBC also adopted a deliberately 'mixed schedule', whereby listeners tuning in for something 'easy on the ear' – say, some light dance music – would then also listen to something more difficult which they had not been seeking: 'a strategy of education by stealth' (Hendy, 2013: p.59).

While it is important not to overstate the elitism of the BBC during the 1920s and 1930s, Reith's BBC certainly gave primacy to the tastes and biases of the upper middle classes, at the expense of ordinary working-class listeners. This point is perhaps best illustrated by noting the popularity of rival broadcasters. Under the agreement between the BBC and the Post Office, no rival stations could be established in Britain itself, but this did not stop programmes being transmitted to British audiences from overseas. Most significantly, from 1933, Radio Luxembourg, transmitting from the tiny European principality of the same name, broadcast an output that was unashamedly populist, with programmes featuring major stars, such as George Formby and Gracie Fields. With programmes funded by and featuring advertising, Radio Luxembourg proved popular with British listeners, particularly on Sundays. In 1935, according to the BBC's own Listener Research, around 22 per cent of listeners were estimated to regularly listen to foreign stations, like Radio Luxembourg, a figure that increased to 66 per cent on Sundays (Briggs, 1965: p.364).

At least partly in response, from around the mid-1930s, the BBC adopted a less elitist approach, with a degree of 'popularisation' to aspects of its programming policy, including the introduction of 'fixed point' scheduling (Scannell and Cardiff, 1982: pp.186–7). The trend towards popularisation gathered pace during the war years. By allocating more time to comedy and popular music, including programmes such as *ITMA* (*It's That Man Again*) and *Music While You Work*, the BBC established itself as 'the nation's comforter and entertainer through its darkest hours' (Stourton, 2017: p.233). At the same time, however, the Corporation remained committed to its underlying public service ethos. In the immediate post-war period, the BBC adopted a new tripartite programming policy, with listeners offered a choice of three different, but overlapping, services, ranging from the populist (Light Programme), to the serious (Home Service), and the highbrow (Third Programme). The intention was, as put by the BBC's new director-general, William Haley, to lead listeners 'from good to better by curiosity, liking, and a growth of understanding' as they scaled the 'cultural pyramid' (quoted in Smith, 1974: p.83). In line with this approach, during the 1950s, an era often regarded as the 'golden age of radio', the BBC launched a host of new formats and popular programmes, including the series' *Journey into Space* and *The Archers*, and the quiz, *Have a Go!*, with the latter attracting around 20 million listeners each week (Crisell, 2002: pp.74–5). At the same time, the Third Programme offered 'highbrow' cultural speech and music, most notably with radio plays from critically acclaimed authors, such as Dylan Thomas and Samuel Beckett (Street, 2002: pp.88–9).

Radio's 'golden age' was short-lived. By the early 1960s, with the growth of television, radio was attracting fewer and fewer listeners. It was around this time that the bulky radio receiver in many households was moved from its prime position in the living room to make space for the television set (Starkey and Crisell, 2009: pp.7–8). However, another technological advance, namely the transistor, ensured radio continued to be used by significant numbers of people. The transistor, an electrical component that allowed large, more delicate components to be discarded from the circuitry of the radio receiver, meant that the physical size of radio sets could be dramatically reduced, 'from the size of a small piece of living room furniture, to that of a box of chocolates' (Starkey, 2017: p.662). By the 1970s, the transistor meant that around 70 per cent of radios were portable and, by the 1980s, radios were also standard equipment in all new cars (Crisell, 2002: p.138). The development of the transistor coincided with a wider socio-cultural change in Britain as teenagers began to express their distinctiveness from other generations in a number of ways, including musical taste. This posed a particular problem for the BBC. The Corporation was wedded to an outdated understanding of 'popular music', which it defined as 'top twenty material', plus one or two other genres, including 'jazz and popular folk' (Briggs, 1995: p.508). By contrast, during the mid-1960s, a host of different 'pirate radio' stations, most famously, Radio Caroline, circumvented the BBC's radio monopoly by broadcasting from specially converted ships anchored off the coast in the Thames estuary. The pirate stations broadcast pop music all day (without paying royalties to record labels) and attracted large numbers of listeners, estimated at between 10 and 15 million, with about 70 per cent of those under the age of 30 (Crisell, 2002: pp.142–3). In response, the BBC lobbied the British government to introduce legislation (the 1967 Marine Broadcasting Offences Act) to effectively ban the pirates (Briggs, 1995: pp.563–7). Just as significantly, only ten weeks after the legislation passed, the BBC also launched a new station, Radio 1, to offer nothing but pop music. At around the same time, the Light Programme was replaced with Radio 2 (offering easy listening music); the Third Programme by Radio 3 (offering mostly classical music); and the Home Service by Radio 4 (offering speech-based programming). Taken together, these changes amounted to a significant shift in the BBC's programme policy. By the 1970s, the Corporation had moved closer to providing a public service that genuinely offered something for all its listeners, albeit across each distinct network, rather than within any one of them. In doing so, however, with the adoption of a collection of distinct generic-based networks, the BBC had also eschewed the element of 'cultural surprise' Reith had so valued in its early days (Street, 2002: p.110). For the BBC, the challenge of upholding its public service ethos while at the same time maintaining its popularity with listeners only intensified with the introduction of commercial rivals.

Commercialisation and Expansion

Driven by a combination of the political priorities of various governments, the interests of commercial media organisations, and new developments in broadcasting technology, since the late 1960s, there has been a steady growth in the amount of radio programming available to British listeners. With support from the Labour government, the BBC began to introduce local radio services, using VHF frequencies, starting with Leicester in 1967. By 1970, there were 20 BBC local stations, reaching around 70 per cent of the public, including major cities, such as London, Birmingham, Leeds, Manchester, Liverpool, and Nottingham (Seymour-Ure, 1991: pp.78–9). Keen to demonstrate their free market credentials, during the early 1970s, the new Conservative government responded with the 1972 Sound Broadcasting Act, which paved the way for the introduction of commercial radio. In accordance with the new legislation, the existing regulator for commercial television, the Independent Television Authority (ITA) (see Chapter 8) had its remit extended to include the licensing and regulation of commercially funded independent local radio (ILR) and was renamed the Independent Broadcasting Authority (IBA). By the mid-1970s, the IBA had issued licences to around 20 commercial stations, including the London-based Capital Radio and the London Broadcasting Company (LBC), offering mostly pop music and talk respectively. More commercial licences were issued during the 1980s and by 1988 46 ILR stations were covering about 85 per cent of Britain (Seymour-Ure, 1991: p.79). A further significant expansion of commercial radio in Britain followed the 1990 Broadcasting Act. In line with their deregulatory approach to the wider economy, during the 1980s and 1990s, the Conservatives oversaw the establishment of a new 'light touch' regulator for radio, the Radio Authority (RA), which licensed a host of new commercial radio stations at the local and regional level, bringing the total number of independent radio stations to 150 (Williams, 2010: p.241). The Radio Authority also awarded three national commercial licences, to Talk Radio, Virgin Radio, and Classic FM. At around the same time, the BBC also launched a new national service, revamped in 1994 as Radio 5 Live: a 24 hours a day news and sport service. During the late 1990s and early 2000s, the development of new digital technology for radio transmission and reception – Digital Audio Broadcasting (DAB) – facilitated the launch of yet more stations. Alongside the simulcasting of existing AM/FM stations, the BBC launched five digital-only UK-wide services, including BBC Six Music and the BBC Asian Network. For their part, commercial broadcasters also introduced a host of DAB stations and by the 2010s there were 172 commercial stations broadcasting on DAB digital radio, albeit around two-thirds of these simulcasts of existing analogue local stations broadcasting only in their existing analogue area (Rudin, 2006: p.164). Finally, most recently, the growing availability of connected devices (e.g. smart phones, tablets, smart speakers, etc.) alongside high-speed fixed and mobile networks for online distribution has given listeners 'more choice than ever in what they listen to and how they listen to it' (Ofcom, 2019a: p.78).

During this period of commercialisation and expansion, four key trends have been clearly discernible within the British radio industry: namely, concentration of ownership within the commercial sector; the dilution of public service regulations originally imposed on commercial stations; increasingly intense competition between BBC and commercial radio; and, finally, most recently, a shift from traditional broadcast radio to audio on demand.

Concentration of Ownership

Concerns over the domination of the British media by large US media corporations and/or existing ITV regional licence holders were reflected in the regulation of commercial radio from the outset. Under the terms of the 1972 Sound Broadcasting Act, no ITV company was allowed a controlling interest in an ILR station in the same area, and vice versa. The IBA could also regulate the extent of foreign ownership, and foreign control was completely forbidden. At same time, however, to be awarded an ILR licence, applicants needed to convince the IBA of their 'financial credibility' to operate the service (Starkey, 2015: p.45). At least partly as a result, the launch and initial growth of commercial radio in Britain was largely supported by investment from local/national newspaper groups and/or commercial broadcasters from Britain and overseas.

For example, LBC was backed by Associated newspapers, publishers of the *Daily Mail*, together with Selkirk Communications, a Canadian broadcasting company. Similarly, Capital Radio's investors included Associated Rediffusion, which operated commercial television in London, and Local News of London, a group controlling 122 local newspapers (Starkey, 2015: p.49). By the late 1980s, several of the 46 stations were 20–30 per cent owned by newspaper groups and only four out of 45 had no press involvement at all (Seymour-Ure, 1991: p.82).

Following the 1990 Broadcasting Act, companies with holdings in other media were allowed to control stations and clusters of ownership soon developed, such as Crown Communications, the Capital Radio Group, and the East Midlands Allied Press (EMAP) (Crisell, 2002: p.225). The 1996 Broadcasting Act permitted further concentration of ownership and there were 14 separate mergers or acquisitions in 1996, as well as a further 13 in 1997 (Devlin, 2018: p.140). By the early 2000s, four leading commercial radio groups – GWR, Capital, EMAP, and Scottish Radio Holdings – owned 47, 20, 18, and 16 separate local stations respectively (Starkey, 2015, p.125). Yet, if anything, facilitated by the 2003 Communications Act's further relaxation of ownership rules, the trend towards concentration of ownership within British commercial radio only intensified during the 2000s. In 2005, Capital and GWR Group merged to form GCAP Media, while EMAP took over Scottish Radio Holdings. In 2007, EMAP itself was taken over by the German publisher group, Bauer, which paid £422 million for EMAP's by then 38 local stations, including the national brands Kiss and Magic. Just a year later, the relatively new GCAP Media was itself taken over, by Global Media, which, in a deal reported to be worth around £375 million, became Britain's biggest commercial radio business, incorporating Global brands, Heart, Galaxy, and LBC, as well as GCap's Capital, Classic FM, Xfm, and Choice. Largely as a result of these takeover deals, the commercial radio landscape in contemporary Britain is dominated by two groups: Bauer and Global, with each group owning a host of leading commercial radio brands (see Table 7.1). Both groups have also expanded their portfolios in recent years, in particular with the introduction of additional national DAB stations such as Heart 80s (Global) and Kiss Fresh (Bauer). Taken together, Global- and Bauer-owned stations reach 58 per cent of the British population each week and account for 20.3 and 14.9 per cent of all radio listening respectively (Ofcom, 2018b: p.74).

Alongside Global and Bauer, a third significant player in the contemporary commercial radio marketplace is Wireless Group plc. Wireless Group is wholly owned by

Table 7.1 Bauer and Global: Leading Commercial Radio Brands

Bauer	Global
Kiss	Capital
Absolute Radio	Heart
Magic	Classic FM
Jazz FM	Smooth Radio
Hit Radio	Radio X
Gem	LBC
Kerrang!	Gold

Rupert Murdoch's News Corp UK and operates talkSPORT and TalkRadio, as well as Virgin Radio, which was relaunched in 2016 as a national DAB station. A notable feature of Wireless Group, since its £220 million acquisition by News Corp, in 2016, has been the use of its commercial radio stations to cross-promote other Murdoch-owned media brands, including *The Sun* and *The Times* (Sweney, 2016). Most significantly, in 2020, Wireless Group launched *Times Radio*, partly to compete against the BBC's speech-based stations, but also to promote the take up of digital subscriptions to *The Times* (Waterson, 2020). Under the auspices of former *News of the World* editor, Rebekah Brooks, News UK has also increased investment in its other radio stations. In 2018, it agreed a deal with popular radio DJ, Chris Evans, to host its Virgin radio breakfast shows, and, in 2019, it outbid the BBC for radio rights to upcoming England cricket tours, as well as exclusive commentary on a host of Premier League football matches (Waterson, 2019b).

Public Service Regulation

As with the introduction of commercial television almost two decades earlier (see Chapter 8), at least to start with, ILR represented the evolution of public service broadcasting in Britain, rather than its abandonment. Following the ITV model, ILR licences were awarded by the IBA for fixed terms on the basis of a public service 'beauty contest', with applicants required to impress the regulator with their (local) programming proposals (Starkey, 2015: p.45). Under the terms of the 1972 Sound Broadcasting Act, each station was required to offer a 'balance of programming', including what the IBA deemed 'meaningful speech', namely: current/social affairs, traffic, weather, competitions/quizzes, religion, education, and serials/drama (Stoller, 2010: pp.103–4). As with ITV, the IBA also drew an absolute distinction between programme content and advertising: sponsorship was not allowed. In effect, ILR stations faced the unenviable task of having to provide the type of traditional public service mix of programming that even the BBC had ceased attempting to provide within a single network. Partly as a result, the early years of ILR in Britain were characterised by financial struggles. Few stations reported profits, with most making a loss. Most notably, in 1974, LBC was reportedly making a loss of £100,000 per month (Starkey, 2015, p.52). For the most part, the programming on offer also fell short of the IBA's aspirations for locally inspired public service broadcasting. ILR was widely criticised for offering little more than 'pop and prattle', with its focus on a narrow range of pop music and listener phone-ins, which were common due to their cheapness and the fact that calls from nearby recognisable locations underlined the localness of ILR stations (Stoller, 2010: p.103.). Ironically, the advertising which was primarily intended to provide the main source of income for the new stations was, and remains, one of the most local aspects of ILR (Starkey, 2015: p.95).

With the introduction of breakfast television, in 1983, commercial radio faced increased competition during one of its peak listening times. Soon after, Centre Radio, in the city of Leicester, became the first ILR station to close, due to ongoing financial problems. In response, in 1984, commercial radio station owners, at what subsequently became known as the Heathrow Conference, demanded increased 'commercial freedom' from the IBA over programming, broadcast hours, advertising shareholdings, and diversification (Starkey, 2015: p.83). The pro-free market Conservative government responded supportively with the 1990 Broadcasting Act. This not only created the RA, but also empowered it to license as many ILR stations as available frequencies would permit. Licences were now to be auctioned as commercial opportunities and awarded to the highest bidder. Furthermore, while bidders were still obliged to outline their programming plans and consider the demands of the local audience, they were no longer required to broadcast a mix of education, information, and entertainment, and could broadcast as much advertising as they wished. In short, commercial radio in Britain was 'no longer... an essentially public service network' (Starkey, 2015: p.119).

By the early 2000s, the combination of increased concentration of ownership combined with the removal of most, if not quite all, local programming requirements gave commercial radio in Britain a distinctly national feel, with 'no more suggestion of localness than Marks and Spencer' (Crisell, 2002: p.248). The last decade has witnessed the continuation of this trend. In 2010, the Global group set about rebranding as many of its locally named stations as possible as Heart, replacing a host of heritage brands and merging them together into a handful of regional Heart 'superstations' (Starkey, 2015: pp.157–8). In the same vein, in 2011, Global also effectively merged the six Galaxy stations it owned in Scotland with a host of other stations across major cities in England so as to extend the Capital brand into another 'quasi-national' commercial pop radio station (Plunkett, 2010b). Following these changes, the breakfast and drive sequences continued to be produced locally in order to preserve some regional distinctiveness from the London output relayed at other times. However, even this concession to localness has since been diluted. Following lobbying from the main commercial players (RadioCentre, 2018), in 2018, Ofcom amended its 'localness guidelines', to enable commercial broadcasters to network all but three hours of programming a day, as long as stations broadcast hourly local news bulletins (James, 2018). In response, in 2019, Global announced that Heart, Capital, and Smooth would each introduce national breakfast shows. For Global, as put by its founder and Executive President, Ashley Tabor, the shift to national commercial services would put it in position to 'properly compete' with the BBC (Martin, 2019).

Commercial Radio versus the BBC

The introduction of ILR during the 1970s made a significant dent in the audience share of BBC radio. By the early 1980s, ILR accounted for 33 per cent of all listening, a figure dwarfed by the BBC's combined national and local services, but only around 10 per cent lower than the combination of Radio 1 and Radio 2 – ILR's main competitors (Starkey, 2015: p.103). The changes to ownership and programming regulation introduced during the 1990s enabled commercial stations to compete more aggressively with the BBC and, by 1993, there had been a 'spectacular falling-off of the Radio One audience', which, in turn, heralded a controversial overhaul of the station's brand (Street, 2002: pp.130–1). By the mid-1990s, commercial radio's audience share had overtaken the BBC's for the first time, with advertising revenues also growing rapidly, from £141 million in 1992 to £270 million by 1995 (Crisell, 2002: p.249). By 1999, there was an almost equal split in terms of audience share between BBC and commercial radio. Driven by the growing popularity of revamped Radio 1 and Radio 2 services, between 1999 and 2014, a gap in audience share between BBC Radio and commercial radio grew to just over 10 per cent in favour of the Corporation (RadioCentre, 2015: p.3). More recently, however, commercial radio has narrowed the gap, primarily due to an increase in listening to national commercial DAB stations (Ofcom, 2018b, p.72). In the first quarter of 2022, the total audience share of listening for BBC and commercial radio was virtually equal, with audience shares of around 50 per cent respectively (RAJAR, 2022b).

Whatever the precise audience share of BBC and commercial radio, it is certainly the case that the BBC retains a much larger share of the radio marketplace than other sectors of the media industries, most notably television. From the perspective of commercial radio stations, the BBC is a 'dominant player', which 'benefits from cross promotion across its multiple networks, crowds out commercial rivals and thereby stifles competition' (RadioCentre, 2015: p.4). On this basis, commercial radio has long called for regulatory intervention to limit the scale and scope of the BBC. Furthermore, this call is part of wider political lobbying from the BBC's commercial rivals, who, particularly since the early 2000s, have consistently complained that the BBC 'crowds out' commercial players by expanding the number and type of services it offers (e.g. BBC iPlayer, digital radio stations, etc.) and/or competing with commercial providers to deliver popular content that would more suitably be provided by the commercial sector (e.g. popular television programming on BBC1, like *Strictly Come Dancing*, or pop music on Radio 1). Largely in response, following the 2006 BBC Charter review, the otherwise broadly supportive of the BBC Labour government required Ofcom to undertake a Market Impact Assessment (MIA) of any newly proposed, or major changes to existing, BBC services, with an emphasis on highlighting possible 'costs' to the commercial sector (Smith, 2013). A decade later, this time under the leadership of an avidly free market Conservative government, the need to ensure the 'BBC is sufficiently distinctive... from commercial providers' had become the 'central objective' of the (2016) BBC Charter review (DCMS, 2016: p.27). The term 'distinctive' or 'distinctiveness' appeared in the government's White Paper on the future of the BBC no fewer than 95 times (Goddard, 2017: p.1090).

In relation to radio, the main areas of controversy have been the output of the BBC's Radio 1 and Radio 2 services. Perhaps most memorably, in 2012, Global's chief executive, Stephen Miron, criticised what he called 'Radio One Direction' (a reference to the successful boy band). Miron complained, 'Radio 1 is squarely up against Capital, Radio 2 is right up against Heart, Radio 3 against Classic' (Plunkett, 2012). In its defence, the BBC has emphasised the 'distinctive services' offered by Radio 1 and Radio 2, claiming that around 90 per cent of the songs played on both Radio 1 and Radio 2 were not played on any other station, and that both stations play a huge range of music (BBC, 2016b: p.6). Independent audience research commissioned by Ofcom has also offered support for the BBC. Most significantly, Radio 1 and 1Xtra were seen by listeners as distinctive for airing new British talent, and for being more relevant for younger listeners than stations provided by commercial providers, with features, such as the Radio 1 Live Lounge, given particular praise (Ipsos Mori, 2017: p.33).

The Corporation's acquisition of exclusive audio sports rights for broadcast on Five Live has also been the subject of regulatory complaint from a commercial rival, namely talkSPORT. In 2018, the owner of talkSPORT, Wireless, formally requested Ofcom to initiate a 'BBC competition review' to scrutinise how the BBC acquires sports rights for BBC Radio. According to Wireless, the Corporation's activities in this area 'harm competition' in the market for sports radio rights (Ofcom, 2018c: p.1). Following an initial investigation, talkSPORT's arguments for regulatory intervention were rejected on the basis that: first, since Charter renewal in 2016, the BBC had, if anything, been spending less, not more, on radio rights for sporting events and competitions; and, second, that the BBC had not prevented talkSPORT from building 'a sizeable portfo-lio' of sports rights (Ofcom, 2018c: p.3). To date then, the BBC has managed to fend off calls for regulatory intervention from commercial radio, but, with the growing choice available for British listeners online, calls from commercial rivals for restriction to be placed on BBC radio are likely to continue.

From Live Radio to Audio on Demand

Over the last decade or so, how listeners access radio programmes has significantly changed. By 2022, almost three-quarters (73 per cent) of listeners were using a digital device, with 41 million adults aged 15+, tuning in to radio via a digitally enabled platform (DAB, DTV, online, or app) each week (RAJAR, 2022a). This is partly because the number of British households with a DAB set has increased markedly over recent years, from 38.2 per cent in 2011 to 65 per cent by 2022, but it is also due to the rapid growth in the number of listeners, particularly young adults, listening via smart phone or tablet (RAJAR, 2022a). Just as (if not more) significantly, more and more of the listening that takes place using digital devices can more accurately be described as audio on demand, rather than traditional (live broadcast) radio. In turn, broadly speaking, audio on demand can be divided into two categories. First, most markedly since around 2013, there has been rapid growth in the use of online streaming music services, like Spotify and Apple Music (see Chapter 9). Perhaps most notably, for younger listeners (15–34), by 2021, live radio accounted for only 24 per cent of their 'audio time', with streamed online music accounting for 43 per cent (compared to 58 per cent and 17 per cent respectively for all adults) (Ofcom, 2021a: pp.79–80). Second, speech-based content is also an important component of audio on demand. There is no firm definition of what constitutes a 'pod-cast', but the term is usually used to refer to 'episodic speech-based pieces of content' available to listen to 'as and when it suits the individual' (Ofcom, 2019a: p.99). What is without doubt is that over the last few years there has been a rapid growth in the amount of time British listeners are spending listening to podcasts, with, by 2021, 15 per cent of adults listening to podcasts each week (Ofcom, 2021b: p.77).

The rise of audio on demand represents a major new challenge for Britain's estab-lished radio broadcasters. For both the BBC and commercial radio broadcasters, competition for listeners is no longer restricted to one another. As put, in 2018, by James Purnell, the BBC's Director of Radio and Education, 'I don't care about share. I don't care about beating Global, Bauer or Wireless in the RAJARs…. the real chal-lenge is from streamers…' (BBC, 2018a). The changing nature of the competitive challenge faced by Britain's established radio broadcasters is arguably most apparent in the burgeoning podcast marketplace. Podcasts are available from a large number of different providers, offering a wide range of content and distributed via a variety of online delivery platforms (e.g. Spotify, Apple Podcasts, BBC Sounds, YouTube, etc.). Alongside traditional radio broadcasters, podcasts are available to British listeners from a host of new entrants to the audio marketplace, including: commercial television broadcasters, e.g. *Sunday Supplement* (Sky); *Love Island* (ITV); *C4 News* (Channel 4); established news brands, e.g. *The Sun Football Podcast* (*The Sun*), *Today in Focus* (*The Guardian*); other media businesses, most notably magazines, e.g. *Appearances* (*British Vogue*), *The Runner's World Podcast* (*Runner's World*); independents, e.g. *The Guilty Feminist* (comedy), *The Anfield Wrap* (football); and, finally, non-media organisations, e.g. *Couch to 5K* (NHS); *Anything But Silent* (British Library) (Ofcom, 2019a: p.100).

Some podcasts are (at least partially) funded via advertising, although the amount of advertiser spending dedicated to podcasts remains relatively small, at around £10 million per annum, a fraction of total radio advertising revenues, which, in 2018, totalled £572 million (Ofcom, 2019a: p.79; p.104). Others use online funding platforms, such as Patreon, to generate regular payments from fans. More significantly, for many podcast providers the underlying value of the podcast is as a relatively low cost supplement to a main product (e.g. magazine, TV show, etc.), which can help to retain/build brand awareness and consumer loyalty in an increasingly competitive media marketplace, rather than as a standalone product (i.e. diagonal integration – see Chapter 2). At the same time, an established brand identity, from either traditional radio broadcasting or the wider media industry, can also provide a competitive advantage within the crowded podcast marketplace. Many of Britain's most popular podcasts are offered by established radio broadcasters and/or other media brands/celebrities (see Table 7.2). In this sense, the growth of podcasting is a product of both technological convergence (i.e. the possibility of online delivery) and industrial convergence (i.e. cross-promotion by established brands).

Finally, it is worth emphasising that while the growth of online delivery has undoubtedly led to increased competition for Britain's established radio broadcasters, the collapse of the British radio industry is far from imminent. Despite the growing popularity of streaming, live radio continues to represent by far the largest proportion of time spent listening to audio each week, including among young people. Listening to live radio accounts for over half (58 per cent) of all audio time across the week (with 44 per cent on a radio set) for the average British listener (Ofcom, 2021b: pp.78–9).

Table 7.2 Britain's Most Popular Podcasts (August 2022)

Chart Position	Apple Podcasts	Spotify
1	*The Rest Is Politics* (Goalhanger Podcasts)	*Archetypes with Megan* (independent/the Duchess of Sussex)
2	*The News Agents* (Global)	*The News Agents* (Global)
3	*The Diary of a CEO by Steven Bartlett* (independent)	*The Joe Rogan Experience* (Joe Rogan/independent)
4	*Empire* (Goalhanger Podcasts)	*The Diary of a CEO by Steven Bartlett* (independent)
5	*Rob Beckett and Josh Widdicombe's Parenting Hell* (Keep it Light Media)	*Empire* (Goalhanger Podcasts)
6	Sh**ged Married Annoyed (independent)	*NearlyWeds* (JamPot Productions)
7	*No Such Thing as a Fish* (independent)	*The Rest Is Politics* (Goalhanger Podcasts)
8	*The Rest Is History* (Goalhanger Podcasts)	*Saving Grace* (The Fellas Studios)
9	*Off Menu with Ed Gamble and James Acaster* (Positive Productions)	*The Fellas* (Spotify Studios)
10	*NearlyWeds* (JamPot Productions)	*Wednesdays We Drink Wine* (JamPot Productions)

Source: Chartable.com

Furthermore, in response to the rise of online delivery, over the last decade, Britain's established radio broadcasters have also made their services available online and most recently via dedicated apps. For example, in 2011, commercial radio and the BBC joined together to launch the UK Radioplayer, providing listeners with access to over 150 radio stations online (Halliday, 2011). In 2018, the BBC also released a new app, BBC Sounds, to provide access to audio content including live shows and catch-up programmes, as well as podcasts and playlists based on user preferences (BBC, 2018b). Or, as put by the then BBC director-general, Tony Hall, to bring 'the best of everything we do in audio into one place' (BBC, 2018b). In the same vein, Global has too launched the Global Player app to offer access to live shows, offline catch-up programmes, and curated playlists from the stations in its portfolio (Ofcom, 2018b: p.74). With these initiatives, Britain's traditional radio broadcasters are likely to be major players within the evolving British audio landscape for at least the foreseeable future.

Conclusion

While the 'golden era' of radio has long since faded, the importance of the radio industry within the British media landscape remains. The underlying values of public service broadcasting carved out during the early/growth years of radio continue to permeate the BBC today (in radio and beyond). The Corporation also retains a significant presence within the contemporary radio/audio industry. Arguably, the BBC is a more important player in the radio/audio sector than any other area of the British media industries. It should not perhaps be a surprise, therefore, that critics of public service broadcasting and/or the BBC have often focused their attention on BBC radio and in particular its most popular services, such as Radio 1 and Radio 2. Such criticisms are likely to continue, but ongoing debates over the BBC and public service broadcasting should not be allowed to create the impression that radio is an old fashioned or fading industry. On the contrary, over the last decade or so, the relatively low cost of audio production coupled with the secondary nature of radio listening have placed radio at the forefront of technological and industrial convergence within the British media industries. As it evolves from live radio to also encompass audio on demand, radio continues to be a key part of the British media industries.

8 Television

Understanding the British television industry used to be fairly straightforward. Until the 1990s, there were three (British owned) national terrestrial broadcasters – the BBC, ITV, and Channel 4 – each with reasonably well defined, albeit slightly different, public service remits, and two main sources of funding: either a compulsory licence fee paid by television owning households (the BBC), or the sale of advertising time (ITV and Channel 4). Each broadcaster also produced, or commissioned in the case of 'publisher-broadcaster' Channel 4, the vast majority of its own programming, supplemented to varying degrees by some popular imports, mainly from the US. In contrast, the British television today is increasingly fragmented and competitive. Since the 1990s, there has been an enormous increase in the number of channels and the amount of programming available to viewers via various distribution technologies, including (analogue then digital) satellite and cable television, as well as, most recently, online via the internet. Just as significantly, these technological developments have been accompanied (and often driven by) the emergence of a new and increasingly important source of revenue, namely direct payments from viewers, mostly monthly subscriptions. Furthermore, the growth of pay television in Britain has been (and continues to be) dominated by a handful of US owned media organisations, most notably satellite and cable operators, Sky and Virgin respectively, alongside more recent subscription video on demand (SVOD) services, such as Netflix and Amazon Prime. These subscription services have been (and remain) largely reliant on a combination of premium content (e.g. Hollywood movies, exclusive sport, and high cost drama), US imports, and/ or archive programming, rather than original British programming. The result is that television in Britain today is a 'mixed broadcasting ecology' of public service broadcasters (BBC, ITV/STV, C4/S4c, and Channel 5) and subscription services (Sky, Netflix, Amazon, etc.), with both increasingly utilising various combinations of traditional (i.e. terrestrial, satellite, and cable) and online distribution (DCMS, 2022: p.5).

It is the 'mixed ecology' of British television that makes it a particularly significant sector for understanding the media industries. The contrasting guiding principles and priorities of public service broadcasters and subscription-based services mean that the television industry has long been the focal point for ongoing political debate over how to best organise the media industries in Britain (i.e. public intervention versus free market competition - see Chapter 3). For example, should the BBC continue to be funded by a compulsory annual licence fee paid by all British television (reception device) owning households? Should Channel 4 be privatised, or remain publicly owned? The British government's position (and decision to focus) on such questions reflects political choices about the relative merits of public intervention versus free market competition.

DOI: 10.4324/9781315396781-11

The contemporary television industry also warrants our attention as it provides another clear example of a sector of the British media industries that has been reshaped by the growth of the internet – a recurring theme of the book. Traditionally, from around the 1950s, television in Britain (and beyond) has been a linear service (or collection of services) broadcasting a schedule of programmes (i.e. channel/s). Since around 2012, with the growth of high speed broadband and the rapid public uptake of a host of internet enabled devices (e.g. tablets, smart phones, smart TVs, etc.), Britain has witnessed the rise of 'online television' (Johnson, 2019). As a result, the television industry in Britain today is increasingly centred around online 'portals', such as Netflix and the BBC iPlayer, which offer 'gateways' to various linear and/or video on demand (VOD) audio-visual content (Lotz, 2017). At the same time, however, it is important to emphasise that traditional linear television has not been replaced by online portals. On the contrary, linear television remains incredibly popular with British viewers. The average time spent viewing (traditional) broadcast television each day in 2020 was 3 hours 12 minutes per person, compared with 1 hour 17 minutes for SVOD/VOD services (Ofcom, 2021b: p.7). In this sense, contemporary television is 'what it has always been and also other things too' (Lotz, 2020: p.802).

This chapter is divided into four main sections. The first two sections provide an overview of the historical development of television in Britain during the 20th century. Part one considers the growth of television as a public service under the auspices of the BBC, ITV, and Channel 4 (1950s–1980s). Part two then details how the concept of public service broadcasting came to be challenged during the 1980s and 1990s on a number of different fronts. The third and fourth parts of the chapter focus on key developments in the British television industry during the 21st century. Part three examines the move from analogue to digital television (1998–2012), while the fourth part details the development of a highly competitive contemporary 'online television' industry.

The Evolution of Public Service Broadcasting

During the 1930s, the development of television was widely seen as an extension of radio broadcasting and it 'slid comfortably into the BBC system' of public service broadcasting (Seymour-Ure, 1991: p.66). The BBC began its television service on November 2, 1936, transmitting from Alexandra Palace in north London and received within a radius of 40 to 100 miles by a few thousand viewers in about 400 households (Crisell, 2002: p.78). Early broadcasts ran for two separate hours per day, but were brought to an abrupt halt by WWII (1939–45) as it was feared that the transmission masts would act as a navigational aid for German bombers. Television resumed in 1946, initially to about 15,000 households, but there was limited support for the new service inside the BBC (Crisell, 2002: p.79). In part, this was due to the relatively high costs of television programme making. In 1939, one hour of television was estimated to cost as much as 12 hours of the most expensive kind of radio programming (Williams, 2010: p.145). There was also a general lack of enthusiasm for the medium of television itself. Television was largely seen as 'illustrated radio' rather than a medium in its own right. For example, until 1948, the news was broadcast in sound only, with an anonymous announcer reading a script behind a picture of the BBC clock (Williams, 2010: p.144). Even worse, the new medium was also often seen as unsuited to public service broadcasting. As described by Grace Wyndham Goldie, a prominent figure in the development of BBC television, there was a fear that 'the high purposes of the Corporation would be trivialised by the influence of those concerned with what could be transmitted in visual terms' (Goldie, 1977: pp.18–19). Consequently, during the immediate post-war period, investment in the new television service came a poor second to the needs of radio (Briggs, 1979: p.208).

Nevertheless, during the early 1950s, the BBC's television service began to grow. By 1954 the Corporation was broadcasting about six hours of television a day, most of it live, to households across Britain (Crisell, 2002: p.79). As with radio, programming was designed to encourage viewers to move up the 'cultural pyramid' (see Chapter 7). There was entertainment, including *Come Dancing* (1950) (the forerunner of *Strictly Come Dancing*) and the popular quiz show *What's my Line* (1951), alongside 'high culture', most notably the science-fiction thriller, *The Quatermass Experiment* (1953) and an adaption of George Orwell's novel *1984* (1954). However, it was the BBC's coverage of the coronation of Elizabeth II on June 2, 1953, that provided a landmark moment in the history of television in Britain. An estimated 56 per cent of the adult population watched the service, around 20 million people, with nearly 8 million watching it in their own homes and another 10 million at the homes of family, or friends (Williams, 2010: p.148–9). The coronation also prompted a boom in the sale of television sets. In 1953, for the first time, more television than radio sets were manufactured and the television audience for the coronation was far in excess of those who listened on radio (Crisell, 2002: p.81). In this sense, the coronation symbolised the arrival of television as a mass medium and the surpassing of radio.

Despite, or perhaps because of the growing popularity of BBC television, the early 1950s witnessed public and Parliamentary debate over the introduction of a rival commercial television service. Fostered by strong economic growth and full employment, the 1950s witnessed the emergence of a new post-war consumer society with labour-saving devices like washing machines and refrigerators becoming increasingly common place. With increased purchasing power in the economy, advertisers began to explore the possibilities of using television to reach potential customers (Wilson, 1961). The introduction of commercial television was also viewed with sympathy by the Conservative Party as it looked to reposition itself in the post-war political landscape. At the 1951 general election, the Conservatives campaigned with the slogan 'set the people free' and presented themselves as the party that would provide greater individual freedom without endangering the central planks of Labour's post-war reforms (e. g. the NHS and the welfare state). However, the idea of commercial television attracted at least as much opposition as support. Opponents argued that maintaining the BBC's monopoly was the only way to avoid the inevitable fall in standards that would result from commercial television's reliance on advertiser funding (Sendall, 1982: p.19; p.31).

In the event, fears that the introduction of commercial television would mark the end of public service broadcasting were unfounded. When, in 1955, commercial television was introduced it was 'an extension of public service broadcasting, not an alternative' (Scannell, 1990: p.18). This was most clearly evident in three key areas. First, the new commercial service, Independent Television (ITV), was regulated by a public authority, the Independent Television Authority (ITA), whose members, like the BBC's governors, were appointed by the government. The ITA was responsible for ensuring ITV provided a 'balanced' (i.e. public service) programme output, including accurate and impartial news (Briggs, 1979: p.919). Second, the sponsorship of programmes was explicitly outlawed and adverts were required to be clearly separate from the rest of the programme. And third, in response to calls for British broadcasting to be decentralised, ITV was established as a regional system with the service in each region the responsibility of a single contractor (e.g. Granada in 'the North').

ITV was soon a popular and financial success. With growing audiences and a regional monopoly on the sale of television advertising, by the early 1960s, holding an ITV franchise was, in the words of one franchise owner, Lord Thomson (Scottish Television), 'a licence to print money' (Williams, 2010: p.152). However, critics accused ITV of achieving its profitability with 'trivial' programming, such as quizzes and American imports (Briggs, 1995: p.16). In 1960, an independent enquiry set up by the government to examine the state of British broadcasting, the Pilkington Committee, 'scolded' ITV for 'failing to live up to its responsibilities as a public service' (Scannell, 1990: p.18). The regulation of ITV was subsequently tightened to ensure more serious programming and quality drama, particularly at peak hours (Williams, 2010: p.159). As a result, during the 1960s, ITV moved closer to fulfilling its public service responsibilities, most notably with news and current affairs programmes, such as *World in Action* and *This Week*. At around the same time, in an effort to regain viewers previously attracted to ITV (and preserve the legitimacy of the licence fee), the BBC itself embarked on a more adventurous programme policy. During the 1960s, the BBC produced: the satirical news programme, *That Was the Week that Was*; a gritty police drama, *Z Cars*; and, the surreal comedy, *Monty Python's Flying Circus*. The Corporation was also awarded the licence for a third national television channel – BBC2 (1964) – which while generally offering more serious programming also provided some populist output, including *Match of the Day*. In this way, the programming of the BBC and ITV converged and during the 1960s and 1970s they came to be seen as 'part of a single public service system', albeit with different (assured) sources of funding (Seymour-Ure, 1991: p.69).

During the 1970s, the BBC and ITV were subject to growing criticism for being a 'cosy duopoly' that no longer represented the increasingly diverse tastes and interests of British society. Perhaps most notably, television news coverage was accused of operating within (and reinforcing) the prevalent middle-of-the-road consensus (see GUMG, 1976). The Annan Committee, which was established by the government in 1974 to examine the future of broadcasting and the allocation of a fourth national television channel, reached a similar conclusion. It claimed that 'there are enough programmes for the majority.... what is now needed is programmes for different minorities which add up to make the majority' (quoted in Williams, 2010: p.165). With this in mind, the Committee recommended the new channel be overseen by a newly established 'Open Broadcasting Authority' (OBA), rather than the BBC or ITV. The OBA concept provided the essential basis for what eventually became Channel 4, which, in turn, marked a significant evolution in the nature of British public service broadcasting. First, Channel 4 was legally obliged to offer programming that would appeal to 'tastes and interests not generally catered for by ITV' as well as 'encourage innovation and experiment in the form and content of programmes' (Broadcasting Act, 1981). In other words, Channel 4's chief public service objective was to produce material specifically targeted at cultural and ethnic minorities, rather than a BBC/ITV type mix of entertainment and serious programming. Second, the new channel was established as a hybrid of public ownership and commercial funding. Channel 4 was publicly owned (originally by the IBA), but funded via an annual subscription paid by ITV companies, who sold advertising on behalf of the new channel in their respective regions. In this way, direct commercial competition between Channel 4 and ITV was avoided. Third, Channel 4 was established as a publisher-broadcaster. Rather than produce programmes itself, the channel commissioned programmes from other programme makers, including a substantial proportion from independent producers. This approach was designed to both 'widen creative access to the airwaves' and foster increased competition for the BBC and ITV companies in the programme production sector (Crisell, 2002: p.208) – the latter being a particular concern of the Conservative government elected in 1979 (see p.121). Finally, in Wales, a separate broadcasting authority, S4C, was established to commission Welsh language programmes to be shown in Wales during peak times, with Channel 4 programming shown at other times.

Channel 4 began broadcasting in November 1982 and during the 1980s provided numerous examples of programming that fulfilled its public service mission, ranging from *Out on Tuesday* (1989), aimed at what was then defined as a 'lesbian and gay audience', to coverage of minority sports, such as American football. The channel also received acclaim for the depth offered by its one-hour-long peak time news coverage and Film on Four supported the production of a host of feature films for both television and cinema exhibition, perhaps most notably *My Beautiful Launderette* (1987), the story of a young Pakistani man living in London. In its own way, by the 1990s, Channel 4 was as much a part of British public service broadcasting as the BBC and ITV.

Multi-channel Television and the Crisis of Public Service Broadcasting

During the 1980s and 1990s, the principles and practices of public service broadcasting came 'under attack' on several interrelated and mutually reinforcing fronts: party political, ideological, and technological (Smith, 2008). The first – party political – challenge faced by Britain's public service broadcasters concerned their approach to news and current affairs. On the whole, before the 1980s, public service broadcasters provided a kind of even-handedness in their political coverage which was viewed as legitimate by both broadcasters and politicians (Negrine, 1989: pp.120–1). During the 1980s, public service broadcasters, and particularly the BBC, came under repeated public attack from the Conservative government (and its supporters) for attempting to apply this approach to coverage of a number of highly controversial issues, most notably the (1982) Falklands/Malvinas conflict and 'the troubles' in Northern Ireland (Negrine, 1989, pp.130–4). As the 1980s progressed, government attacks also extended to the mundane reporting of day to day politics and widened to include other public service broadcasters and their supporters, most notably ITV's London regional licence holder, Thames Television, and the IBA (Schlesinger, 1987). By the mid-1980s, the Conservative Prime Minister, Margaret Thatcher, had concluded that it was 'time the BBC put its house in order' (Schlesinger, 1987: p.xviii). To begin with, this meant challenging the public service broadcasting tradition of appointing BBC Governors on a bi-partisan basis. In 1986, the government appointed Marmaduke Hussey, the Thatcher supporting former Chairman of Times' Newspapers, as BBC Chairman, and then 'packed' the Board of Governors with political supporters (Curran and Seaton, 2010: p.206). In the long term, it meant a fundamental ideological challenge to the concept of public service broadcasting itself.

During the 1970s, the established political consensus about the beneficent role of the state – as planner, direct producer of goods and services, and employer – began to crumble. Against this background, key figures within the Conservative Party, including the leader, Margaret Thatcher, began to be influenced by the ideas of New Right theorists, such as Milton Friedman and Freidrich Von Hayek (Selsdon, 1994). Drawn largely from the principles of classical liberalism, New Right thinking amounted to a restatement of the case for a minimal state. During the 1980s and 1990s, the making of British public policy drew heavily on such thinking and a host of flag ship policies from successive Conservative governments were driven by a commitment to free market principles, including the privatisation of publicly owned industries (e.g. British Telecom and British Gas), the sale of publicly owned (council) housing, and the establishment of an 'internal market' within the National Health Service (NHS). In the same vein, the Conservatives' overriding approach to British television during the 1980s and 1990s was to make it 'more a matter of the marketplace, and less a matter of public service' (Goodwin, 1998: p.166).

The Conservatives' willingness to challenge the public service traditions of British broadcasting was first demonstrated in their approach to new cable and satellite technologies. These technologies were perceived largely in terms of the industrial benefits their successful development could produce for the British economy, rather than as the means to achieve any wider public service objectives. Furthermore, it was reasoned that these industrial benefits could best be exploited through the stimulation of free markets, which, in turn, would only be possible if new broadcasters were kept free from extensive public service commitments (Goodwin, 1998). However, perhaps the clearest articulation of the free market challenge to the principles of public service broadcasting came with the report of the Peacock Committee (1986). The Committee had been established by the government with a deliberately narrow mandate – to consider the future financing of the BBC – and was widely expected to approve the government's favoured policy option, namely for the BBC to take advertising. Instead, it put forward a far more radical vision for the future of television in Britain. Peacock concluded that, 'British broadcasting should move towards a more sophisticated market system based on consumer sovereignty' (Peacock, 1986: para.592). According to Peacock, advances in broadcast technology would enable the BBC to become a subscription service and, if particular public service programmes were still required, these could be provided via explicit public subsidy to a Public Service Broadcasting Council, much like the Arts Council. In the event, relatively few of the committee's policy recommendations were implemented (Wheeler, 1997), but this does not detract from its long term significance. The Peacock Committee placed the goal of creating more competition firmly at the heart of British television policy and in one way or another it has remained there ever since.

In the immediate aftermath of the Peacock report, ITV was the main focus of Conservative attempts to increase competition in British television. In 1990, the IBA was replaced by a new 'light touch' regulator, the Independent Television Commission (ITC), which was responsible for regulating all commercial television services, including cable and satellite. The way that ITV licenses were allocated was also changed. The IBA's traditional public service 'beauty contest', which awarded ITV regional licence on the basis of the range and quality of programming, was replaced with an auction, albeit with a programme quality threshold, overseen by the ITC. At the 1991 franchise round, while a number of highest bids were rejected for failing to pass the quality threshold, two major existing ITV broadcasters, TV-AM (Breakfast) and Thames Television (London Weekday) were replaced by higher bidders, Sunrise and Carlton

Television respectively (Davidson, 1992: p.218). Just as significantly, the requirement of the successful bidders to make considerable annual payments to the Treasury led the biggest ITV companies to lobby for the relaxation of ownership rules originally designed to prevent concentration of ownership within ITV (see Chapter 3). Keen to move closer to free market competition, the government's response was favourable and in the mid-1990s there was a flurry of merger activity. By 1995, three ITV groups – Granada, Carlton, and MAI – accounted for 82 per cent of ITV's total advertising revenue (Gibbons, 1998: p.227). Rather than 15 public service focused regional broadcasters, ITV was now in the hands of three commercially minded heavyweights.

Changes to the BBC and Channel 4 during the early 1990s were also designed to produce a more competitive British television industry. The BBC's licence fee was preserved, but with no real increase in the level which, when taken together with the changes in BBC management already instigated by the Conservatives, made cost reductions and efficiency savings the Corporation's main priorities. This was seen most clearly in the BBC's adoption of Producer Choice, an internal market within the BBC, whereby 'cost-centres' bought and sold their products, services, and expertise to each other, and were free to go outside the BBC, if their requirements could be purchased at a lower price (O'Malley, 1994: pp.163–5). To introduce more competition in the television advertising market, in 1990, Channel 4 was given the responsibility to sell its own advertising time. As a result, during the 1990s, Channel 4's schedules took on a more populist slant and increasingly employed popular US imports, such as *Friends* and *ER*, to 'swell the ratings' (Crisell, 2002: p.255).

The Conservatives' commitment to free market principles was even more evident in their approach to the development of satellite television. During the early 1990s, Britain's officially licensed satellite service, British Satellite Broadcasting (BSB), faced intense competition for satellite viewers from Rupert Murdoch's News Corporation owned satellite television service, Sky. By employing a far less sophisticated transmissions technology and a 'medium' powered satellite (Astra), originally intended for telecommunications use, Sky was able to broadcast to Britain without the need to obtain an official British licence. Instead, as the service was merely up-linked from Britain, before being relayed to British viewers via the Astra satellite, Sky was legally defined as a 'non-domestic' satellite service, and faced none of the public service obligations imposed upon BSB (Gibbons, 1998). In fact, far from facing public service regulations, Sky was able to benefit from a carefully constructed and deliberately placed legal loophole designed to enable Murdoch to retain both his satellite television and British newspaper interests (Smith, 2007: p.64).

Following a brief period of expensive competition, in 1990, Sky and BSB merged. In reality, however, the merger was in all but name a takeover of BSB by Sky (Horsman, 1997). The newly formed company, British Sky Broadcasting (BSkyB), was 50 per cent owned by News Corporation (later reduced to 40 per cent), controlled by Sky's management team, and continued to use the non-domestic Astra satellite. Given the Conservatives' positive predisposition towards Sky, there was no government attempt to prevent the merger, or even to initiate an investigation by the Monopolies and Mergers Commission (Negrine, 1989).

Over the next few years, based largely on big money exclusive rights deals for premium content, such as English Premier League football, BSkyB developed into a highly profitable subscription-based broadcaster (Evens, Iosifidis, and Smith, 2013: p.199). By 1995, BSkyB had over 4 million subscribers and recorded annual profits of

£155 million (Horsman, 1997). The cable television industry also benefited from BSkyB's success. By the mid-1990s, mainly by relaying BSkyB channels, the number of cable subscribers had increased to around 1 million. Taken together, by 1995, about one in five British households was able to receive BSkyB's subscription service, either direct or via cable (Smith, 2007: p.66). Just as importantly, BSkyB's success did much to further the overall commercialisation of British television. First, BSkyB itself became an institutional embodiment of the government's belief in free market values, such as competition and consumer choice (King, 1998). Second, BSkyB's very existence acted as a commercialising force on the established public service broadcasters. Britain's established public service broadcasters now faced intense competition for viewers, programme rights, and advertising finance. By the mid-1990s, British television was more competitive than ever and public service broadcasters were part of a mixed television ecology, rather than the whole system.

Digital Switchover and the Growth of Pay Television

The invention of digital television stemmed from rivalry between European, Japanese, and US consumer electronics firms. In 1990, engineers at the US laboratory of the General Instrument Corporation discovered that television pictures could be encoded and transmitted digitally, in the form of a 'bit stream' (a series of noughts and ones) and then compressed so as to allow the transmission of much more information (Smith, 2007: pp.70–1). The development of digital technology provided (terrestrial, satellite, and cable) broadcasters with the potential to offer many more channels, as well as better quality pictures and sound. By taking advantage of digitalisation, broadcasters could also offer extra services based on interactivity, including internet access. After all, television pictures, transmitted merely as a series of noughts and ones, were interchangeable with other forms of digital communications, such as telecommunications and computing. Digitalisation therefore raised the prospect of television itself becoming a far more flexible communications medium, hence the much heralded convergence of television, telecommunications, and computing technologies (see Chapter 1).

The British government also had much to gain from the digitalisation of television. The development of digital technology raised the possibility of a switch from traditional analogue to digital television transmission, which would free up valuable electromagnetic spectrum for auctioning off to either broadcasters or other users, such as mobile phone operators. As early as 1994, the British government estimated that auctioning the spectrum freed up by a switch from analogue to digital television could raise as much as £5 billion per annum for the British Treasury (DNH, 1994). Problematically, however, digital television transmissions could not simply be received by the existing analogue television sets owned by most households. To receive digital television required either a new fully integrated digital television set, or a set-top-box digital decoder. The underlying British television policy issue for much of the 1990s and early 2000s was therefore how to switch from analogue to digital television without depriving millions of viewers of their existing television services.

In October 1998, BSkyB became the first British broadcaster to launch a digital television service, Sky Digital. Within a few years, BSkyB had managed to convert its existing analogue subscribers to digital (satellite) and had also added a significant number of new subscribers. By 2002, around 6 million British households received digital television via Sky Digital. However, partly as a result of BSkyB's success, the launch of digital terrestrial television (DTT) was a commercial disaster. From the early-mid-1990s, the ITC and the British government were concerned with trying to prevent BSkyB from translating its domination of analogue pay television into a domination of the whole of digital television. Consequently, the Broadcasting Act (1996) obliged the ITC to award licences to operate commercial DTT services on the basis of whether applicants would 'promote the development of digital television services in the United Kingdom otherwise than by satellite' (Part I, Section 8). This provision led to the exclusion of BSkyB from the successful bidder for commercial DTT licences, a consortium called British Digital Broadcasting (BDB) that was originally made up of BSkyB and the two largest ITV companies, Carlton and Granada. Over the next few years, digital television in Britain was dominated by a pay television battle between the renamed BDB, ONdigital (later renamed ITV Digital), and BSkyB. For a number of reasons, ranging from problems with DTT reception to the fact that BSkyB remained ITV Digital's main source of premium programming, this battle was only ever likely to have one winner: BSkyB. In 2002, with around 1.2 million subscribers, ITV Digital was declared bankrupt with losses of over £1 billion (Smith, 2008: p.140).

With the British government's plan to switch off analogue television transmissions in disarray, the BBC provided a new strategy. A few months after the collapse of ITV Digital, DTT was relaunched in Britain as a free-to-air service offering around 30 channels under the banner of Freeview, a joint venture led by the BBC, but also including BSkyB and Crown Castle. At least in part, the establishment of Freeview was instigated by the BBC as a means to safeguard its own future. First, the BBC reasoned that by establishing DTT as a universally available free-to-air service it could maximise the audience for its own channels, including new digital channels, such as *CBeebies* and *BBC Three*. Second, the BBC knew that Freeview boxes could not easily be adapted to receive (encrypted) pay television services. The widespread adoption of Freeview would therefore protect the Corporation against Peacock-inspired calls for the BBC to be funded by subscription (Dyke, 2005: p.187).

Freeview was an instant success, with around 3.5 million households receiving digital television via Freeview within 18 months of its launch (Smith, 2008: p.140). It was also particularly popular amongst older viewers and pay television sceptics. Furthermore, Freeview provided an easy way for households to convert second or third television sets to receive digital television. Almost single handedly, the BBC had rescued the government's digital television policy. For the BBC, this was particularly good timing because it coincided with the government's review of the Corporation's Charter and Licence. The BBC was already under attack on a couple of fronts. First, from summer 2002 until early 2003, the BBC and the government were embroiled in a bitter dispute over the Corporation's coverage of the 2003 Iraq War and in particular an accusation made on the BBC's radio news programme, *Today*, that the government had misleadingly 'sexed up' the case for war by suggesting that Iraq possessed chemical weapons. The subsequent publication of a damning, if much disputed, independent judicial inquiry on the BBC's coverage of the war, the Hutton Report (2004), led to the unprecedented resignation of both its Chairman, Gavyn Davies, and its director-general, Greg Dyke (Wring, 2006). Second, the BBC faced repeated criticism from those who argued that in the digital era of 'spectrum plenty' there was little, or no, need for a publicly owned broadcaster funded by a regressive tax, like the licence fee (BPG, 2004). However, in contrast with the Conservatives during the 1980s, there remained within the Labour government a residue of ideological support for the BBC and the principles of public service broadcasting. When the government launched the BBC's Charter review, it described the BBC as a 'quintessentially British institution' and likened it to the National Health Service, arguably the greatest achievement of any Labour government (DCMS, 2003). Despite the antagonism over the BBC's coverage of the Iraq War, there was no government desire to oversee a wholesale dismantling and restructuring of the BBC.

Against this backdrop, the BBC set out a new vision for its own future in the digital age, *Building Public Value* (BBC, 2004). At its heart, this was a reformulation of traditional public service principles in terms of 'public value', which the BBC contrasted with the 'shareholder value' pursued by commercial broadcasters (BBC, 2004: p.28). To deliver 'public value', BBC programmes and services would seek to contribute towards five 'public purposes': active and informed citizenship; British culture and creativity; a revolution in learning; connected communities; and the UK's voice in the world (BBC, 2004: pp.12–14). Finally, the BBC also pledged to play 'a leadership role' during the transition period from analogue to digital television to ensure that everyone in Britain has access to 'digital public service television' (2004: p.61). In 2007, the BBC's Charter and Licence was officially renewed (2007–17) on broadly favourable terms. Subsequently, the continued rapid growth of Freeview enabled the 'switch off' of analogue terrestrial television to be completed in 2012, with little, if any, disruption for the vast majority of viewers. Since the early 2000s, the British government has received over £20 billion from mobile phone companies to use the freed up spectrum (Fildes, 2021).

Alongside the BBC securing its own immediate future, the early 2000s also witnessed significant growth in the take up of pay television. Between 1998 and 2012, the proportion of households subscribing to a pay television service increased by over 20 per cent. By 2012, just over half of all British households subscribed to a (digital) pay television service (Ofcom, 2013: p.127). BSkyB remained the clear market leader with over 10 million subscribers, followed by the cable broadcaster, Virgin Media, with around 3.5 million, but heavily reliant on premium channels supplied by BSkyB (e.g. Sky Sports) (Ofcom, 2013: p.179). From around 2006, pay television subscriptions had also become the British television industry's most important source of revenue, surpassing both advertising and public funding (mostly the licence fee) (Ofcom, 2010a: p.97). By 2012, the relative importance of subscription revenue was stark, with subscriptions accounting for 43 per cent of total television revenues (£12.3 billion), compared to 29 and 22 per cent for advertising and public funding respectively (Ofcom, 2013: p,127). As during the 1990s, the growth of pay television, and BskyB in particular, was built on providing premium content, most notably live English Premier League football and other popular sports. In 2012, sports channels accounted for 56 per cent of the total amount invested in programming by pay television broadcasters, more than double the amount spent on other entertainment programming (Ofcom, 2013: p.156).

Against this background, during the 2000s, the regulation of the pay television market became an increasingly important (and controversial) feature of the British television industry. This trend was most clearly illustrated, in 2003, by the establishment of Britain's new communications regulation, Ofcom. Ofcom replaced five separate broadcasting and telecommunications regulators, including the ITC and the Office of Telecommunications, largely on the grounds that technological convergence made the continued separate regulation of television and telecommunications increasingly problematic (Smith, 2006). Just as significantly, however, Ofcom was also explicitly introduced to 're-base broadcasting regulation upon modern competition law principles' (DCMS and DTI, 2000). Ofcom's legal duties require it to further the interests of both 'consumers' and 'citizens', but critics have argued that in practice it has tended to prioritise the former set of interests (Lunt and Livingstone, 2012). It is certainly the case that during the 2000s the dominant position of BSkyB in the pay television market was subject to almost constant investigation by Ofcom, as well as Britain's other general competition regulators, the Office of Fair Trading (OFT) and the Competition Commission. Ofcom's regulation of BSkyB focused on two key bottlenecks within the pay television industry: first, ensuring 'fair, reasonable and non-discriminatory' access for channel owners (e.g. MTV) to its delivery platform (i.e. Sky Digital) (Ofcom, 2006); and second, ensuring access to premium content/channels (e.g. Sky Sports) for rival delivery platform (e.g. Virgin Media) (Ofcom, 2010b). In each of these areas, Ofcom's attempts to promote competition in the pay television market were only partially successful (Smith, 2013). In a similar vein, and with arguably more long term significance, in 2009, the Competition Commission blocked a joint venture between the BBC, ITV and Channel Four to offer a 'one-stop shop' for video on demand services (known as Project Kangaroo) on the grounds that it would lead to a 'substantial lessening of competition' in Britain's emerging video on demand market (Competition Commission, 2009: p.7). The Competition Commission's decision cleared the way for major US media corporations, such as Netflix, to launch their SVOD services in Britain with only limited competition from public service broadcasters.

The Era of Online Television

Over the last decade, television and the internet have become 'indelibly intertwined' (Johnson, 2019: p.1). By 2021, over 90 per cent of all homes in Britain had a broadband internet connection; 63 per cent had a television connected to the internet (either a Smart TV or a TV with a streaming stick); over 80 per cent of adults owned a smart phone; and, over half of all adults had access to a tablet (Ofcom, 2021d, pp.9–11). Taken together, these technological developments have enabled the internet to become a medium for the distribution of audio-visual content, including, but not limited to, television. Furthermore, the same devices used to view television programmes via the internet are also used to access audio-visual content from countless other online services, such as social media platforms and digital news brands. A significant consequence of this technological convergence (see Chapter 1) is that the definition of television itself has become less certain. With this issue in mind, online television services, such as Netflix and the BBC iPlayer, can be distinguished from other audio-visual content delivered online in two crucial ways: first, online television services acquire (through producing or licensing) content to offer to viewers; and second, their services are provided within 'closed ecosystems' that are designed to provide a controlled and structured viewing experience (Johnson, 2019: p.48). By contrast, social media platforms, like YouTube and TikTok, depend on open platforms to which users can easily contribute (audio-visual) content. On this basis, online television is defined as 'services that facilitate the viewing of editorially selected audiovisual content through internet-connected devices and infrastructure' (Johnson, 2019: p.48).

The first online television services to launch in Britain were provided by the established public service broadcasters, namely Channel 4's 4oD player (2006), the BBC's iPlayer (2007), and ITV's ITV Player (2008) (D'Arma, Raats, and Steemers, 2021). These VOD services were directly tied to their respective broadcaster's traditional linear channels and offered viewers the opportunity to 'catch up' with programmes previously broadcast. Within a few years, VOD catch up services had become an established part of the British television landscape. In 2012, around 25 million people were using catch up VOD services every month, with the most popular, the BBC iPlayer, consistently receiving over 150 million programme requests each month (Ofcom, 2012: p.173; Ofcom, 2013: p.203). At the same time, however, online television still only accounted for a relatively small proportion of total television viewing, around 5 per cent (Ofcom, 2013: p.145). At this stage, online television was a supplement to traditional television, rather than a replacement.

Since around the mid-2010s, the rapid growth of SVOD services has represented a more significant change to Britain's television landscape. Launched in Britain in 2012, US-based Netflix has established itself as Britain's leading SVOD provider, ahead of rivals Amazon (2014), Disney+ (2020), and Apple TV (2020) (see Table 8.1). Each of these (and countless other specialist) SVODs have their own unique commercial strategies. For example, while Netflix is focused solely on online television, Amazon offers online television as part of a wider strategy designed to drive take up of its retail service, Amazon Prime. Nevertheless, online television 'portals' share a number of distinctive features (Lotz, 2018: pp.492–3). First, online television can be 'non-linear'. Portals, like Netflix, provide viewers with on demand access to curated libraries of content, rather than traditional channels organised through a schedule. Second, portals make much more use of 'pure subscriber' funding, as distinct from the mixed (advertising and subscription) model of cable and satellite television services. Third, by collecting rich viewing behaviour data, online portals target 'taste communities', rather than traditional 'blunt demographics' (e.g. mens, teens), or 'simple genres' (e.g. sports, news). Fourth, while not a new strategy within the television industry, vertical integration is a particularly important feature of online television portals. Increasingly, online portals operate as both content producer and as distributor via direct to consumer streaming. For example, the exclusive availability of Disney's various content brands (e.g. Marvel and Star Wars) via Disney+ is a defining feature of Disney's SVOD

Table 8.1 SVOD Service Take Up: Number of SVOD Households (millions)

Year	Netflix	Amazon Prime	Now	Disney +	Apple TV	Any SVOD
2014	1.21	2.79	0.24		–	3.83
2015	4.37	1.15	0.52		–	5.43
2016	5.94	1.65	0.85		–	7.24
2017	6.89	3.64	1.08		–	8.92
2018	9.11	4.83	1.46		–	11.16
2019	11.47	5.96	1.62		–	13.33
2020	13.01	7.86	1.94	3.37	0.96	15.00
2021	16.79	12.57	2.06	5.49	1.24	19.07
2022 (Q1)	17.29	13.35	2.13	6.53	1.57	19.57

Sources: Ofcom (2021b); Ofcom (2021c); BARB (2022b)

service, as are Netflix Originals (e.g. *Bridgerton* and *Stanger Things*) for Netflix. Taken together, these features have made SVOD services 'a new and disruptive phenomenon' for Britain's established (pay television and public service) broadcasters (D'Arma, Raats, and Steemers, 2021: p.684).

The term 'cord cutting' is used within the television industry to refer to households that cancel their traditional cable/satellite television subscriptions in favour of SVOD services, and a degree of 'cord cutting' has certainly been evident in the British television industry. Between 2015 and 2021, the number of households subscribing to a traditional cable/satellite pay television service declined by around 4 million, from a peak of over 18 million (around 60 per cent of households) to just under 14 million (48 per cent of households) (Ofcom, 2016: p.54; Ofcom, 2021b, p.63). Since the early 2020s, many more households have been subscribers to at least one SVOD than a traditional cable/satellite pay television service (Ofcom, 2021b: p.4). At the same time, however, a notable feature of pay television in contemporary Britain is the relative resilience of traditional pay television services, particularly when compared with other countries, such as the US, where 'cord cutting' has been a far more dramatic phenomenon (Wayne, 2018: p.726).

The continued popularity of traditional pay television in Britain owes much to the strategic response of BSkyB (in 2014, rebranded, and referred to from here as 'Sky') to the competitive threat posed by SVOD. First, in 2013, Sky launched its own SVOD service, Now TV, which offered access to Sky content for non-subscribers via flexible payment options (e.g. daily/weekend Sports, Movies and Entertainment passes) akin to those offered by SVODs, like Netflix, rather than the traditional long term contracts (e.g. one year) associated with satellite/cable television. With over 2 million regular subscribers by 2022 (see Table 8.1), the success of Now TV has gone some way to make up for the loss of subscribers to traditional pay television. Second, Sky has also pursued a strategy of integrating SVODs into its own satellite service. Following a series of individual distribution deals, since 2020, Sky has been able to offer its satellite subscribers access to all of the leading SVODs 'in one place' (Sweney, 2020b). Finally, and perhaps most importantly, Sky has also continued to invest heavily in premium content, most notably exclusive sports rights. In 2021, Sky agreed to pay over £3.5 billion to renew its exclusive rights deal for Premier League football (seasons 2022–3 to 2024–5) (Nair, 2021).

Britain's public service broadcasters may not compete with SVODs for subscribers, but they do compete for viewers. The share of total television viewing accounted for by public service broadcasters (BBC, ITV, Channel 4, and Channel 5) has long been in decline (see Table 8.2). Since the launch of digital television during the late 1990s, audiences have fragmented across the hundreds of available channels. Between 1997 and 2013, public service broadcasters suffered a dramatic 38 per cent decline in their audience share. Over the last decade the audience share of public service broadcasters has stabilised, at just over 50 per cent, but the growth of SVODs has presented a new challenge, namely a reduction in the amount of time viewers are spending watching traditional broadcast television. Between 2014 and 2019, average broadcast television viewing fell from 3 hours and 41 minutes to 3 hours and 3 minutes, with a particular sharp decline of 1 hour and 6 minutes amongst younger (16–34) viewers (Ofcom, 2020b: p.27). By contrast, albeit boosted by Covid lockdowns, between 2017 and 2020 the average amount of time viewing SVOD services increased from 18 minutes to 65 minutes per day (Ofcom, 2021c). For the BBC, any significant loss of viewers

Table 8.2 Channel Share of all Broadcast Television Viewing (%): 1989–2021*

Year	BBC One	BBC Two	ITV	Channel 4	Channel 5	Main Five PSB Channels	PSB Portfolios**	Multi-channel TV
1989	39	11	42	8	–	100	–	–
1993	33	10	40	11	–	94	–	6
1997	31	12	33	11	2	89	–	12
2001	27	11	27	10	6	81	–	20
2005	23	9	22	10	6	70	7	23
2009	21	7	18	7	5	58	16	26
2013	21	6	15	5	4	51	21	28
2017	22	6	15	5	4	51	19	30
2020	21	6	16	5	4	52	18	30

Sources: Ofcom (2018d); Ofcom (2021b); Ofcom (2021c)

*The main PSB channels include HD channel variants but exclude viewing to +1 variants.
**PSB portfolio channels are all family channels operated by the PSBs other than the main PSB channels, e.g. ITV2, BBC4.

undermines the legitimacy of the licence fee and the case for the Corporation's very existence. For advertiser funded public service broadcasters, the loss of viewers to SVODs and/or other online services has had a more immediate financial impact. Between 2015 and 2019, ITV, Channel 4, and Channel 5 saw a collective decline of over £500 million in advertising revenue across their broadcast channels (Ofcom, 2020b: p.48).

In response to the rise of SVODs during the mid-2010s, Britain's established public service broadcasters each revamped their online television services. In 2013, the BBC's new director-general, Tony Hall, set out his vision for the reinvention of public service broadcasting in a digital media world based around a transformation in the role and function of iPlayer: 'from being catch-up TV to online TV' (BBC, 2013). Hall argued that the iPlayer was positioned to become 'the best online TV service in the world – and the front door to many people to the whole BBC'. As well as an extended 'catch up' window to view previous broadcast programming, Hall's vision for the iPlayer included new programming available 'first on iPlayer' and access to 'classic programming'. The new iPlayer would also offer a 'personalised service based on recommendations' with a distinctly public service twist. As put by Hall, the new iPlayer will suggest 'more of what you might like. But also more of what you wouldn't have guessed you'd like. We'll surprise you. Challenge you' (BBC, 2013). The BBC's 'new iPlayer' was officially launched in 2014 and in the same year Channel 4 adopted a similar approach, relaunching its on-demand service, 4OD, as an 'integrated brand platform' called All 4. In 2014, ITV also announced a digital strategy for developing the ITV Player as 'a destination for live television viewing', which, in 2015, led to the relaunch of its on-demand player as the ITV Hub (Johnson, 2017).

The revamped VOD services launched by Britain's public service broadcasters have been a qualified success. In 2021, Ofcom estimated that around three-quarters of British households used these services, around the same proportion as SVODs (Ofcom, 2021b: p.8). For some viewers at least, these VODs have also become 'destinations' to watch new programming. For example, in 2020, the iPlayer recorded a record number of requests for programmes not previously broadcast on BBC channels, including *Normal People* and *Killing Eve* (BBC, 2020). The opportunity to view archive programming has been another popular feature of the VODs of public service broadcasters. In April 2021, almost half of all viewing across their combined VOD services was 'library content and box sets' at least five years old (Ofcom, 2021b, p.44). However, while, in 2020, the BBC's iPlayer recorded 5.8 billion streams, making it Britain's second most popular online television service, it was still much less used than Netflix, which recorded 15.53 billion streams during the same year (Ofcom, 2021b: p.17). To date at least, the VOD services provided by Britain's public service broadcasters have not, therefore, been able to offset the decline in viewing for their traditional broadcast channels. Between 2014 and 2019, average daily viewing per person to the main five public service channels fell by 24 minutes, but viewing of their respective VOD services accounted for less than 11 minutes of an adult's daily viewing time (Ofcom, 2020b: p.32).

In a similar vein, for Britain's advertiser funded public service broadcasters, while advertising revenues from their respective VOD services have grown rapidly, reaching £523 million in 2020, this has not been enough to fully counteract the much larger decline in revenue from 'spot advertising' on their traditional television channels (Ofcom, 2021b: p.56). Between 2015 and 2020, annual revenue from spot advertising on British television fell from £5.1 billion to £3.5 billion (Ofcom, 2021b: p.56). In response, Britain's advertiser funded public service broadcasters have looked to pursue alternative sources of revenue. During the mid-2010s, ITV and Channel 4 both launched advertising free subscription services, ITVHub+ and All 4+, but neither have achieved anything more than a modest take up, with 3 and 2 per cent of British households subscribing respectively (Ofcom, 2021b: p.46). In a joint venture with the BBC, in 2017, ITV also launched a SVOD service offering classic British comedies, dramas, and documentaries called BritBox. BritBox was first established in North America, before expanding to Australia and South Africa. By 2021, it had 1.7 million international subscribers (BBC, 2021: p.68). In 2019, a version of BritBox was also launched in Britain, but, with only around 2 per cent of British households subscribing, it has not provided meaningful competition for Britain's leading SVODs (Ofcom, 2021b: p.46).

A more successful commercial strategy for Britain's public service broadcasters has been to increase revenue from the production and licensing of programming. Over the last decade, ITV Studios, the production and distribution division of ITV, has grown to become the largest commercial producer in Britain, with total revenues, in 2021, reaching £1.76 billion, around half of ITV's total revenue (ITV, 2021: p.4). As well as selling programmes to other British broadcasters, including Channel 4 (e.g. *Come Dine with Me*) and the BBC (e.g. *Line of Duty*), ITV Studios also sells programmes/formats to broadcasters around the world. For example, the ITV Studios' formats *Love Island* and *I'm A Celebrity...Get Me Out of Here* have been sold to 21 and 15 countries respectively (ITV, 2021: p.36). Furthermore, a growing part of ITV Studios business is producing programmes for SVODs, such as *Cowboy Bebop* for Netflix and *Physical* for Apple+. In 2021, the proportion of ITV Studios' total revenue from streaming platforms reached 13 per cent and ITV aims to double this figure to 25 per cent by 2025 (ITV, 2021: p.28). Faced with its own financial challenges (see the following paragraphs), the BBC has pursued a similar approach through its production and distribution business, BBC Studios. In 2021, BBC Studios achieved revenues of around £1.2

billion (BBC, 2021: p.66). As with ITV, a growing source of revenue for BBC Studios is commissions from SVODs; however, providing new programming (and/or licensing existing programming) for SVODs is not without risk for public service broadcasters. To position itself as the audience's 'principle point of identification' Netflix often conceals the 'branded origins' of programmes commissioned or licenced from other broadcasters (Wayne, 2018: p.735). This can lead to 'brand dilution' for public service broadcasters (D'Arma, Raats, and Steemers, 2021: p.685). For example, Ofcom has found that young audiences are often unaware that some of the programmes they are watching (e.g. *Peaky Blinders*) on SVODs were originally made for and broadcast on a public service channel. Consequently, they tend to give credit for these programmes to the platform or service they are watching them on, rather than public service broadcasters (Ofcom, 2020b: p.57).

To withstand the competitive challenge posed by SVODs in the era of online television, Britain's public service broadcasters require political support. However, since 2010, there has been little evidence of any such support from successive Conservative led governments. Since 2010, the BBC's ability to invest in programming and services has been eroded by repeated cuts to its funding. In 2010, as part of the newly elected Conservative led coalition government's plans to cut public spending, the BBC agreed to make annual savings of around £700 million for the next five years (Kanter, 2013). In 2015, the Conservative government then decided that the BBC should take on from the government the £600 million-plus annual cost of providing free television licences for people aged over 75 (Martinson and Plunkett, 2015). In 2022, the Conservative government also announced that the annual cost of a television licence would be frozen for the next two years (at £159), which against a backdrop of rising inflation, equates to a significant real terms funding cut and requires the BBC to find annual savings of around £285 million (Waterson, 2022a). The accumulative impact of these funding cuts has been over a thousand job losses, service closures, and reduced investment in virtually all areas of BBC programming.

Since the mid-2010s, reduced funding for the BBC, combined with falling advertising revenues for ITV, Channel 4, and Channel 5, has led to a significant reduction in spending on original programmes by Britain's public service broadcasters. Between 2010 and 2020, the amount spent on original programming by public service broadcasters declined by almost £1 billion, from £2.99 billion to £2.07 billion (Ofcom, 2021b: p.67). In contrast, as global corporations with far greater financial resources, Britain's most popular SVODs have been able to significantly increase their spending on original programming, including programmes made in Britain. For example, in 2020, Netflix spent $1 billion (£750 million) on original programming produced in Britain (Sweney, 2020c). However, the programmes produced in Britain for SVODs tend not be as distinctly 'British' as those commissioned by Britain's public service broadcasters. While describing or quantifying 'Britishness' is inherently subjective, research commissioned by Ofcom has found that British-produced programmes commissioned by SVODs had far fewer 'British touchpoints' (e.g. culturally loaded references to places or people) than similar shows commissioned by public service broadcasters (Ofcom, 2021b, p.76). Furthermore, even if British made programmes on SVODs are considered 'British', British made programming remains a relatively small proportion of the total amount of programming hours offered by SVODs, ranging from 3 per cent (Disney+) to 26 per cent (NOW) (Ofcom, 2021b: p.36).

With the growth of online television, public service broadcasters have become increasingly concerned that existing regulations designed to ensure their channels are given 'prominence' on (terrestrial, cable, and satellite) television delivery platforms do not cover their

VOD services and/or the availability of their VOD services on new delivery platforms, such as smart TVs and smart sticks (House of Commons, 2021a: pp.24–5). Without regulatory oversight, public service broadcasters need to negotiate the 'access and prominence' of their VOD services with individual delivery platforms and are therefore vulnerable to the risk of their services not being carried, or carried on unfavourable terms (Ofcom, 2019c: p,29). For example, Amazon's Fire TV standard terms require 30 per cent of advertising revenue in return for favourable positioning on the platform (Ofcom, 2020b: p.41). In its White Paper on the future of British broadcasting, *Up Next*, the British government has declared that it plans to support public service broadcasters by legislating for a new 'prominence regime for on-demand television' whereby 'designated TV platforms' (i.e. those used by a significant number of British viewers) will be required to give appropriate prominence to the VOD services of public service broadcasters (DCMS, 2022: p.24).

On other key issues, however, government plans for the future of British broadcasting have been less encouraging for public service broadcasters. First, the government recently announced that it will 'carry out a review of the licence fee funding model' (DCMS, 2022: p.17). Given the thinly veiled underlying ideological hostility to the licence fee within the Conservative government (Waterson, 2022b), the BBC may face renewed calls for the abolition of the licence fee and/or increased financial insecurity. Second, the government also plans to privatise Channel 4. According to the government, privatisation will 'free the channel to respond to the challenges and opportunities' of the 'changing broadcast market' (DCMS, 2022: p.19). The proposed privatisation of Channel 4 has been widely opposed within the television industry, not least from Channel 4 itself, but the Conservative government remains intent on privatising one of Britain's leading public service broadcasting institutions.

Conclusion

This chapter has provided an overview of how the television industry in Britain has been shaped by a combination of technological, economic, and political factors. In a sense, the contemporary British television industry offers a mix of each of the different periods discussed, namely, public service broadcasters, satellite/cable pay television operators; and VOD and SVOD services. Television viewers in Britain today can access more programming than ever before and have the option to watch via a host of different distribution technologies and/or reception devices. At the same time, however, much of this increase in choice is dependent on the ability and/or willingness to pay. In this context, debates over the future of public service broadcasting remain as important as ever. The continued value of public service broadcasting in contemporary Britain was underlined during the Covid 19 pandemic lockdowns of 2020 and 2021. While SVODs increased their subscriber numbers, the BBC was by far the public's most important source of reliable information/news about the pandemic (BBC, 2021: p.5). Almost overnight, the Corporation also provided a comprehensive mix of online and broadcast 'Lockdown Learning' material to support children, parents, and teachers (BBC, 2021: p.14). Together with other public service broadcasters, the BBC also provided an unrivalled mix of original and archive British programming, offering everything 'from arts and culture to escapism and distraction' (BBC, 2021: p.19). For Britain's public service broadcasters to survive and prosper in the era of online television will require financial and regulatory support from the British government.

9 Music

The contemporary music industry is best understood as a 'copyright industry' (Wikström, 2020: p.14). Copyright legislation is what makes it possible to commodify a musical 'work', be it a song, or a recording. For example, in 2022, the estate of David Bowie (who died in 2016) sold the publishing 'rights' for his catalogue of songs to the publishing arm of Warner Music Group, one of the major corporations that dominate the global music industry, for £185 million (Beaumont-Thomas, 2022). This sale was one of a host of similar deals in recent years for the (song and/or recording) rights of high profile artists, including Bruce Springsteen, Bob Dylan, The Killers, and Neil Young, to either major music companies, or corporate investors. The rationale is that the ownership of such rights is likely to provide a reliable long term source of income (i.e. the 'long tail' – see Chapter 2) via royalties paid from streaming services and a host of other licensed users (e.g. radio broadcasters, film companies, advertisers, etc.). While important for all sectors of the media industries, the concentration of commercial value in ownership of copyright is particularly acute within the music industry. This explains another recent trend within the sector, namely major artists, such as Ed Sheeran and Taylor Swift, facing 'copyright battles' in court to (successfully in both of these cases) prove they have not plagiarised other musicians (Music Week, 2022). Various copyright agreements and licensing arrangements are also at the heart of an ongoing heated public debate between music streaming services (e.g. Spotify and Apple Music), major music corporations (e.g. Sony, Warner, and Universal), and artists/ musicians over the distribution of streaming revenues. For example, in 2021, over 150 artists, including Paul McCartney, Chris Martin, Noel Gallagher, Sting, and Kate Bush, signed an 'open letter' to the British government urging it to 'fix streaming' by amending copyright law to ensure more streaming income 'is put back in the hands of artists' (Beaumont-Thomas, 2021). This chapter examines in more detail how and why the issue of copyright is (and has long been) at the epicentre of the music industry.

The music industry is made up of three segments – music publishing, music recording, and live music (Wikström, 2020: p.50). The focus of this chapter is the first and second segments, but it is worth acknowledging the inherent links between music publishing/recording and live music. Not least because, since the early 2000s, when revenues from sales began to be diluted by digital piracy (see p.139), live performances have been an increasingly important source of revenue for most, if not all, artists (Leyshon and Watson, 2021: p.268). Some contemporary artists even claim that the relative lack of income they receive from music streaming platforms, like Spotify, means streaming is more akin to a 'promotional tool' for live performances than an independent source of revenue (House of Commons, 2021b: p.30). Nevertheless, the British music market is

DOI: 10.4324/9781315396781-12

the third largest in the world, behind only the US and Japan (IFPI, 2022: p.10). In Britain, in 2021, recorded music generated over £1.6 billion from retail sales (including streams), plus around £225 million from licensed uses (e.g. radio broadcasts, films, etc.) (ERA, 2022: p.66; UK Music, 2021: p.17). Britain is also the second biggest exporter of recorded music (after the US). In 2019, British record labels generated around £500 million in export revenues, with one in every ten tracks streamed globally by a British artist (BPI, 2020: p.9).

Many large music companies have both 'publishing' and 'recording' operations, but they are usually organised as autonomous entities, even if they are part of the same corporation. For example, Sony Music Publishing and Sony Music Entertainment (recording) both operate under the auspices of the Sony Music Group (in turn part of the Japan-based Sony conglomerate). This reflects the fact that under the terms of copyright law, publishing and recording are distinct activities (with different associated rights). The first owner of the copyright in a song is its 'creator', the people (or person) who wrote it (Frith and Marshall, 2004: p.7). Music publishers, so called because they historically published sheet music books, work with creators to license their works for various purposes, such as live performance, recording, or background music in a film. Traditionally, music publishing royalties are split 50/50, with half going to the publisher as payment for their services and the rest going to the creator/s (Wikström, 2020: p.62). With the growth of recorded music during the 20th century, the right to record the work (known as the 'mechanical right') became a creator's most valuable right, but also led to a new kind of music copyright subsisting in the recoding itself, rather than the underlying musical work. This 'neighbouring right' (i.e. the right to license use of a recording) is usually owned not by the creator, but by the company that organises and publishes the recording: the recording company. The recording company, often referred to as a record label, is an important 'gatekeeper' in the music industry, who 'stands between' consumers and recorded music (Shuker, 2010: p.207). Record labels make decisions about what artists to sign (i.e. record), promote, and market. For signed performers, the contract with a record label usually transfers all recording rights to the label in exchange for a percentage royalty payment (and/or an advance). Historically, the amount paid by record labels to signed artists in royalties has been very low – 5 percent of the suggested retail price was standard for much of US music history (Stahl, 2013: p.121). In the contemporary British music industry, recording contracts still heavily favour the record label, with artists estimated to receive between 12 and 30 per cent in royalties, depending on when they signed and their prior popularity and success (House of Commons, 2021b: p.19).

As well as shaping the contours of the music industry itself, the issue of copyright (and piracy) is also a key reason why music is often regarded as a particularly significant sector within the contemporary media industries. Music was the first sector to be disrupted and then transformed by the growth of the internet. Largely due to online piracy, between 1999 and 2014, global revenues for recorded music fell from US$24.1 billion to US$14.2 billion (IFPI, 2022: p.11). However, with the growing popularity of music streaming services, from 2015, global revenues began to grow again and, in 2021, had reached £25.9 billion (IFPI, 2022: p.11) (see Table 9.1). The same pattern has been replicated in Britain, with industry revenues from recorded music falling from just over £1.2 billion, in 2001, to under £800 million by 2014, before returning to over £1.2 billion in 2021 (BPI, 2020: p.9; UK Music, 2021: pp.16–7).

The remainder of this chapter is divided into two main sections. The first part provides an overview of the emergence of the music industry during the 20th century as a sector focused on the sale (and licensed use) of recorded music, rather than live performance. The second and main part of the chapter then examines the reformulation of the music industry in the era of online distribution. This section begins by discussing the growth of online music piracy during the early 2000s and the response of key players within (and outside) the industry. It then focuses on the rise of music streaming services and how they have transformed the music industry, for the benefit of some more than others.

The Rise of the Music Industry

The origins of recording technology can be traced back to the mid-late 19th century, but the emergence of the gramophone record as 'the predominant music commodity' took place following the end of WWI (Frith, 1988: p.13). In the early 1920s, in the US and Europe, there were dozens of companies involved in the production of gramophone players and gramophones (from here on referred to as records). In a similar way to the early years of radio (see Chapter 7), these companies were part of the electrical goods industry, with records manufactured and sold largely to facilitate sale of gramophone players. For example, in Britain, in 1914, the Decca Gramophone Company (Decca) marketed the first portable record player, the Decca Dulcephone, which became 'an iconic item' through its popularity with troops in the trenches of WWI (Barfe, 2004: p.122). In the 1920s, with gramophone player ownership increasingly widespread, the market for records boomed. In 1924, 24 million records were sold in Britain and this increased to 59 million just six years later (Barfe, 2004: p.81). It was during this period that the music industry became increasingly focused on the sale of recorded music, rather than live performance. An integral part of this shift was the way that leading gramophone player/record manufacturers evolved to become music publishers and recording labels. In Britain, during the 1930s, two companies came to dominate the record industry: Electric and Musical Industries (EMI) and Decca. Like Decca, the origins of EMI were in the gramophone manufacturing industry, as The Gramophone Company. When the word 'gramophone' became more of a generic term, the company rebranded itself as His Master's Voice, or HMV, which, of course, remains a recognisable brand within the music (retail) industry today (Barfe, 2004: p.81). EMI itself was established in 1931, following a merger between the Gramophone Company (HMV) and the Columbia Gramophone Company. The new company immediately set about expanding its interests in the music industry. During the 1930s, EMI bought into Chappell & Co, Britain's largest song publishing and concert promotion company (Frith, 1988: p.17). At around the same time, Decca was also developing a commercial strategy to maximise revenues from the sale of recorded music. Decca was the first company to realise that investment in advertising and promotion was more than justified by the resulting increase in record sales (see 'Economies of Scale' in Chapter 2). Using this logic, Decca invested heavily in the promotion of artists, such as the coveted band leader, Jack Hylton, and the banjo playing Lancashire comedian, George Formby (Barfe, 2004: p.128). Largely through the acquisition of various other companies, Decca also acquired the British recording rights for various Hollywood stars, including Bing Crosby (Barfe, 2004: p.130–1). By the end of the 1930s, EMI and Decca manufactured and sold nearly all the records made in Britain (Frith, 1988: p.17). Just as significantly, with interests that spanned music publishing, recording, and distribution (accompanied by a heavy emphasis on marketing and promotion) EMI and Decca had established a blueprint for the 'major' record company – a defining feature of the music industry ever since.

The ending of wartime austerity and the advent of rock'n'roll music saw the record industry continue to grow during the 1950s. In Britain, Decca and EMI remained at the forefront. Decca subsidiary (Brunswick) recorded the (1954) hit 'Rock Around the Clock' by Bill Haley & His Comets, which is often seen to mark the arrival of the rock'n'roll era. Through licensing deals with various US labels, Decca also secured the British distribution rights for the recordings of popular US artists, including Buddy Holly and Chuck Berry (McGuiness, 2022). Between 1946 and 1956, Decca's turnover increased eight-fold (Frith, 1988: p.20). EMI was just as, if not more, successful during this period. In 1958, it acquired the US-based Capitol Records, which featured artists such as Frank Sinatra and Nat 'King' Cole and, in 1962, it signed a recording deal with a little known 'Merseybeat' group called The Beatles (Barfe, 2004: p.188). The success of The Beatles contributed heavily to the rise of EMI to become the biggest record company in the world at the time. In 1964, one in every four records sold around the world was an EMI record and half of the world's top ten singles of 1964 were by EMI artists (Simonelli, 2013: p.210). With the lucrative teenage market now firmly established, by the end of the 1960s and into the 1970s, the British record industry was repeatedly making profits in excess of £100 million, with Decca, who by now had signed The Rolling Stones, as well as EMI, achieving record revenues (Simonelli, 2013: p.210).

Paradoxically, the success of EMI and Decca during the 1960s and 1970s provided an opening for the growth of smaller rival companies, known as independents, or 'indies', due to their independence from the majors. With their 'monolithic and hierarchical organisational structures' the majors had become overly reliant on established artists and ill equipped to identify new talent and/or music genres (Wikström, 2020: p.71). Consequently, during the 1970s, independent recording labels, like Virgin and Island Records, were able to achieve commercial success with new artists/genres, such as progressive rock (e.g. Mike Oldfield) and reggae (e.g. Bob Marley) respectively. Similarly, the growth of punk music during the 1970s was driven by a host of independent record labels, including Stiff Records, with artists such as Ian Dury and The Damned. Since the 1970s, independents have continued to play an important role within the British music industry, mostly linked to innovative artists/genres, including 'Britpop' (e.g. Blur: Food Records) during the 1990s and 'drum and bass' (e.g. Ram Records) during the 2000s. In this sense, the term 'independent' (or 'indie') denotes not just a type of economic entity, but a 'musical attitude' with authenticity at its core and 'diametrically opposed to a stereotyped mainstream' (Shuker, 2008: pp.21–2). Faced with increased competition from independents, the majors adopted a number of different commercial strategies, ranging from 'upstream' deals, which gave them the opportunity to acquire promising artists, to partial, or complete, takeovers (Wikström, 2020: p.72). For example, in 1992, Virgin (publishing and recording) was purchased by EMI in a deal worth over £500 million (Barfe, 2004: p.310). Often, even following takeovers, however, the majors allowed (former) independents a large degree of autonomy over their artist portfolios in order to be able to respond more quickly to changing musical trends and preferences.

From around the mid-1960s onwards, the growth of the music industry in Britain was also supported by an expansion in the number of media outlets available for recorded music. During the 1960s, the BBC's initial reluctance to deviate from Reithian public service principles was exploited by pirate radio stations, such as Radio Caroline, who offered their (mainly younger) audiences a diet of wall to wall pop music (see Chapter 7). Pirate radio stations amounted to an 'extended sales pitch' for EMI and Decca recordings, but did not pay royalties (Crisell, 2002: pp.143–4). Largely as a result, the record industry was happy to support the launch of official pop-based radio stations, including the BBC's Radio One, in 1967, and a host of local commercial stations during the 1970s and 1980s, which became increasingly centred on pop music. The growing popularity of (commercial and BBC) television during this period and the subsequent introduction of multi-channel television during the 1990s provided a similar boost for the music industry. Television provided a mass audience for specialist music programmes, such as the BBC's *Top of the Pops*, as well as never ending opportunities for artist promotion via general entertainment shows. The 1980s also witnessed the rise of the 'music video' as essentially 'pop promos', commissioned and released by record labels to accompany audio singles (Caston, 2021: p.382). Music videos were the main diet of specialist music channels during the 1990s, such as MTV, and soon became an increasingly significant part of how record companies promoted their artists. By 1998, the British record industry was spending £36.5 million on approximately 850 music videos, a substantial increase on the estimated £10 million spent in 1984 (Caston, 2021: p.383).

The development of new technological formats for the recording and sale of music, such as cassette tapes and compact discs (CDs), provided another significant source of growth for the British music industry. Despite Britain's general economic downturn during the early 1970s, in 1975, the popularity of the cassette tape enabled the British record industry to make sales of £170 million, a major increase from £150 million in 1973 (Simonelli, 2013: p.212–3). During the 1980s and 1990s, the introduction and popularity of the compact disc proved even more lucrative. For industry insiders, the volume of CD sales was 'astonishing' (Barfe, 2004: p.301). The CD format did not just replace vinyl records and cassettes, it created a vast number of new sales. In 1977, the British record industry sold 101.3 million 'units', the bulk of which, 81.7 million, were albums. In 1998, total unit sales more than doubled, reaching 210.3 million, at a retail value of £1.86 billion, with CDs representing 175.7 million of those units and £1.47 billion of the value (Barfe, 2004: p.310). Some of this growth was driven by new music, but the vast majority came from record labels repackaging their old back catalogues and effectively selling people what they already had (on tape or vinyl) again.

As well as a booming domestic market, during the 1960s and 1970s, British record labels enjoyed unrivalled commercial success in America, by far the largest national music market. During the mid-1970s, British artists, such as Elton John, The Rolling Stones, David Bowie, The Bee Gees, and numerous others, dominated the American charts, both singles and albums (Simonelli, 2013: p.213). This made British record labels subject to growing interest from overseas investors. In 1979, Decca was sold by its aging founder, Sir Edward Lewis, for around £10 million, to Polygram, a major record company based in the Netherlands and jointly owned by the giant German and Dutch electronics companies, Siemens and Phillips, respectively (Barfe, 2004: p.288). Driven by the enormous growth in CD sales, during the 1980s and 1990s, the music industry beyond Britain was also increasingly viewed by various corporate interests as an investment opportunity. During this period, the global music industry was characterised by numerous mergers and acquisitions. In 1988, the Japanese-based electronics company, Sony, acquired the US-based label, CBS Records, and established Sony

Music Entertainment, which, in 1995, expanded by acquiring a 50 per cent stake in the ATV label, owned by the American artist, Michael Jackson, and including (publishing) rights to the songs of The Beatles (Wikström, 2020: p.75). In a similar vein, in 1990, the Japanese electronics company, Matsushita, acquired the US major record label, MCA, which was, in turn, purchased by a Canadian conglomerate, Seagram. In 1998, Seagram also purchased Polydor and merged it together with MCA to form the Universal Music Group. With this series of mergers, by the end of the 1990s, the global music (publishing and recording) industry was dominated by a small group of global majors, namely: Bertelsmann Music Group (BMG) (Germany); EMI (Britain); Sony Music Entertainment (Japan); Universal Music Group (Canada); and Time Warner (US) (Shuker, 2008: p.19).

The Fall and Rise (again) of the Music Industry

The CD may have changed the way that listeners experienced recorded music, but for the most part the sale of CDs still relied on the same distribution infrastructure that had supported the sale of tapes and vinyl records for decades. By contrast, from around the late 1990s, the ability to distribute music online provided a completely new challenge for the music industry. The fundamental problem (for the music industry at least) was that, rather than a pre-planned industry sanctioned format change, like the move to CDs, the distribution of music online was the culmination of a number of interrelated technological innovations developed within the computing and telecommunications industries, including: the MP3 compression standard, which allowed vast amounts of digital audio information to be compressed into manageable sizes; the spread of high bandwidth connections, such as ISDN and ASDL, particularly in workplaces and universities; the introduction of multi-media computers, with increased storage capacity, CD players, and speakers; and the development of easy to use software that could 'rip' CDs into MP3 files and could find and download these files (Hesmondhalgh, 2009: p.59). In this sense, the rise of online music distribution was a by-product of 'convergences in multimedia computing' (Morris, 2015, p.12). The fact that music requires much less disk space and bandwidth than audio-visual content meant that it was the first sector within the media industries to experience an upheaval prompted by convergence.

Launched in 1999 by a teenage computer student, Shawn Fanning, while at Northeastern University in Boston, a file sharing software called Napster is synonymous with the enormous growth of online music piracy at around the turn of the century. Downloadable for free, the Napster software facilitated online music file sharing by granting users access to all other Napster users and the MP3 files they chose to share. Within a few months, transfers of music files using Napster reached millions per day, and, at its peak, it was estimated that as many as 60 million people, mainly in the US and Western Europe, were using the service (Shuker, 2008: p.23). The rise of Napster did not go unnoticed by the major record labels. Before the end of 1999, numerous legal cases had been launched against it in the US for violation of copyright law and loss of revenues, by artists, such as the heavy metal rock band, Metallica, and the rap star, Dr Dre, as well as the record labels themselves. The legal battles lasted several years, but, in 2001, Napster was ordered to filter all copyrighted files out of its network. Following an unsuccessful appeal, a year later Napster faced bankruptcy (Morris, 2015, p.97). Albeit with a relatively small market share, the Napster brand still exists today as a legal music streaming service. However, it remains most famous for when it facilitated

Table 9.1 Global Music Revenues (US$ billions)

Year	Total Physical (e.g. CDs and Vinyl)	Total Streaming	Downloads and other Digital	Performance Rights (e.g. radio broadcasts; shops, etc.)	Synchronisation (use of music in advertising, film, games and TV)	Total Revenues
1999	24.1	–	–	–	–	24.1
2004	19.4	–	0.3	0.9	–	20.8
2009	10.5	0.3	3.8	1.3	–	15.9
2014	6.0	1.9	4.0	1.9	0.3	14.2
2019	4.5	11.4	1.5	2.6	0.5	20.4
2021	5.0	16.9	1.1	2.4	0.5	25.9

Source: IFPI (2022)

music piracy on 'an industrial scale' (House of Commons, 2021b: p.9). Napster is also often seen as marking the 'beginning of the end of the twentieth century music economy' as it (and numerous other similar providers, e.g. Limewire and Pirate Bay) was the catalyst for a decline in global physical sales of recorded music (Wikström, 2020: p.78) (see Table 9.1).

Apple and Digital Downloads

For at least some Napster users, sharing music freely through the site was viewed as a form of protest against the commodification of music and in particular the role of the majors (Hesmondhalgh, 2009: p.60). In reality, however, Napster was a commercially driven entity, backed by venture capitalists to grow and commodify an audience (via the sale of advertising on the site). With this in mind, the legacy of Napster may be interpreted slightly differently. Albeit illegal and short-lived, Napster demonstrated the existence of a market for digital music. Or, as put later by Steve Jobs, the founder and chief executive of Apple, 'Napster demonstrated that the internet was made for music delivery' (quoted in Morris, 2015: p.141). The dilemma facing the music industry during the early 2000s was how to commodify digital music. An (at least partial) solution was provided by the computer industry, or more precisely Steve Jobs' Apple. Following negotiations with the majors (see p.140), in 2003 (in the US and then 2004 in Britain), Apple launched its music service, iTunes. iTunes offered all songs from the majors (and eventually numerous independents) as single song downloads for 99 cents/ 79 pence and was an immediate success. Just three years after its launch, iTunes sold its billionth download worldwide. In Britain, in 2004, 5.7 million tracks were downloaded, which increased to 26.4 million in 2005, and, by 2006, 1 million tracks were being downloaded every week, mostly (around 80 per cent) via iTunes, but also via other similar services (e.g. Virgin Digital and MSN, owned by Microsoft) (Coughlan, 2006). By 2006, in all the world's largest music markets, including Britain, legal buyers from sites like iTunes were outnumbering illegal file swappers (Shuker, 2008: p.25).

The commercial success of iTunes was built on four main features. First, iTunes was intrinsically connected to Apple's overarching business model as a computer hardware company. Apple used a proprietary copy-protection technology (DRM) called FairPlay, which restricted consumers from playing music acquired on iTunes on any portable device other than the Apple iPod, the company's portable digital music player launched a couple of years earlier. If consumers decided to switch to another manufacturer's MP3 player (e.g. Sony) they had to purchase the same songs all over again. This was a 'system lock-in' strategy designed to maximise the sales of hardware (the iPod) via relatively cheap and accessible software (i.e. music from iTunes) (Wikström, 2020: p.106). Second, with the iTunes online store, Apple went some way towards dissolving the barrier between the personal music collection and the retail outlet. The iTunes store 'fused the moments of purchase and playback' and in doing so encouraged further consumption 'as part of digital lifestyle' built around Apple products (Wade-Morris, 2015, p.134). Third, iTunes championed a single song download model – the 'unbundling' of the album – which provided a clear and (more) flexible way for users to purchase music. In this way, iTunes was able to appeal to the evidently large number of music consumers, who would rather pay (a reasonable price) to download music from a legitimate provider than use illegal file sharing sites that they do not fully trust (Hesmondhalgh, 2009: p.61). Fourth, Apple was able to reach agreement with the majors over the division of aggregate revenues from iTunes sales, with a 30:70 split between Apple and the rights holder respectively (Wikström, 2020: p.106). At least in part, it was Apple's main focus on the promotion of the iPod that enabled it to offer this ratio to the majors, who, in turn, were eager to explore ways to rescue some of the revenues lost to online piracy. Subsequently, this revenue sharing model/ratio became the template for agreements between record labels and music streaming services.

In 2008, music sales on iTunes constituted more than 70 per cent of the global legal online music market, with billions of songs and millions of iPods sold worldwide (Wikström, 2020: p.106). With the dominance of iTunes, Apple had the music industry 'in its grip', but this grip was short-lived (Hesmondhalgh, 2019: p.298). First, in 2008, Amazon launched Amazon MP3, which competed with iTunes by offering songs to download without any proprietary DRM and at a range of price points. Faced with this competitive threat, Apple opted to abandon its use of the FairPlay DRM and also adopted a more flexible approach to song pricing. Second, as already noted earlier, for Apple, music was always just one small piece of its wider corporate strategy and, following the successful launch of the iPhone in 2007, in 2008, Apple introduced the App store (Hesmondhalgh and Meier, 2018: p.1564). The App store enabled 'third party' (i. e. not Apple) software developers to offer their programmes/applications (apps) to iPhone users and led to a rapid growth in the number of apps available, offering access to a seemingly endless range of products and services. With revenues from apps downloaded from the App store divided 30:70 between Apple and third parties respectively, control of the app ecosystem has proved hugely lucrative and 'strategically advantageous' for Apple (Hesmondhalgh and Meier, 2018: p.1564). Nevertheless, in relation to the music industry, an important by-product of the launch of the App store was that it provided an infrastructure that enabled major record labels (and other investors) to explore new ways to generate revenue from digital music.

The Rise of Music Streaming Services

The growth of the digital music download market reinjected some of the value that had 'seeped out of the music commodity' due to online piracy (Morris, 2015: p.25). At their peak, in 2012, download sales totalled $4.4 billion, around 30 per cent of total global music revenues (IFPI, 2022: p.10). Similarly, in Britain, in 2012, digital downloads accounted for just under half of total recorded music revenues, at around £400 million (BPI, 2020: p.9). However, overall revenues for the music industry continued to fall. Digital downloads had not come close to compensating for the loss of revenues from declining physical sales (see Table 9.1). Against this background, between 2008–10, a number of new companies launched digital music services based on the potential of revenues from advertising and/or subscription, rather than direct sales of music. The most successful (or at least long lasting) of these was Spotify. Founded in 2006 in Stockholm by Daniel Ek and Martin Lorentzon, Spotify was first launched in Sweden and several other European markets in 2008. A year later it launched in Britain, followed by the US (2011) and subsequently national markets throughout the world (Simon, 2019: p.536). By utilising technological developments linked to 'cloud-based computing', Spotify offered users access to music on demand with an 'all you can eat' model (CMA, 2022: p.63). In doing so, Spotify heralded a significant reconfiguration of the recorded music industry, from being a 'product-based' business to an 'access-based' business (Wikström, 2020: p.113). To begin with, Spotify had to overcome scepticism from the major record labels, who were concerned that access-based music services would cannibalise the digital download market. In response, Spotify claimed that it would compete with online music piracy, rather than downloads, and would thus provide an additional source of revenue. Even so, to secure access to their music catalogues, Spotify offered the majors particularly favourable terms, including: a guaranteed fee for each 'play' served by the platform; a substantial share of advertising revenue generated; and equity in Spotify itself, amounting to shares worth a combined 18 per cent of the company (House of Commons, 2021b: p.59). Partly as a result, for much of its existence, Spotify has been heavily reliant on funds secured form corporate investors. Between 2008 and 2015, Spotify raised $1.6 billion in seven rounds of investment from 26 investors, including Coca-Cola and Goldman Sachs (Vonderau, 2019: p.9). In 2015, it also raised US$500 million via the US financial securities market in the form of a loan convertible into Spotify shares, and, in 2016, another $1 billion in convertible debt (Vonderau, 2019: p.9). The rationale is that heavy investment is needed to launch and promote the service across the world, before the 'economies of scale' and 'network externalities' (see Chapter 2) established during this growth phase provide ample long term returns on the initial investment.

During the 2010s, Spotify achieved impressive growth, particularly in Europe, including Britain. By 2015, it had 60 million users and was by some distance the most popular music subscription service in the world (Dredge, 2015). At this stage, around 45 million of Spotify's users were signed up to the free version of its service, including advertising, while the remaining 15 million were paying a monthly subscription for the advertising free version. This two tiered approach has been a key part of Spotify's growth strategy. While industry observers have long doubted the value of the advertiser funded tier as an independent source of revenue, it is considered to provide a strategically important 'stepping stone' for users to sign up to the paid subscription service. It has been estimated that around 60 per cent of Spotify's paid subscribers started on the ad-funded tier (House of Commons, 2021b: p.87). Since 2015, Spotify has faced competition from Apple and Amazon, who have launched their respective (paid only) music streaming services, Apple Music (2015) and Amazon Music Unlimited (2016). By 2022, Apple and Amazon were estimated to have 78 and 68 million subscribers respectively, far behind Spotify's 422 million total global users, including 182 million paid subscribers (Dredge, 2022). In Britain, Spotify is the clear leader in the digital music streaming market. Measured by market share, at the end of 2021, Spotify accounted for close to 50 per cent of total revenues, with Apple, Amazon, and YouTube (including YouTube's paid subscription music service, YouTube Music, launched in 2018) each accounting for between 10 and 20 per cent (CMA, 2022: p.13). However, purely in terms of 'audience reach', YouTube's User Uploaded Content (UUC) platform is just as popular as Spotify, with each service used by about two-fifths of British adults to access music online (Ofcom, 2021b: p.93).

Winners and Losers in the Age of Streaming

Since around 2016, the growing popularity of music streaming services has returned total global music revenues to growth (see Table 9.1). In Britain, over the last five years, music streaming services have become firmly established as the dominant source of revenue for the recorded music industry (see Table 9.2). By contrast, the digital downloads market has all but disappeared and in a symbolic move, in 2019, Apple announced the replacement of the iTunes store, with separate apps for Apple Music, Apple Podcasts, and Apple TV (Kleinman and Russon, 2019). For the music industry at least, another clear indication of the success of music streaming services has been the continued decline of music piracy. According to a (2018) YouGov *Music Report*, the number of people illegally downloading music in Britain fell from 18 per cent, in 2013, to 10 per cent, in 2018, and 63 per cent of those who had stopped using illegal sites were instead using streaming services (House of Commons, 2021b: p.12). While piracy has not completely disappeared, it is no longer an existential threat to the music industry. In no small part, this is testament to the popularity of the 'all you can eat' access model offered by music streaming services, which typically offer catalogues with more than 75 million tracks (CMA, 2022: p.10). In Britain, by the end of 2021, there were 39 million monthly active users of music streaming services; and, in total, tracks were streamed more than 138 billion times in 2021 (CMA, 2022: p.9). With rival streaming services competing to attract new subscribers, over the last decade, the cost of subscribing to a music streaming services has also remained remarkably stable, at £9.99, meaning that in real terms (i.e. taking inflation into account) the cost has reduced. On this basis, it is difficult to disagree with the Competition and Markets Authority (CMA), which, following an investigation into 'music and streaming', concluded that the market was working 'reasonably well' for consumers (CMA, 2022: p.69).

Whether the rise of music streaming services has been as beneficial for others involved in the music industry is more debatable. Artists, musicians, and song writers have long complained about the low royalty fees they receive from streaming services.

Table 9.2 Retail Music Sales in Britain (£ millions)

Year	Subscription Streaming	Compact Discs	Vinyl (LP and singles)	Digital Downloads (albums and singles)	Total
2017	602	368	90	168	1,229
2018	812	288	94	125	1,321
2019	1,046	217	100	90	1,454
2020	1,120	156	113	72	1,544
2021	1,331	150	139	55	1,677

Source: ERA (2022)

Perhaps most memorably, in 2014, Taylor Swift criticised Spotify and Apple for giving away music for free and withdrew her catalogue from Spotify, only to relent three years later as streaming grew in popularity (Sweney, 2017). In Britain, in 2020, Tom Gray, of the band Gomez, launched a public campaign group, #BrokenRecord, which argued that artists were not getting a 'fair deal' from streaming services and the major record publishers (Gray, 2020; Bakare, 2020). The focal point of artist complaints against music streaming services is often that they receive only a tiny fraction of a penny per stream. For example, Gray has noted that the estimated average pay out to a song writer per stream on Spotify is £0.0004, meaning that 2,500 streams are required to earn £1 (Gray, 2020: p.4). In a similar vein, the CMA estimated that a million streams per month are required for an artist to earn £12,000 per year (CMA, 2022: p.16). However, focusing on the rate per stream paid to explain the relatively low income of musicians can be misleading (Hesmondhalgh, 2021). Music streaming services do not actually pay according to a per-stream rate. This 'rate' is an 'analytical construct', an average produced by taking the income generated by an individual recording, by an artist, or by a label, and dividing that income by the number of streams achieved by that recording, artist or label (Hesmondhalgh, 2021: p.3599). As summarised by Headmondhalgh (2021: pp.3599–600), the income received by music creators from streaming services under the current 'pro-rata' system is determined by three key factors:

i   the total amount of revenue generated by the streaming service (i.e. the size of the pot);
ii   how much of that pot goes to rights holders, which is determined by licensing deals between the streaming service and rights holders (mainly the major recording companies and music publishers) and by the share of total streams that is achieved by each recording; and
iii how much of the money going to rights holders (again, predominantly the majors) is then passed on to musicians, which is mainly dependent on contracts between rights holders and musicians.

Some musicians have called for this 'pro-rata' system to be replaced by a 'user centric system', whereby each subscriber's fee is 'isolated' and then allocated exclusively to the tracks streamed by that particular subscriber (House of Commons, 2021b: p.91). An advantage of this system would be a clearer link between the listening choices of sub-scribers and the revenues paid to musicians. Under the current system, even if a sub-scriber does not listen to any music from a popular artist, such as Ed Sheeran, a proportion of that user's subscription fee (i.e. from the 'total pot') goes to the rights owners of those recordings. Some researchers have also suggested that a 'user centric' approach may also increase the income received from streaming services by 'non-superstar' artists (Hesmondhalgh, 2021: p.3609). However, any such change would not impact the total amount of revenue allocated to artists. Some would benefit from such a change, others would not. To produce a more significant change to the amount of income received by musicians from music streaming services would require an increase in their relative share of total streaming revenues.

In 2022, the CMA (2022) calculated how total revenues from music streaming have been shared between the main industry stakeholders (see Table 9.3). The proportion of revenues received by song writers and recording artists is clearly far lower than that

Table 9.3 Share of Streaming Revenues (%)

Year	Music Streaming Services	Recording Company	Publishing Company	Recording Artist	Songwriter
2017	27	40	4	16	13
2018	28	40	3	16	13
2019	28	39	3	16	13
2020	30	38	3	16	13
2021	32	37	3	16	12

Source: CMA (2022)

received by streaming services, or recording companies. Alongside growing the total size of 'the pot' (something some streaming services are more motivated to do than others – see p.146), this suggests that there are two ways in which musicians might receive greater income: first, streaming services pay more to record/publishing companies, who then pass on (a proportion) to musicians; and/or, second, record labels offer more favourable terms to their artists. As regards the former, music streaming services are themselves struggling to achieve profitability and are therefore unlikely to countenance a major reduction in their revenue share (see more on p.145). In terms of the latter, as already noted, the relatively low percentage of royalty payments paid by record labels to artists is a long standing feature of the music industry. Compared to physical sales, under streaming, the share of revenues received by artists and song writers has actually increased (IPO, 2021: pp: 132–6). All of this suggests that the rise of music streaming services has highlighted the issue of low royalty payments for musicians, rather than caused it.

The major record labels have been the chief beneficiaries from the rise of music streaming services. Over the last couple of decades, there has been significant consolidation in the (already concentrated) global music industry. In 2004, BMG merged its recording operations to form a joint venture with Sony, Sony BMG. Four years later, in a $1.2 billion deal, Sony took full control of Sony BMG, to (re)establish Sony Music Entertainment (House of Commons, 2021b: p.54). From the perspective of the British music industry, a more significant development was the disappearance of EMI from the music industry. From 2012 onwards, EMI's recording and publishing operations were variously acquired by Universal, Sony, and Warner, with Universal acquiring its recorded music operations, for $1.9 billion (some of which was later sold on to Warner), and Sony acquiring its publishing operations, for $2.2 billion (House of Commons, 2021b: p.55). Since the mid-2010s, the global music (recording and publishing) industry has therefore been dominated by three major corporations: Sony Music (Japan), Warner Music Group (US), and Universal Music Group (US). A significant proportion of the rights payments paid out by music streaming services are paid directly to these three corporations. In 2021, these global major music corporations were estimated to be making more than a million dollars per hour from streaming revenues (Page, 2021). In Britain, in 2021, the majors accounted for over 70 per cent of total streams and collectively they had some form of rights (recording or publishing) in 98 per cent of the top one thousand singles (CMA, 2022: p.15).

The dominant position of the majors in the recorded music industry is also reinforced by two important features of music streaming services. First, with the 'full catalogue' of music made available by music streaming services, the 'back catalogue' (defined as music older than 12 months) is readily available and represents a very high proportion of streams, calculated to be as high as 86 per cent in 2021 (CMA, 2022: p.10). This means that the value of the 'back catalogue' has increased considerably in recent years. In this sense, streaming services have thickened (i.e. added value to) the 'the long tail' within the music industry (see Chapter 2). While individual artists may benefit from increased royalties, or the sale of their rights, the main beneficiaries are those with large collections of rights assembled over decades, i.e. the majors. Second, playlists are a popular feature of music streaming services. As well as playlists created directly by the user/s, playlists are also provided by streaming services, either as curated lists based on certain themes/genres (e.g. summer hits), or an algorithm-based recommendation system. Around 20 per cent of streams are from playlists created by the streaming service (CMA, 2022: p.43). Some researchers claim that playlists provided by streaming services 'tend to favour more mainstream, established and international music, in particular that which appears on major labels, and to disadvantage the more niche, the more independent, the more locally-focused' (Antal, Fletcher, and Ormosi, 2021: p.9).

Alongside the majors, music from hundreds of 'indies' is also available via streaming services, including some new types of providers, such as 'DIY' distributors that focus on putting new music onto streaming services at low cost. Partly as a result, since Spotify launched in 2009, the number of British recording artists has grown by 145 per cent, to 115,000 (Page, 2021). This development gives some credence to long held hopes for the 'digital democratisation' of music, but its significance should not be overstated (Hesmondhalgh, 2019: p.299). While hundreds of indies make music available from thousands of artists via streaming services, they account for only around a quarter of all streams, and only two indies have a market share in excess of 1 per cent (CMA, 2022: p.15). The majors also continue to acquire any indies deemed commercially valuable. For example, in the last few years, the majors have acquired a number of successful British indies, including: Ministry of Sound Recordings (by Sony Music); ZTT, Stiff Records and Perfect Songs (by Universal); and First Night Records (by Warner) (House of Commons, 2021b: p.55). When considered alongside the demise of EMI, it could well be argued that, in the words of the iconic British singer, Sandie Shaw, 'there is currently no such thing as the [British] record industry' (House of Commons, 2021b: p.55).

Music streaming services themselves are also subject to the market power of the major music corporations. With millions of users, streaming services may well receive significant subscription revenues, but around 70 per cent of these revenues are immediately paid out to rights holders, most notably the majors (see Table 9.3). As a result, to date at least, music streaming services have proved far from profitable. Most notably, in the decade up until 2020, Spotify's cumulative annual losses totalled €2.62 billion (Ingham, 2020). For Spotify's main rivals, Apple and Amazon, music streaming services are 'loss leaders', used to attract consumers to other parts of their respective businesses, rather than being profitable operations in their own right (House of Commons, 2021b: p.76). Faced with such rivals, Spotify has sought help from European competition regulators. In 2019, Spotify lodged an official complaint with the European Commission about the 30 per cent fee it is obliged to pay to Apple for any sales made via the Apple App store, including when Spotify users upgrade from its free to its subscription service (Sweney, 2019). Spotify argues that this 'tax' provides Apple's own music streaming service with an unfair competitive advantage over rival music services, including Spotify. In 2021, the European Commission officially charged Apple with breaching EU competition law and Apple may face a large fine and/or be forced to change its App store rules if it is unable to convince the Commission that it operates in accordance with EU law (Wakefield, 2021).

While a change to the way the App store operates may provide a competitive boost for Spotify, its long term profitability remains far from certain. One approach could be to increase the price charged to consumers, but while this option might be attractive to a standalone music streaming service, such as Spotify, for 'multi-sided' platforms, such as Apple and Amazon, a low price for consumers is the basis of their 'loss leader' strategy (Towse, 2020: p.1465). With the major music streaming services all offering an almost identical 'full catalogue', a unilateral price increase would no doubt result in a significant loss of subscribers. Alternatively, Spotify (and other music streaming services) may opt to focus on increasing their subscriber numbers and/or the proportion of subscription revenues they retain. The former has obviously been the main focus of streaming services since their inception and, as a result, if anything, subscriber growth is likely to slow in the coming years as the market reaches saturation point. However, there are possibly more grounds for optimism in relation to revenue distribution. Over the last few years, music streaming services have managed to gradually increase the proportion of revenues they retain, mainly at the expense of record labels. Between 2017 and 2021, the share of music streaming revenues retained by streaming services has increased from 27 to 32 per cent (see Table 9.3). This has no doubt been particularly welcome for standalone music streaming services, like Spotify, but question marks remain over the long term commercial viability of music streaming services.

Conclusion

The music industry was the first sector of the media industries to be disrupted and then reshaped by convergence. The music industry of the 2020s is certainly very different to the one that emerged during the early part of the 20th century and, by the 1990s, had grown to become a multi-million-pound business. The digitalisation of music distribution has seen (existing and new) corporate interests from the consumer electronics and information technology sectors, such as Apple, Spotify, and Amazon, become key players in the music industry. At the same time, however, the commercial value of the music industry remains located largely in the control of music (recording and publishing) rights. For this reason, while the global major corporations that dominate the music industry today – Sony, Universal, and Warner – are very different to their predecessors, such as EMI and Decca, the source of their market power remains intrinsically linked to the control of large portfolios of rights and the ability to market and promote their signed artists and musicians. In this sense, the music industry of the 2020s is characterised as much by continuity as change.

10 Videogames

As has been discussed at various points throughout this book, the idea around what constitutes a 'media' industry has often been a rather narrowly focused one in the academic literature, dominated by broadcasting (television in particular) and newspapers. Even as processes such as convergence and the move online made that narrow focus ever more problematic, media studies continued to be structured around these core media. Yet, as the book has shown, even veering only slightly outside of these dominant media, such as into film or magazines, reveals both the similarities and differences across and between sectors. The videogame industry is barely 50 years old and despite having grown to be a substantial media sector over the last decade or so, the level of attention to aspects of its politico-economic impact, both in academic but also in terms of wider public discourse, remains comparatively marginal. In 2000, the games industry had a 17.8 per cent share of the British entertainment market, lagging behind video and music, but by 2020 it had overtaken them, worth four and half times more than it had done in 2000, and accounting for almost half of the entire entertainment market in Britain (ERA, 2021). Yet, as Newman notes, in that wider discourse, videogames have routinely been categorised as little more than a 'worthless diversion' (2008: p.1), and debate has centred mainly on videogame violence, and how the popularity of violent games are 'both symptomatic of and the partial or even sole cause of social, cultural and educational decline' (ibid.: p.2). Within that explicit critique lies a more implicit acknowledgement, however, that the videogame industry can be seen as an important part of the wider cultural industries (Kerr, 2017: p.5), though much of the academic literature on the videogame industry comes more from business studies and computing/technical fields than from the political economy of the media area. This chapter will explore the industry in terms of this position, and these debates, but will also consider the really distinctive role that Britain has occupied within the various stages of the development of the global videogame industry, as part of that wider body of media and cultural industries. A consideration of videogames sits as a really useful counterpoint to the accounts of the traditional media industries in previous chapters, particularly as it is so often left out of accounts of the British media. Some parts of the narrative around the British videogames industry align well with those of other media industries, reflecting the same kinds of structural issues, but there are also distinctive features that will be considered in this chapter, and are worth considerably more attention than they usually garner.

Britain is one of the largest videogame markets in Europe, with 2021 revenue over £6 billion (Clement, 2022). Unlike some other media industries, Covid 19 did little to halt the overall rise of the videogame market value, achieving a record market value of £7

DOI: 10.4324/9781315396781-13

billion in 2020, up by over a quarter on the previous year, as many locked-down Brits turned to home consoles and online gaming (Ukie, 2020). European countries are some way behind the biggest markets in terms of value, with China having rapidly expanded in recent years to become the biggest market, worth around $46 billion, followed by the two countries that have dominated the industry since its inception, the United States ($40 billion) and Japan ($22 billion). South Korea is some way behind the big three, and a small amount in front of Germany, Britain, and France (Newzoo, 2022). None-theless, both globally and within countries, the videogame industry is now much bigger than most other media industries, in terms of revenue. There are many reasons for this, though the multi-faceted means through which games can now be consumed continue to play a role in the growth of the industry, and whilst there have been peaks and troughs, as technologies and habits have changed, its overall onward march has made it an ever more central element of the media industries. It is in those, sometimes dra-matic, changing circumstances through the short history of the videogame industry that the notable and distinctive role Britain has played becomes apparent and illustrates many of the key themes of this book. Whilst videogames arguably display a 'relative immaturity as an accepted cultural form' (Webber, 2020: p.136), their role as an increasingly significant cultural form has played into both industry-specific and broader media policy and regulation formation, within which there are distinctive patterns of debate and development in the British context. Videogame regulation in Britain has paralleled the regulatory structures of the British film industry (Webber, 2020), for instance. Whilst in its early days the outputs of the industry might not seem to have much in common with culture akin to films (or broadcast media for that matter) in terms of content, as the sophistication of games has increased over time, the promi-nence of videogame representations within them, and impact on wider culture, has become ever more evident. As such, at least in part, regulation has begun to diverge from the structures inherited from traditional media in some regards. Moreover, both in terms of content, in global franchises like the *Tomb Raider* series with its British protagonist Lara Croft, and production, in franchises like the *Grand Theft Auto* games, British videogame developers have been at the centre of many of the most significant contributions of the videogame industry to wider culture, seeing other aspects of videogame industry structures becoming more substantial elements of wider cultural and economic policy in Britain.

The Hardware and Software Symbiosis

Perhaps the most immediately distinctive feature of the videogames industry lies in the intersection between hardware and software. Some scholars have preferred 'digital games' (Kerr, 2017) as a catch-all term to cover games available across a range of dif-ferent hardware platforms, and depending on what is included or excluded in the term used, authors have offered a range of both different models of industry structures, and also the classification of games industry phases (Izushi and Aoyama, 2006; Zack-ariasson and Wilson, 2010; Tsang, 2021). For the purposes of simplicity in this chapter, the term videogames will be used to cover the whole sector. As pointed out in Chapter 1, at least for some media forms, the issues around hardware have either retreated fully into the background of academic debates or only crop up on occasion. Studies of newspapers, for example, might discuss the shift to tabloid formats but purely in terms of editorial quality not printing technology. Major technical developments in screen media, the rise of the talkies, or the shift to streaming formats for broadcast media, for instance, do garner attention but again the focus is more on implications for content production, reception, and policy associated with those elements. The political economy of the production of radios or televisions, however, barely feature in typical studies of media industries, and whilst hardware format wars are prevalent at times, such as the battle between Betamax and VHS in the 1980s, or Blu-Ray and HD-DVD in the 2000s, or the varied formats for recorded music (see Chapter 9), they're rarely a central focus of discussions of those industries. The key reason for that is, brief format wars notwithstanding, most of these technologies end up with standard hardware used globally. So, changing your television set from a Samsung to a Sony, say, hasn't been particularly consequential for the political economy of television production, or rather it hasn't to an extent that features prominently in either political or academic discourses around television thus far. For the videogame industry, however, the role of hardware remains a significant component of discussions of the industry alongside software to the time of writing, and makes it a good example of a dual product or two-sided market, as explained in Chapter 2. Switching from a Sony PlayStation to a Microsoft Xbox is a substantial choice for consumers, with different hardware architectures, different software landscapes, and so on. As such, videogames are a two-sided market as there are games hardware manufacturers, selling things like consoles to consumers, but there are also videogame developers who produce games both for consumers but also for consoles (Lee, 2012, Cabras et al., 2017). The market between hardware manufacturers and videogame developers is a particularly significant one for the games industry overall, for a range of reasons, not least how differences in particular nations' industry structures led to different historical developments in terms of this hardware/software relationship and, as mentioned, Britain has a distinctive position in this regard.

In Chapter 1 we introduced the concept of convergence, and the idea that the shift to digital across media industries was a key technological factor in media convergence. The videogame sector is a fascinating counterpoint to that narrative of convergence as, despite being an intrinsically digital medium from the outset, its history is one of near constant upheavals of hardware technologies, and a 'diversification of devices and channels' persists up to the time of writing (Kerr, 2017: p.35). Videogames have gone through phases of physical machines in arcades, home consoles, home computers, a return to consoles, the rise of online gaming (via PCs then another phase of consoles), and handheld and then networked mobile devices (both bespoke devices, and gaming for mobile phones/tablets, etc.). These hardware phases have also impacted on other aspects of industry structures, particularly in terms of movements between more and less vertically integrated markets, and changes in the patterns of market dominance both within and between hardware and software firms (Lee, 2012).

Whilst there are antecedents, the first videogame proper, in the sense of one that entered public use and public consciousness, was *Pong* in 1972. *Pong* initiated the first, and oldest, hardware format for videogames – the videogame machine. By the early 1980s, arcades, previously full of pinball and slot machines, had been largely replaced by videogame arcades and were a familiar feature of screen culture at the time, such as the arcade in *Tron* (1982), a Disney film imagining computer coders getting trapped in a videogame world. Today a common evocation of the 1980s in retro screen fiction incorporates videogame arcades, such as in *Stranger Things* (2016–). However, it was just three years after *Pong* launched that its founding company, Atari, developed a second platform/channel for videogames in the home videogame console (their first being the Atari 2600). There was a relatively brief explosion of the home console market between 1975 and 1983, as Atari became a major business and other companies developed their own rival systems. In the US, a largely flooded market of competing systems using different underlying hardware, often with poor quality hardware and software, saw the home console market crash in 1983. A key reason behind the crash was that the business model started by Atari was not sustainable across multiple companies in a number of senses. The first arcade machines and home consoles were typically produced within wholly vertically integrated companies. Atari, for instance, built the consoles, wrote the games, and then distributed them (Zackariasson and Wilson, 2010: p.144). Rival companies initially tried the same approach, but there were then problems of costs of console development and production, as well as games production. Formed by disgruntled developers within Atari, unhappy with a lack of recognition and autonomy, Activision in 1979 was the first of what became known as *third-party developers* – independent companies producing games for different systems. Rather than welcome diversification for videogame development, Atari sued claiming stolen trade secrets, though the case was settled with Activision able to operate paying royalties to Atari (ibid.: p.145). For consumers, although each console was comparatively cheap, there was no logic to having to buy multiple consoles to play multiple games, and for producers, game cartridges were a single point of sale. Arcades functioned because it was possible to have an array of games from different producers in a single arcade, and each individual game machine could generate continuing revenue through coin slot payments. Ever since, the global markets for home consoles have tended to end up with only two or three viable systems at any one time, impacted both by the symbiotic relationship between consumer choice and, crucially, the range of game production possible across each system (and thus consumer choice of games).

In Britain, however, the late 1970s and early 1980s had seen a growth in interest in home computers – distinguishable from games consoles in being programmable by the consumer. They were also multi-functional, not unlike the emerging home computer market in the US that would eventually lead to the behemoths of Microsoft and Apple, but distinguishable from those in two key regards. First, those early US computers were centred on hobbyists for bespoke, home assembly requiring some level of technical skill, whilst the microcomputers came as fully built machines. Second, they were substantially cheaper, the cheapest coming in under £100 (Lean, 2012). Sinclair computers, the ZX80, ZX81, and then especially the ZX Spectrum, launched in 1980, 1981, and 1982 respectively, became a central space for the development of the home computer industry in Britain, and enabled a games market to persist and flourish in Britain despite the console crash in the US (Izushi and Aoyama, 2006). The perceived future importance of computing was also recognised by British governments in the late 1970s and early 1980s. Aligning with the Thatcher administration's neo-liberal modernisation agenda, there were various publicly funded schemes aimed at developing computer literacy education across industry and in schools at the time (Lean, 2012: pp.549–50). Whilst it wasn't central to the games market specifically, another important player in the wider home computer environment in Britain was the BBC. As Lean explains 'with a public service mission, nationwide reach, and recent experience of a large-scale education project from the Adult Literacy Project, they were in a unique position to introduce computing to the nation' (ibid.: p.550). At a time when the BBC was still very much operating in its self-perceived role as the dominant paternalistic media organisation in Britain, the resulting Computer Literacy Project didn't just involve an education television series, *The Computer Programme* (1982), but an actual computer used in the show, and distributed to the majority of schools, as well as being available for home purchase (albeit much more expensive than Sinclair computers). The hardware was produced by British company Acorn Computers, at the insistence of the government Department of Industry, and the machine was branded as the BBC Micro. It was an innovative computer as well, not a cheap knock-off, and in combination with the multi-format materials produced in the project (the TV show, books, materials for schools), it played a significant role in normalising computing and defusing the 'fearful modernity of the personal computer' (ibid.: p.552). But ultimately it was games that were by far the largest driver of home computer ownership and usage in the 1980s in Britain. Alongside the Sinclair machines, others become significant as well, such as the VIC-20 and Commodore 64 from the US and, alongside a few other machines (e.g. from Amstrad, another British company), it was home computer gaming that maintained the videogame industry in Britain. Indeed, the proportion of homes with computers was actually higher in Britain than in the US for most of the 1980s and into the early 1990s (ibid.: p.555). It was this phase that is crucial to the initial development of the first wave of the British videogame software industry, of which more later in the chapter.

In Japan, videogames had also taken off. Taito's 1978 arcade game *Space Invaders* remains one of the most successful and iconic videogames of all time, for instance, and a range of Japanese companies had gradually begun to dominate the production of arcade games. Prior to the videogame boom, many Japanese companies were at the forefront of arcade game machine manufacture and distribution (e.g. pinball and slot machines) whilst others had moved from things like toy production into games production (e.g. Bandai). Strong domestic engagement with arcade games, and innovative games like Namco's *Pac-Man* (1980) and Nintendo's *Donkey Kong* (1981), helped sustain a largely independent videogames sector from that of the US and elsewhere. The lack of a domestic crash enabled Japanese companies to continue to successfully develop home consoles, building success through the home versions of their own arcade games as exclusives to their machines. The most significant companies with regard to hardware have been Nintendo, Sega, and Sony. The Nintendo Famicom, or Nintendo Entertainment System (NES), was launched in Japan in 1983, and its domestic success led to distribution to the US by 1985 and to Britain by 1987, where it, for a time, became the dominant home console (with implications for software producers, we'll come to later). Whilst Atari was comparatively struggling along for the rest of the 1980s, continuing to release consoles in the US, much of its international assets, particularly in Japan, had been swallowed up by Japanese companies. The only other console manufacturer to meaningfully compete with Nintendo at this time was Sega. Whilst its Master System, as it was branded and launched to the US and Europe in 1986 and 1987 respectively, hadn't significantly impacted Nintendo's dominance in Japan, it was comparatively successful in Europe in particular.

A key development in this period centred on relationships between console-makers and game producers, particularly in Britain. As mentioned, third-party developers were initially not especially welcomed by console manufacturers like Atari, but the potential for 'a horizontal disintegration of the industry's value chain, creating significant market space for videogame developers' (Cabras et al., 2017: p.307) remained, and evolved notably in Japan. Nintendo was the first to embrace third-party developers (Bossom and Dunning, 2016: p.186) through a system of tight licensing of development for their consoles, often through exclusive deals, and also with a literal piece of hardware in their console's cartridges that would lock out games from working if they didn't have official Nintendo licensing. In this way, console manufacturers could consolidate a level of both physical and quality control over the games that featured on their systems. This phase began to see the shifts in the separation and consolidation of videogame companies as focused more (or exclusively) on hardware *or* software, and the narrowing down of the hardware side of the market, not least because many companies recognised the relative costs in creating their own hardware compared to concentrating on software for other companies' machines. By the early 1990s, in terms of hardware this was effectively down to just two companies, Nintendo and Sega, and because both companies retained a lot of first-party development, and controlled third-party access to their machines, they were investigated in Britain by the Monopolies and Mergers Commission, as British developers were essentially forced into the deals dictated by Nintendo and Sega (Cabras et al., 2017: p.309). Under increasing political scrutiny, internationally not just in Britain, Nintendo dropped its technological block on third-party production in 1990 (Lee, 2018).

Sony's entry into the console market with the PlayStation in 1994 was the game-changer here, though. Selling 100 million units in its first decade, the first console to do so, Sony's mix of first- and third-party development to rapidly generate a large library of games made a huge impact on the industry. Sony had built its business primarily on media and communication hardware technologies, like the Compact Disc, and consumer technology like the Sony Walkman for instance, another iconic bit of technology from the early 1980s. The PlayStation's use of CDs, rather than bespoke cartridges as the games format, was also a key factor in the system's success. As part of a wider strategy of horizontal integration, and with convergence explicitly in mind, the company expanded in the 1990s and early 2000s into hardware and software, such as buying out Ericsson mobile phones in 2001, as well as adding film studios (Columbia in the early 1990s, MGM in the mid-2000s) alongside its ever larger Sony Music division. It's notable as well as an example of wider consolidation in the videogame developer industry, as many of the smaller developers were being incorporated into ever larger publishing companies and/or being bought out wholly by the console manufacturers like Sony, a trend that was particularly noticeable in Britain (Tsang, 2021). *Grand Theft Auto*, for instance, originated with the Scotland-based DMA Design, an independent developer that produced the first of the series in 1997 for PlayStation. Later that year it ended up being owned by the multi-national games publisher, Take-Two Interactive (Tsang, 2021: p.556), and its games since 2002 have appeared under the banner of the subsidiary Rockstar Games label, with the developers now dubbed Rockstar North. In many cases then, the independence and autonomy of the videogame developer sector in Britain was substantially diminished through the 1990s, even as the return of consoles and the growth of PC gaming saw many British-originated game franchises becoming global successes, due to this consolidation of videogame development and publishing into larger, multi-national companies.

Sony's PlayStation success meant Sega was eventually pushed out of the hardware market altogether, though it remains a huge software brand, and titles like *Sonic the Hedgehog* continue to be successful, just now across multiple platforms. Nintendo has diversified into different types of console-based entertainment, with the motion-sensor-based gaming of the Wii (launched 2006), and the dual-use, home and mobile Switch (launched 2017). The challenge to Sony's seeming march to home console monopoly was only halted by the entry of Microsoft into the market with the original X-Box in 2001. By 2001, Microsoft was one of the largest companies of the world in any sector, and despite its concentration on business software, its huge dominance of both office and home personal computing software, and predominance in internet browsing through MS Explorer, gave it the capital to consider entering the console hardware market. By the 1990s, microcomputers had enabled a wide array of game genres to develop but the technical requirements for even conversions of arcade and console games were rapidly outstripping their capabilities, and the relative costs of home PCs, that ran Microsoft Windows for the most part, started to become a major platform for videogame players and developers. PCs, in the early 1990s, had memory capacities measured in Megabytes, rather than Kilobytes like the microcomputers, and PCs have continued to outstrip consoles in terms of CPU power, memory, and the like in succeeding decades. Like the microcomputers, the multi-functional nature of home PCs also meant that the development of games was intrinsically easier for third-party developers and as the market for home PCs grew, fostered by growing interests in the internet for home use, so that the market became an ever more lucrative one.

The idea of games being playable by multiple players across computer networks was not in itself a new idea. The trend for fantasy-based role-playing games, started with Dungeons & Dragons in the early 1970s, had been an inspiration for text-based adventure computer games in the late 1970s, and in Britain in 1978 *Multi-User Dungeon* was developed that allowed multiple players across a university network (Tsang, 2021: p.548). By the late 1990s, the capacity of the internet for an ever larger scale, and ever more sophisticated games, started to see online games become major avenues for revenue that hardware manufacturers wanted to tap into. The success of massively multiplayer online role-playing games (MMORPGs) like *Ultima Online* (1997) is presented by some as a key shift in the global games industry (Zackariasson and Wilson, 2010: p.145), but arguably the key structural shift was in the hardware changes that brought both PCs and home consoles into the market for online gaming, and in particular with regard to digital distribution of games. The videogame developer Valve established the Steam online service in 2003, initially as a platform for digital distribution for their own games' updates, but by 2005 they were serving as a platform for independent developers to distribute their games, and the next generation of games consoles for PlayStation, Xbox, and Nintendo, as well as spaces like the Apple and Google application online stores, all emerged in the latter half of the 2000s (Tsang, 2021: p.561). This development has been of global significance, of course, but its specific impact in Britain has been to see a rapid expansion of independent videogame developers in Britain again, from around 600 companies in 2007 to 2,261 by 2018 (ibid.). The current generation of home consoles is potentially the last to have hardware elements, e.g. the PlayStation 5 comes in two formats, one with a 4K Blu-ray disc drive and one with games solely downloaded (or streamed) via the PlayStation online store. With mobile phones having CPU and memory capacities far bigger than the early consoles and microcomputers, the predominance of digitally distributed games aimed at mobile, online markets are the direction of travel for the whole sector, and where the biggest recent gains in the sector have occurred – such as the rise to dominance of the Chinese company Tencent, who built their revenues through online services and moved into games in the later 2000s, and by July 2022 had a market capitalisation of over $400 billion (i.e. its estimated total value according to shares markets). Some of that value stems from being heavily involved in the Esports sub-sector of the games industry that, whilst having been around since the late 1990s in East Asia, has exploded in the last decade to become a multi-billion-dollar sector in its own right (Zhao and Lin, 2021). Esports are where videogames are played competitively, usually for prize money, with competitions screened live via specialist online sites like Twitch or, in several countries, via television, and often with live audiences in stadiums in some countries (Bossom and Dunning, 2016: p.34). By 2015, the top professional Esports teams were earning millions in prize money each year (ibid.: p.176). In turn, this demonstrates the continued dramatic potential inherent in game development, a feature that has persisted across the many twists and turns of the hardware side of the industry.

Software: Bedroom Coders to Corporate Boardrooms

Given the billion-dollar, global scale of many videogames in the 2020s, played by tens of millions, and intrinsic parts of wider popular culture, it is quite something to note the beginnings of videogame development, particularly in the British context. As mentioned earlier, a distinctive phase in the British industry occurred when home microcomputer ownership took off in the early 1980s, and in terms of games production, this period is often referred to as the 'bedroom coder' phase of the industry (Izusho and Aoyama, 2006: p.1852; Tsang, 2021: p.551). Many of the most successful British companies were founded by bedroom-coding brothers at that time including Rare, that started as Ultimate Play the Game, founded by Tim and Chris Stamper; Codemasters started by Richard and David Darling; and Traveller's Tales founded by Oliver and Paul Collyer. The bedroom coder era is captured with some authenticity in the Netflix series *Black Mirror*'s interactive episode *Bandersnatch* (2018). Another real-world example of this era of tiny, home-based, teams was Quicksilva, a company founded in 1979 that initially made peripheral equipment for the Sinclair ZX80, and then made games, the earliest of which needed the extra bit of kit to run (Eyles, 2016: pp.3–4). Whilst in both the US and Japan, the console manufacturers were tapped into the standard big business strategies of marketing and traditional advertising for their games (Cabras et al., 2017: p.308), in Britain the bedroom coder outfits relied on word of mouth through specialist computer shops, trade shows, and in particular the emerging specialist computer magazine market. As discussed in Chapter 5, the capacity of the magazine sector to identify and exploit emerging niches is particularly well demonstrated with regard to computer and videogames, as a range of titles like *Sinclair User* (founded 1982), and *Computer and Video Games*, or *C&VG* (founded 1981), provided spaces where developers could advertise their games (peripherals and other accessories). This was a reciprocal relationship – as magazine readerships grew so did potential developer customers and so on, and several sources identify this relationship as key to the growth of the industry to a point where major high street retailers began to see a market in stocking and selling games (Izushi and Aoyama, 2006; Eyles, 2016). It is estimated that during its lifetime, somewhere between 6,000 and 7,000 games were made for the ZX Spectrum, and probably more than 10,000 for its big rival the Commodore 64 globally (Izushi and Aoyama, 2006: p.1852).

A key feature of the bedroom coder phase is the dramatic variety of game genres that evolved on what were, by comparison to today's systems, really quite limited machines. Many initial games were essentially copies of, or very similar games to, prominent arcade and console games. Some of Quicksilva's games, for instance, had titles like QS Asteroids, QS Invaders, and QS Defenda (Eyles, 2016: p.8). The small coding teams of the era ensured a lot of distinctive, localised game content. So, whilst platform games, for example, were made, games like *Manic Miner* (1983) and *Jet Set Willy* (1984) had a distinctive look, tone, and feel that reflected their British origins. Relatively quickly, though, game companies started developing more distinctive and complex games, such as *Elite* (1984), a space trading game with wire-frame 3D graphics, originally developed for the BBC Micro. Ultimate Play The Game developed a series of celebrated games like *Sabre Wulf* (1983) and *Knight Lore* (1984) which turned the traditional 2D platform game format into an isometric 3D format, and alongside game sophistication, developers started to become more sophisticated in terms of marketing and promotion. A distinction between publishers and developers began to emerge, where the development teams concentrated on writing the games, and the publishers concentrated on the promotion and marketing.

Ultimate Play the Game changed its name to Rare in 1985, and when the tide began to shift back towards the console market in the early 1990s, they made an exclusive deal with Nintendo in 1993 and became, effectively, a second-party developer – that is, independently making games, but with Nintendo owning a big stake to ensure its premier games were for Nintendo machines. This deal was indicative of two features of the industry into the 1990s. First was the spate of buyouts of British developers, either wholesale into the console manufacturers, or into ever larger, multi-national games publishers (Izushi and Aoyama, 2006; Tsang, 2021). Second, these structural changes were an economic reflection of what had been a distinctive feature of the videogame industry almost since its inception – the prominence of Japan, alongside the US, as a key *cultural* influence on videogames, making it quite distinct from other cultural industries like film or music (Consalvo, 2006). As an example, Consalvo notes the global success of the *Final Fantasy* series of games, turn-based role-playing games with an intrinsically Manga/Anime inspired look and narrative, but with global appeal across diverse cultural markets (2006: p.118). Japan had continued to make distinctive and successful arcade games and their consoles also gave the world many iconic games, shaping the context in which game production elsewhere in the world has operated over time.

It is striking, also, how many of the top ten UK companies since 1995 (shown in Table 10.1), reflecting this economic trend, have been subsumed into multi-national, mainly US, publishers, into first-party studios within hardware companies or have closed altogether. A factor in that has been the extraordinary growth in the costs of game production, and how the game production process, at least for major home consoles and physical media production (i.e. games on disc), now involves vast teams of people. To get a sense of that scale, Team17, isted in Table 10.1 as the tenth biggest company by sales over the last 25 years or so, almost exclusively through its *Worms* series of games for multiple platforms, was able to become publicly listed, with a market capitalisation of around £580 million as of July 2022 (finance.yahoo.com). By the time of *Grand Theft Auto IV* in 2008, at that point in time one of the most expensive games ever developed, it cost around £62 million, but just five years later, its successor *Grand Theft Auto V* cost more than double that at £164 million (Bossom and Dunning, 2016: p.157). These Hollywood film levels of production costs can be worth it, however, indeed more so than in the film industry. The first *Avengers* film, for instance, was the highest grossing film globally in 2012, taking just 19 days to reach $1 billion in revenue. *GTA V*, the following year, reached $1 billion in just *three* days (ibid.: 158).

Table 10.1 Top Ten UK Videogame Developers (1995–2018)

Company*	Founded	Current Status	Most Successful Boxed Game*
Rockstar North	1987 (as DMA Design Ltd)	Owned by Rockstar Games (US) since 2002	*Grand Theft Auto V* (2013)
Traveller's Tales	1989	Owned by TT Games (UK, holding company of Warner Bros) since 2005	*LEGO Batman* (2008)
Codemasters	1986	Owned by Electronic Arts (US) since 2021	*Colin McRae Rally* (1998)
Sony Studios (PlayStation London)	1994 (as Team Soho)	Closed 2002, team moved to London Studio (first-party developer for Sony PlayStation Studios)	*The Getaway* (2002)
Sports Interactive	1994	Owned by Sega (Japan) since 2006, and part of Sega Europe	*Football Manager* (2007)
Core Design	1988	Closed 2010	*Tomb Raider 2* (1997)
Eurocom Entertainment	1988	Closed 2012	*James Bond 007: Nightfire* (2002)
Criterion Games	1996	Owned by Electronic Arts since 2004	*Need for Speed: Hot Pursuit* (2010)
Rare	1985 (from Ultimate Play the Game, 1982)	Owned by Xbox Game Studios (US) since 2002	*Goldeneye 007* (1997)
Team17	1990 (merger of UK publisher 17-Bit Software and Swedish developer Team 7)	Became a Public Limited Company in 2018	*Worms* (1995)

*Source: Ukie/GfK via www.gamesindustry.biz/articles/2019-04-11-revealed-the-most-successful-uk-game-developers

With the spiralling of costs, the dominance of the Japanese consoles, and US/Japanese publishing multi-nationals, British developers created a representative trade body, The Independent Game Developers' Association (TIGA) in 2001 (Tsang, 2021: p.559). TIGA has campaigned for state action to support the industry. Interestingly, other industry bodies in the sector, such as Ukie (the association for UK Interactive Entertainment, which reflects more publishers, and their multi-national interests) haven't always agreed with the proposals of TIGA, mainly concerned about potential restrictions on market access that might result from some kinds of preferential treatment for local developers (Webber, 2020: p.137). After some initiatives linked to tax credits and labour flows, the most notable economic measure achieved by TIGA has been the introduction of the Video Games Tax Relief (VGTR) in 2014 (ibid.). Following the same format and requirements as the tax relief scheme for film, discussed in Chapter 6, and produced in essentially the same context of both international industry pressures for access to markets, and EU restrictions on state-aid for industries, British videogame developers have to pass a similar cultural test to film-makers to qualify for the tax relief. Just as in film, however, the real cultural as opposed to economic value of the tax relief scheme remains an open question. The extent to which a blockbuster videogame series like *Grand Theft Auto*, for instance, set wholly in a fictionalised America, and distributed through a US publisher, qualifies for tax relief as a 'British' game through being produced by a British-based development team suggests more economic than cultural motivations.

Content Regulation

The cultural test for tax relief mirrors that of film, and also of some forms of television production subjected to a parallel test since 2014, but there are other areas of video-game regulation where the underlying issues are distinctive, even if the resulting reg-ulation is not. Some of these have been moments of wider public controversy and discourse both in Britain and globally, indeed some aspects of videogame regulation have emerged in relation to such controversies. One that has yet to be directly addres-sed in regulatory terms in Britain is the specific concern around videogames and addiction. Concerns about the physiological (as well as psychological) impacts of media are common, and indeed some never quite go away (e.g. claims over extensive television watching and heart disease risk (Davis, 2022)) but the specifics of videogame *playing* have generated concerns about addiction pretty much ever since videogames first appeared in the 1970s. Scholars in medicine, and psychology in particular, have routinely presented concerns in this vein; for example, some relatively recently calling for a specific videogame regulator in Britain in relation to their perceptions of addic-tion risk (Zendle et al., 2019). So far, in Britain at least, regulatory measures in relation to concerns about addiction have not specifically emerged, but have been to some extent arguably subsumed into regulatory frameworks focused more on content and implied impacts on games players, in line with responses that have developed over time in other media, specifically concerns about videogame violence (and other kinds of adult content).

For videogames, concerns about violence have not just been about representations of violence but the apparent agency of the games player in generating violence within the game, and the nature and acceptability or otherwise of those acts (Tavinor, 2009). Even very early on in the history of videogames, barely a few years after *Pong* and with game graphics highly simplistic and crude, games were generating controversy, such as *Death Race* (1976) which required players to run over 'gremlins' in a car that critics took to be running over people, though the controversy increased sales of the game (Kent, 2001). *Custer's Revenge*, from 1982, involved a sequence where the player's character (based on General Custer) finishes a level by raping a native American woman tied to a post, generating a substantial outcry in the US (Kent, 2001). In Brit-ain, however, videogames did not generate any specific regulation for more than a decade after they first appeared, essentially because 'they were unsophisticated and graphically crude so were not perceived as either a sufficient threat or benefit to society to warrant policy interventions' (Reynolds, 2015: p.113).

The first signs of potential British policy intervention came in 1981 with a private member's bill aimed at 'control' over electronic games (ibid.: p.117), reflecting that persistent trend of public anxieties emerging over new technologies. Although over-shadowed in terms of public focus by the moral panic over the 'video nasties' controversy, videogames did find themselves incorporated into the Video Recordings Act in 1984. Although that Act explicitly exempted videogames from being required to be submitted for approval by the British Board of Film Classification (BBFC), it did so only if they were deemed not to contain imagery relating to sex, violence, and crime (Black, 2013: p.552). If they did, then they would need certification by the BBFC though it was up to videogame publishers to decide whether they needed to submit games for consideration by the BBFC who had, via the statutory establishment of the Video Standards Council in 1989, already begun to work with the industry in the planning and organisation of this system of self-regulation (Reynolds, 2015: p.118).

In order to make sense of why initial videogame regulation for content was incorporated into existing film regulation, as opposed to either developing bespoke regulation or drawing on some other regulatory set up from other media, it's worth going back a little to briefly consider film regulation in the UK. The 1909 Cinematograph Act gave local authorities power over film exhibition, established with a focus on public safety, due to the flammability of early film, but it would then become the basis for potential restriction of film exhibition for issues relating to, the previously entirely unregulated, content. The London County Council, for instance, banned a film depicting the world heavyweight boxing match won by the first African American world champion Jack Johnson, beating the white boxer James J. Jeffries in 1910 (Richards and Robertson, 2009: p.67). Indeed, power over film exhibition remains with local authorities, seen most notably in several councils' decision to ban the biblical satirical comedy Monty Python's *Life of Brian* (1979), some bans of which remained in place as of 2021 (Adams, 2021). In order to limit what could have been a chaotic situation across the hundreds of local authorities making local decisions, the industry voluntarily established the British Board of Film Censorship in 1912 (Richards and Robertson, 2009: p.67). Although an industry-funded, self-regulatory body, the BBFC was very much an establishment body, and local councils generally followed their decisions around which films could be exhibited, whether films needed to be cut before exhibition, and the classification of films, initially distinguishing between films for a general audience and those for adults only. The BBFC argued that consideration 'has to be given to the impression made on the average audience which includes a not inconsiderable proportion of people of immature judgement' (ibid.: p.68). Before WWII, close association with the Home Office saw the BBFC being a vehicle for political censorship, but an intrinsically moralistic focus to film censorship was prominent from the outset, with concerns around the depiction of sex, violence, crime, and religion being amongst the most persistent instances of controversial cuts and outright bans over the decades. Gradual liberalisation has occurred in the post-WWII period, and by the early 1980s, the BBFC shifted to become the British Board of Film Classification, nominally as classification of films had become more of its function than censoring films. However, home video was initially exempt from BBFC classification, and a number of internationally made horror films, like *Driller Killer* (1979), *Cannibal Holocaust* (1980), and *I Spit on Your Grave* (1978) were released on video uncut, despite cuts for film exhibition being required by the BBFC. So, at the same time as changing its name, the BBFC, under the 1984 Video Recordings Act, became a major censor of home video releases – and one that had statutory force for the first time. Since then, film classification has continued to be gradually liberalised, and many of those video nasties have been released (though often with still substantial cuts). The BBFC today regularly adjusts its criteria for cuts through large scale public consultation, rather than relying solely on the judgement of the compliance officers who rate the films, and controversies are a lot less apparent in recent decades.

It wasn't until the mid-1990s that global developments in regulatory attention to videogame content started to come to greater prominence, prompted partly by the increasing visual sophistication of games, and the rhetoric around the 'risks' of games very much parallel those of the justifications for the censorship/classification of film some decades earlier. *Night Trap* (1992), which contained filmed sections with actors (depicting scantily-clad sorority girls being attacked by vampires), and the first in the still running *Mortal Kombat* series from the same year, with its bloody depictions of 'fatality' attacks in a martial-arts fighting game, led to US Senate hearings on videogame violence (Kent, 2001). As a result of those hearings, and under the risk of Federal regulation, the US games industry introduced the Entertainment Software Ratings Board (ESRB) in 1994, which utilises a similar ratings system to that used for film (Black, 2013). In Britain, the Criminal Justice and Public Order Act, also in 1994, carried provisions that updated the Video Recordings Act to extend the need for classification of videogames that depicted crime in a way that might lead to criminal offences, a legacy of the ongoing moral panic around media violence in Britain at the time (linked to the shocking murder of a toddler by two school age boys that was, quite inaccurately, associated with video violence by the murder trial's presiding judge). At the same time, a distinctive ratings system for games was introduced, developed between the industry and the Video Standards Council, essentially mapping to the BBFC's film ratings (Reynolds, 2015: p.119). One notable incident at this time was the first game to be refused a classification, *Carmaggedon* in 1997, a game which co-opted elements of the earlier *Death Race* with much the same kind of public controversy, although it was eventually altered sufficiently to be rated and released (ibid.).

In Britain, the system of self-referral to the BBFC continued through the 1990s and early 2000s as it did for film and video, until the establishment of the Pan European Game Information (PEGI) rating system in 2003. PEGI, now used in some 41 countries, and signed up to by the big three global games companies, Sony, Nintendo, and Microsoft, was again an industry initiative, so a form of self-regulation (Black, 2013: p.543). PEGI was initially aligned with the British system through its process of requiring videogame developers to respond to a questionnaire to generate game classifications, by asking an additional question for the British market as to whether there was a need for separate BBFC classification. The Video Recordings Act provision still held, so in effect every game with a PEGI rating of 16 or over pretty much needed to be also rated by the BBFC. This resulted in games essentially having two ratings, one from PEGI and one from the BBFC. It also remained the case that the BBFC had the ultimate say, as in the case of the 2007 game *Manhunt 2* which they refused to review making it impossible to release in Britain. The ESRB in the US classified the game as 'Adults Only' highly limiting its potential market (Campbell, 2013: p.256). *Manhunt 2* placed the player in the role of a convicted criminal tasked with murdering others in a variety of gruesome ways for a chance to escape if the player satisfies an unseen audience watching the killings as entertainment. The first game had been controversial but released without any ratings issue and received much critical acclaim, but the sequel was judged initially to have taken the concept beyond acceptable bounds before it, like *Carmaggedon*, was significantly altered and then eventually rated and released.

This system was simplified in 2012, with PEGI ratings now used as the sole ratings used in Britain, and a discrete arm of the Video Standards Council, named the Games Ratings Authority, was set up to act as the PEGI classifier in Britain (Black, 2013: p.554). The BBFC can still play a role where games have, for instance, substantial live action filmed sequences, or for how game footage is used in advertising (ibid.), so it is not completely removed from the regulatory process. Nonetheless, the system remains one of essentially industry self-regulation, though fines can be issued for games released without classification. Whether such self-regulatory ratings systems work, particularly with regard to concerns about the impact of videogames on children and young people, is still a matter of some debate (see Dogruel and Joeckel, 2013), and, with the ever-growing visual capacity of games on the one hand, and their increasing prominence across media platforms on the other, may well be an area of media regulation that is yet to be largely settled as controversies continue to emerge on a pretty regular basis (Campbell, 2013; Bossom and Dunning, 2016).

Conclusion

In January 2022, Microsoft announced plans to buy the publisher-developer company Activision Blizzard, with the *Call of Duty* series of games amongst others in its stable, for a staggering $69 billion, a deal which has attracted the attention of regulatory bodies around the world, including the British Competition and Markets Authority (CMA) (Browning and Lanxon, 2022). Of course, a combination of the global scale and reach of such deals means that the interventions of any one country's regulatory frameworks are challenged to a substantial degree. Frameworks intended to try and support internal industry structures, such as the cultural test-based tax relief scheme, as seen in other industries as well, may offer some elements of help but also don't necessarily prevent, and arguably even enable, consolidation of multi-national predominance in terms of games production. As Kerr notes, in the last decade or so there have been expansions, through digital distribution mainly, of producers into new markets, new channels for growth in independent production, including in Britain, but at the same time consolidation of ever greater proportions of the global market into the dominant companies, those able to afford the expensive franchises and brands (like FIFA) that have come to dominate the games market (2017: pp.43–4). Whilst aspects of the development of the videogame industry, such as the *cultural* as well as economic influence of Japan alongside America, are distinctive from other media, in other ways, such as the trend towards concentration and conglomeration, it demonstrates some of the more common patterns across the media industries. Not least amongst these is the substantial contribution the British videogame industry has made to global videogame culture, and Britain's exit from the European Union might be particularly keenly felt in this sector, depending on the level of attention post-Brexit governments decide to give the industry.

11 Social Media

In Chapter 1, the point was made as to how understanding media industries, particularly 'new' media industries, depended upon understanding aspects of the wider politico-economic and social-cultural context in which media industries emerge, develop, and exist today. Across the chapters so far, it should have become clear that whilst there might be distinctive features of specific media forms, at the same time some broad patterns in relation to technology, politics, and economics provide a clear context and framework within which new forms of media emerge. Issues around ownership and control, for example, are common concerns across different media, influenced both by ideological debates around public and private ownership, and around national versus international interests, amongst other issues. As such we can trace a range of policy interventions of greater (e.g. the establishment of public service broadcasting and the founding of the BBC) or lesser (e.g. tax relief schemes in film and videogames) extent in terms of the organisation of the media. But we can also see how often these debates overlap with concerns about the socio-cultural impact of media industries as well, whether around moral considerations (e.g. video nasties, music sub-cultures, lad's magazines, violent videogames, and so on) or concerns around information and democracy (e.g. press partisanship or due impartiality in broadcasting). Whilst many of those issues have never fully gone away, even when nominally addressed through policy and regulation, the last decade or so has seen much of the same kind of attention beginning to be focused on the newest discrete area of the media industries, social media. Like many media forms before them, much of the public discourse around social media relates to questions of ownership and control and how that relates to questions of societal impact, not least around questions of harm – harm to individuals, harm to social groups, harm to institutions, and particularly harm to democratic institutions. Whilst social media platforms are barely two decades old, and have exploded in terms of British citizens' use of them over the last decade at an extraordinary rate (see more on p.166), how debates around them are playing out at the time of writing closely align with the predominant themes of this book in a way that enables us to understand social media in context. Just as with each medium covered in this book, social media also generate distinctive new features and structures to the media industries as a whole.

Defining Social Media

Social media have developed within what is known as the second substantive phase of the internet, dubbed Web 2.0. In the first phase of the internet's development as a mass

DOI: 10.4324/9781315396781-14

public medium with the establishment of the World Wide Web in 1991 (rather than as the more military-academic series of networks that proceeded the Web), it was essentially distinguishable from traditional media by being a 'pull' rather than 'push' medium. In other words, whilst media like radio, say, pushes material out into the world, literally broadcasting to anyone with a receiver to listen to, Web 1.0 internet users had to actively seek out content to find material. Internet search engines and Web browsers became a key arena for sector growth and dominance, as a result, as these were the platforms through which ordinary internet users searched the Web for content. Initially an array of search tools with names like Lycos, Excite, Yahoo!, and Alta Vista competed for users, and whilst other search engines are still available, the founding of Google in 1998 was a key moment in consolidating the majority of internet searching through a single platform. Search engines' techniques for searching the Web for content could be exploited in ways to ensure the web sites of individuals and organisations came up near the top of people's searches, and Google's system that increasingly individualised people's search results based on what they had searched before, gave rise to the concept of the 'filter bubble' (Pariser, 2011). Search Engine Optimisation (SEO) remains a crucial feature of the internet today, but in Web 1.0, whilst online communities began to emerge and reach quite large scales, they were ones that people tended to actively have to seek out and find to participate in, and this developed differently in different countries. Online political campaigning, for instance, was already notable in the US by the early 2000s, not really impacting British political campaigning till a decade or so later. Having said that, however, some marginalised and extremist groups have found online spaces useful back into the Web 1.0 era, with such groups' exclusion from mainstream media providing a key incentive for them to develop online networks as alternative spaces. Both Jihadi groups like Al Qaeda or ISIS, and far right-wing groups in the US and Britain, have been shown to have developed quite sophisticated strategies for the use of the internet for communication and organisation, with real-world offline consequences as a result of quite rapid adoption of the affordances of social media platforms as they have emerged (Ahmed and Pisiou, 2019; Europol, 2021). Alongside the idea of search engine filter bubbles, another concept emerged in relation to these online communities, and their potential associated risks as 'echo chambers' where people increasingly seek out and participate in online content communities expressing only views and beliefs they themselves hold, and thus blocking themselves from alternative points of view. Though the term is in common usage today, in research terms it's a contested concept (Dubois and Blank, 2018). The big change in Web 2.0 was the rise of platforms that enabled a much more serendipitous engagement with a wide array of content in everyday online activity via interactive, social spaces, rather than millions of mostly lone cyber-surfers in their filter bubbles and echo chambers. Fuchs' overview of a range of definitions of social media from different sources summarises the various identified elements of social media as 'various forms of online sociality: collective action, communication, communities, connecting/networking, co-operation/collaboration, the creative making of user-generated content, playing, sharing' (2014: p.37). As Fuchs' discussion shows, how one defines social media, or perhaps which of these elements becomes of central interest, depends upon the perspective from which they are being observed. Social media, like many other media, are often considered primarily in terms of their socio-cultural and socio-political impact, but whilst these are extremely important perspectives, from a media industries perspective, there are key features that arguably help define and distinguish social media from other media, and a big part of that is how they radically alter the notion of a media 'audience', and the transactional relationship between media companies and their users.

Rethinking the Audience

In Chapter 2 we outlined how the traditional media can be thought of as semi-public goods. Whilst many forms of media have involved tangible goods, like a newspaper, vinyl record, or videogame cartridge, even those specific goods have semi-public characteristics that are mostly unavoidable and usually costed into the production process. For instance, when it was more common for newspapers to be sold as physical copies, the industry standard was to assume around three to four for readers for every one newspaper copy sold. Instead of seeing that as lost revenue, to free riders reading a paper they did not pay for, the claimed reach of a newspaper became a mechanism for attracting advertisers and getting them to pay large amounts to reach those readers. In broadcasting, whether analogue or streaming services, the solutions to trying to monetise audiences in spite of the free rider problem have settled on either some form of licensing or subscription system, or content free to audiences, with the audiences, then, in effect, sold to advertisers. In the videogame sector, in its early history it was partly through the coin-slots of arcade machines, then through the sale of some kind of hardware object – cartridges, CDs, etc. Even before online media arrived, these traditional sectors experienced challenges to these revenue models, from unstamped newspapers avoiding the taxes on knowledge, pirate radio stations, bootleg music albums, pirate video, and also more overt, legal alternative markets like second-hand sales. In the videogame market, whilst the second-hand market was great for gamers, it was a significant loser for games publishers. The game *Heavy Rain* (2010), for instance, sold around 2 million copies on initial release, but the publishers noted that data from PlayStation's Trophy system (that archived gamers' performances on games) suggested some 3 million had played the game by 2011, something like a million players without the company getting money from them (Purchese, 2011).

As this book has shown, however, the challenge of online to traditional media from the point of view of audience revenue has far out-stripped things like bootlegs, and second markets. In some ways, the disruptions have settled into familiar solutions to familiar problems, such as the rise of online subscription services for newspapers, magazines, and music. In television streaming services, as more competitors join early market leaders like Netflix, some are experimenting with cheaper services with some content advertising-funded, thus seeing a return to advertising breaks in non-premium services, not unlike linear television of old. In videogames, aside from later generations of consoles and PC games largely eradicating the second-hand market by requiring online registration of games locking them to single individuals, another tactic has been to make games increasingly cheaper at first purchase, or even entirely free (so called 'freemium' games), but then with regular in-game purchases either to make the game easier, to prolong gamer engagement, or even necessary to just continue or complete the game. So-called microtransactions, particularly in mobile gaming, have become a major point of contention amongst gamers, and has started to put videogame companies and the big online platforms into conflict with each other. In 2020, Epic Games, publisher of the online game *Fortnite*, filed a lawsuit against Apple, due to Apple requiring a 30 per cent cut not only of every game sold through its App store but also of every microtransaction within games sold through its App store, which Epic regarded as an illegitimate levy on its own, independent revenue streams (Bostoen, 2021).

The reason for mentioning these kinds of developments is that they are, in some way or other, all premised on generating revenue from audiences either directly from them paying for content, or indirectly from selling the audiences' attention to advertisers who, then in turn, pay for the content. At the root of everything here are notions of some kinds of products, content essentially, that is the focus of revenue generation, how media companies make money. With social media, however, content is not generated by the social media companies, rather it is generated (created) *by* audiences. Indeed, the very idea of social media users as an audience (consuming content) rather than as producers (making content), or something in between, is one that has featured in much academic discourse around social media. Concepts such as 'prosumption' and 'prosumers' to describe what people do with social media in creating, sharing, and commenting on the content they produce themselves have emerged to try and make sense of this breakdown between producers and audiences. In some critical political economy accounts, this content producing role is categorised as 'free labour' (Fuchs, 2014: p.117). There are some who have managed to monetise their social media presence, as in the new category of social media 'influencers', people who've built such substantial follower numbers that commercial brands are willing to pay them for their endorsements, or who can attract enough advertising revenue to, say, their YouTube channel to sustain them not just as financially independent, but in some cases to become part of the wider media celebrity class. British examples of this would include Zoe 'Zoella' Sugg, who at her peak had some 10 million subscribers to her YouTube channel, and featured on a range of television programmes including a celebrity edition of *The Great British Bake Off* (D'Emilio, 2021). Her brother, Joe Sugg, also had a successful YouTube channel with millions of followers, and was a runner-up on *Strictly Come Dancing*. For many traditional media professions, the rise of these online celebrities, often without any evident talents in performance, or in more specific media roles like journalism, for instance, has generated major challenges. Significant consequences for debates around news and information have emerged in the wake of so-called citizen journalists and online political commentary, for example. But for the vast majority of social media users, all the content that we create and post on these platforms – posts, comments, photos, videos, etc. – is activity that we do for nothing, financially speaking anyway, and not as a means of constructing some kind of online career or celebrity status.

On the one hand, like earlier media that provided content free to the consumer, the core revenue stream for social media platforms is advertising, both the more obvious things like adverts before and during YouTube videos, but also less obvious strategies like promoted posts, content paid-for by companies to be put on users' timelines and recommendation lists. On the other hand lies one of the most contentious aspects of social media company practice – the use of the content users put online as marketable and saleable data. Some of this is the kind of basic information needed to start accounts in the first place, sometimes seemingly logical and innocuous information, like name, gender, age, location, education, job, hobbies and interests, and so on. On top of this information though comes an array of metadata – underlying information that is collected automatically by the platforms that can be extremely useful to them, and monetisable for an array of external companies. This can be information like what times of day you log on, how long you're logged on for, how long you spend on particular videos, posts, etc. Unlike traditional advertising where, by comparison, it is always a bit of a hit and hope with an advert put out into the public domain and only limited means of checking whether it reached the intended target audience, and whether they've reacted to it in the way you hoped, social media provide extremely precise amounts of data on user behaviour. A step further from that is the use of a range of algorithms that also monitor everything you do online, including tracking your reactions (likes, shares, etc.), and your written comments, looking for patterns of behaviour, again monetisable data. In 2012, for instance, it was claimed that the US department store Target had devised a model that could predict, from social media behaviour, whether its customers were pregnant or not, alarming the father of an allegedly pregnant teenage daughter when vouchers for baby products arrived in his mailbox. Whilst that story is unlikely to be true (Fraser, 2020), and the veracity and efficacy of such tools is much discussed, this notion of monetising people's self-generated content is at the core of the social media business model. It creates something of an interesting paradox in that users have arguably more control over what content appears on social media than on any other media formats, and yet in doing exactly that, they are arguably providing social media companies (and others) ever more precise information that is both monetisable in itself, and of great value to providers of other goods and services (as mentioned in Chapter 1, see Chang, 2016). And yet, even with ever-growing awareness and concern about social media's power, whether real or exaggerated, in this sense of consumer surveillance and control, the rate of expansion and reach of social media in Britain is quite extraordinary.

Social Media Use in Britain

Over the last decade or so, arguably the most significant change to the British media landscape has been the growing use of social media platforms. To at least some extent, this growth has been facilitated by increased access to the internet more generally, and particularly the widespread take up of smart phones and tablets. Between 2011 and 2021, ownership of a smart phone in Britain grew from 27 to 82 per cent of the adult population and tablet ownership increased from 2 to 52 per cent (Ofcom, 2020c: p.6). By 2021, 94 per cent of British adults used the internet and a growing proportion, over 20 per cent, relied solely on their smart phone to do so (Ofcom, 2022b: p.10). Whether accessed via smart phone or other devices, the use of social media is virtually universal amongst internet users in contemporary Britain. For example, in 2021, 98 per cent of the online population accessed Facebook, Britain's most popular social media platform (Ofcom, 2022b: p.60). Social media use also accounts for a significant proportion of the total time spent online by internet users in Britain. In 2021, online adults in Britain spent an average of 42 and 35 minutes a day respectively on Meta (Facebook, Instagram, and WhatsApp) and Alphabet (YouTube, Google) owned platforms and apps, which were by far the most heavily used online services (Ofcom, 2022b: p.18). At the same time, however, despite the prominence of social media in contemporary debates about the (social, political, and/or economic) impact of the media (see p.170), it is worth noting that, on average, adults in Britain spend far less time using social media than they do watching traditional linear television, which albeit slowly declining, was, in 2021, viewed for an average of 144 minutes per day (Ofcom, 2022c: p.5).

Social media platforms are used for a host of different purposes, depending on both the nature of the platform and the priorities of the user. Ofcom (2019b: p.119) lists a dozen different 'functions' of social media commonly offered by social media platforms, including: a curated/personalised feed; friends/contacts/connections; followers/subscribers; photo sharing; video sharing; comments; direct/private messaging; group messaging; hashtags; likes; and dislikes. While many of these functions are common across numerous social media platforms, some platforms have tended to specialise in offering some functions more than others. For example, since around 2019, the growth of TikTok in Britain has been based largely on the popularity of its (short length) video sharing function and related 'For You' algorithm that curates a personalised feed for the individual user. By contrast, social media platforms, like Twitter and Facebook, at least to begin with, were focused more on individual messages and/or text focused functions. Individual users also engage with social media platforms in a variety of different ways. For example, some Instagram users may use the platform to follow celebrities and/or friends, but never post any content themselves (sometimes referred to as 'lurkers'), whereas others may opt to upload new content every day, or even more frequently, and also regularly comment on others posts. In this sense, 'whether a service is considered "social media" can often depend on the user using it' (Ofcom, 2019b: p.118).

A host of different social media platforms are widely used in Britain. These include specialist platforms, such as: Strava, a fitness tracking service; Twitch, commonly used to watch and stream videogames; and LinkedIn, a business and employment orientated service. However, the most popular social platforms tend to offer more generic functions, which then facilitate the growth of specialist communities/networks within them. Table 11.1 lists Britain's most popular social media platforms. For over a decade, social media use in Britain has been dominated by a handful of popular platforms, namely Facebook, YouTube, Instagram, and Twitter. As illustrated in Table 11.1, each of these services has close to double, or more, users than the other leading platforms. However, it should be noted that significant differences exist in the popularity of social media platforms between different age groups. Most notably, Facebook is most popular amongst older adults and is used regularly by around 90 per cent of those over 55 years old with a social media account, whereas it is used by only 69 per cent of 16–24 year olds. By contrast, Snapchat and TikTok are particularly popular amongst younger adults, with 72 and 54 per cent of 16–24 year olds using these platforms respectively and hardly any older (55+) users (Ofcom, 2021d: p.32).

Table 11.1 Britain's Most Popular Social Media Platforms*

Social Media Platform	Parent Company	Total Monthly Adult Reach (millions)	Online Adult Reach	Average daily audience
Facebook and Messenger	Meta	46.7m	94%	34.3m
YouTube	Alphabet	45.6m	92%	20.9m
Instagram	Meta	36.3m	73%	17.6m
Twitter	Twitter	30.8m	62%	11.4m
LinkedIn	Microsoft	18.8m	38%	4.6m
Pinterest	Pinterest	16.6m	33%	2.7m
TikTok	Bytedance	15.4m	31%	5.4m
Reddit	Reddit Inc	14.1m	28%	2.9m
Snapchat	Snap	11.8m	24%	6.9m
Nextdoor	Nextdoor	9.2m	18%	2.4m

Source: Ofcom (2022b)

*Figures based on Ofcom survey data from September 2021.

The Economics and Ownership of Social Media

While social media may be unique in the way it relies on user generated content, one similarity it shares with other sectors of the media industries is concentration of ownership. As noted on p.165, the most popular social media platforms in Britain are controlled by a handful of organisations, with two of the most popular, Facebook and Instagram, owned by a single organisation, Meta. A further illustration of Meta's dominance of the social media industry can be seen in relation to advertising revenues generated by social media platforms in Britain. Advertising is by far and away the most important source of revenue for the social media industry as a whole and is the only source of revenue for many platforms. In 2021, advertising made up 91 per cent of total social media revenues (£7.06 billion), with subscription comprising the rest (Ofcom, 2022a: p.34). Meta's combined social media platforms generate by far the largest advertising revenues of any social media platform (Ofcom: 2022a: p.34). For example, in 2019, total spending on digital display advertising was worth £5.5 billion, of which more than half went directly to Meta (CMA, 2020: p.62).

Facebook (and/or Meta) has not always been the dominant player in the social media industry. Founded in 2004 by undergraduate Harvard University student Mark Zuckerberg, together with a couple of fellow students and roommates, Facebook grew by offering a superior product to its main rival, Myspace. In the early 2000s, the market leader in the emerging social media sector was Myspace. In 2005, Myspace was bought by Rupert Murdoch's News Corp for $580 million, but News Corp failed to invest in the development of the platform, leaving it with a 'cluttered interface' and 'overloaded with advertising' (Barwise and Watkins, 2018: p.37). In 2008, Myspace was overtaken in popularity by Facebook and then quickly lost its user base, with numbers falling from its peak of 100 million users to 63 million users in February 2011 (CMA, 2020: p.122). In June 2011, Myspace was sold by News Corp to an online advertising company for just $35 million (Rushe, 2011). Facebook has claimed that its replacement of Myspace shows that its position as market leader is not unassailable (CMA, 2020: p.123). In a similar vein, the rise of TikTok over the last few years could also be seen to suggest that new entrants can make a significant impact in the social media industry. For the most part, however, it is difficult to disagree with the conclusion of CMA, which, in its report on *Online Platforms and Digital Advertising* concluded that, unlike in the case of Myspace, 'rival social media platforms do not act as a material threat to Facebook's competitive position' (CMA, 2020: p.12). For over a decade, Facebook has been the most popular social media platform in Britain. Globally, Facebook has in excess of 2 billion monthly active users (compared to Myspace's peak of 100 million) and has also successfully monetised its platform for much of this period (CMA, 2020: p.123). In 2021, Meta generated annual revenues of £66 billion (MRC, 2021: p.3).

Meta's continued domination of the social media industry can at least in part be explained with reference to some of the interrelated underlying economic characteristics of the media industries (see Chapter 2). As discussed throughout this book, these features are present across the media industries, but some are particularly acute in the realm of social media. First, social media companies are 'platform businesses', creating value by matching customers with complimentary needs, most notably advertisers and consumers. Bringing together advertisers and consumers is, of course, a common commercial strategy across the media industries, most notably in areas such as newspapers, magazines, commercial free-to-air television, and radio. In the case of the social media industry, however, platforms offer not just a dual-sided (i.e. advertisers and consumers) but a multi-sided market, whereby social media platforms position themselves as the middleman connecting a host of different users and interests. For example, Facebook can be seen to connect at least six distinct groups: friends as message senders, friends as message receivers, advertisers, app developers, and businesses as both message senders and receivers (Barwise and Watkins, 2018: p.27). A second related economic feature of social media platforms is the particular importance of network effects, sometimes referred to as network externalities. In a direct sense, the value of a network, or platform, is increased as more users join the network as it enables, for example, the existing members of the network to message, or receive messages from, more users. The growth of the platform also produces an additional (indirect) network effect because as more users join a certain platform, that platform becomes the standard for a certain activity (e.g. posting messages, or video sharing), which, in turn, results in a more and more popular network. In relation to social media, the importance of the accumulation and use of user data means that network effects are particularly significant. More users produce more data, which enables the development of more sophisticated algorithms for sorting content, which leads to better services. In this way, a large scale social media platform, like Facebook, benefits from a 'network effect-driven data feedback loop' (Verdegem, 2021: p.308). Taken together, these network effects mean that users face what economists refer to as 'high switching costs'. In other words, once a user has adopted a social media platform as their main platform, or one of their main platforms, they are unlikely to switch to a new platform. The third key economic characteristic of the social media industry is that it is characterised by a particularly extreme case of economies of scale, not least because its focus on user generated content enables it to operate more easily across national boundaries than many other media sectors (e.g. newspapers or television). For social media platforms, the initial costs of development are very high, but the marginal cost of distribution (i.e. adding an extra user) is low or close to zero. Taken together, these economic characteristics of social media platforms mean that once a dominant position is established it is very difficult for a new entrant to challenge it. The social media industry can therefore be described as an example of what economists sometimes refer to as a 'winner-take-all' market (Barwise and Watkins, 2018: p.22).

The 'winner-take-all' nature of the social media industry means that a dominant player, such as Facebook, is very difficult to displace from leadership in its core product market. Instead, the main threat to market dominance is that they will be 'eclipsed' by another company dominating a new, and maybe eventually bigger, adjacent market with similar winner-take-all qualities (Barwise and Watkins, 2018: p.24). This goes a long way to explaining Facebook's acquisition of potential rival companies over the last decade. Most notably, in 2011, Facebook paid $1 billion to buy Instagram, which had only launched a year earlier and had just 13 employees, but was perceived as offering a service that could pose a long term challenge to Facebook (BBC, 2012). In 2014, the same logic informed two other high value acquisitions by Facebook. First, in a deal reported to be worth around $19 billion, Facebook acquired the mobile messaging company, WhatsApp, which had around 280 million active users (Smith, 2014). Second, around a month later, Facebook also bought the virtual reality gaming company, Oculus, for $2 billion (Lee, 2014). Another strategy adopted by Meta's social media platforms to preserve their market dominance has been to replicate the successful features of other rival platforms. For example, in 2018, with the growing capacity of mobile phones to access audio-visual content, not least from rival social media platform, YouTube, Facebook launched its own Facebook Watch service, which enabled users to access (select publishers) and post long form and short form video content (Kelion, 2018). Similarly, in 2020, in response to competition from rival social media platforms, TikTok and Snapchat, Instagram launched its 'Reels' feature, allowing users to make short (15-second long) videos that can then be upload to their profile (Smith, 2020).

Economists would typically expect a company with a dominant position in a market to exercise its market power by increasing the price charged to consumers and/or restricting supply to reduce costs. However, with most social media platforms, including Facebook, not charging users to access their platform and close to zero costs for increasing supply of 'the product', the social media industry is far from typical. Nevertheless, it is certainly possible to detect evidence of the impact of Meta's market power within the social media industry, and, in particular, in relation to the market for advertising on social media. First, Meta's dominant position has arguably manifested itself in high prices charged to advertise on Facebook. Between 2011 and 2019, Facebook's average revenue per user increased from under £5 to more than £50, and the cost of advertising on Facebook is more than ten times higher than other social media platforms (CMA, 2020: p.314). While some of this discrepancy could be due to the particularly sophisticated use of targeted advertising by Facebook, it seems likely that 'weak competition' in the social media advertising market has allowed Facebook/Meta to charge advertisers more than 'would be expected in a more competitive market' (CMA, 2020: p.313). This is important because, if advertisers have to pay more to advertise their goods and services (e.g. holidays, hotels, cars, etc.), then over the long term this will be reflected in higher prices charged to consumers. Second, some studies have also suggested that 'there are signs that the volume of advertising consumers are exposed to is also on the rise' (Furman, 2019: p.43). A third area of concern is Meta's potential to use its market power for 'value capture' in the advertising market (Furman, 2019: p.46). Social media platforms are an increasingly important means for accessing news and current affairs in Britain, particular for younger adults. Facebook, Instagram, and WhatsApp are each ranked (third, eighth, and tenth respectively) in the top ten of the most used news sources in Britain across all delivery platforms (i.e. including television, radio, etc.) (Ofcom, 2022a: p.18). However, a number of news outlets, such as *The Guardian* and the *Daily Mail*, have complained that they can receive as little as 30 per cent of the advertising revenue when stories are accessed via social media (Furman, 2019: p.46).

In response to these types of concerns, in 2020, the British government announced its intention to establish a new Digital Markets Unit within the country's main competition regulator, the CMA. The new unit is intended to ensure that digital platforms with 'strategic market status' (e.g. Facebook) deal with third parties (e.g. news brands) based on 'fair trading, trust and transparency' and could issue significant fines if they fail to do so (Sweney, 2020d). To date, however, legislation is still required to legally establish the new authority and set out its precise powers and remit.

Social Media and the Regulation of Online Harms

For the most part, concerns over the growing presence of social media platforms have focused more on their political and social impact, rather than their market power.

Perhaps most notably, the last decade has witnessed repeated concerns over the impact of social media on the conduct of elections in Britain and beyond. For example, in 2018, with reference to the role of online media during the 2016 Referendum on Britain's membership of the EU, the House of Commons' Culture, Media and Sport Select Committee declared that 'our democracy is at risk' from 'the phenomenon of "fake news", distributed largely through social media' and 'the relentless targeting of hyper-partisan views, which play to the fears and prejudices of people, in order to influence their voting plans and their behaviour' (House of Commons, 2018: p.1). The Committee concluded that 'in this rapidly changing digital world, our existing legal framework is no longer fit for purpose' (House of Commons, 2018: p.1). The availability and impact of various other illegal and/or harmful forms of content on social media (e.g. material promoting terrorism, hate crime, self-harming, and/or suicide, etc.) have also long been the focus of public and political debate. For example, in 2019, the suicide of teenager, Molly Russell, 14, and her father's claim that Instagram 'helped kill my daughter' after she had viewed content about suicide, prompted widespread public debate and led the then Culture secretary, Matt Hancock, to warn that social media platforms 'could be banned' if they did not remove harmful content (BBC, 2019).

In an attempt to limit the availability of harmful content, social media platforms have long operated their own 'community standards' rules, with options for users to flag content that breaches these rules. More recently, at least partly in response to the type of concerns cited here, major social media platforms have also committed to a number of joint initiatives in an attempt to reduce the availability of harmful content. For instance, in 2016, in conjunction with the EU, Facebook, YouTube, Twitter, and Microsoft agreed to an online 'code of conduct' designed to tackle 'hate speech', which included a commitment to review 'user notifications' related to 'hate speech' in less than 24 hours (Hern, 2016). Such initiatives have certainly led to the removal of significant amounts of potentially harmful content from social media platforms. For example, in 2018, Facebook announced that, using a combination of algorithms based on artificial intelligence and human moderators, over a period of just three months, it deleted, or added warnings to, about 29 million posts that broke its rules on hate speech, graphic violence, terrorism, and sex (Lee, 2018). But, relying on online media companies to regulate their own platforms (i.e. self-regulation) is problematic for a number of reasons. First, there is a clear disparity between the claims of online media companies to be willing and able to remove harmful content from their platforms and the experiences of ordinary users. Research commissioned by Ofcom has revealed that around two-thirds of British adult internet users 'are concerned about content people view, read, or listen to online' and 45 per cent 'have experienced some form of online harm' (Ofcom, 2018e: p.4). Second, the growth of online media has led to what Ofcom's then chief executive, Sharon White, has described as a 'standards lottery' for British viewers, whereby the same content can be subject to different rules – or none at all – depending on the service through which it is consumed (Waterson, 2018). For instance, the same programme broadcast on ITV's television channel might face different regulatory requirements when appearing on its on-demand platform ITV Hub, or on Netflix, and no regulation if accessed through YouTube (Ofcom, 2018a, p.17). For many politicians and regulators, this inconsistency underlines the need to incorporate online media, including social media platforms, within broadcasting's existing legal and regulatory framework (Parker, 2018). A third objection to the self-regulation of social media platforms stems more from democratic principles than practical concerns. This is that decisions over what constitutes harmful content, and thus by implication the limits of media freedom/freedom of expression in Britain, are inherently political ones (i.e. they reflect value judgements about the type of society we want to live in). As such, these decisions should be made by democratically elected representatives, or at least legally accountable regulators, rather than the executives of commercially driven companies based in Britain, or beyond.

With at least some of these concerns in mind, in 2018, the British government declared its intention to legislate for the introduction of a statutory 'code of practice' for social media, which would cover 'the full range of online harms, including both harmful and illegal content' (DCMS, 2018). However, the regulation of social media is particularly challenging for a number of reasons (Ofcom, 2018a). First, there is the sheer volume of content (text audio-visual) that is generated or shared by online platforms. It has been estimated that over 400 hours of video are uploaded to YouTube every 60 seconds, which equates to a staggering 576,000 hours of content per day (Tran, 2017). To regulate online content in the same or a similar way to broadcast content would be particularly arduous, if not practically impossible. Second, the 'variety of content' available via social media also makes it difficult to simply apply regulatory approaches used for traditional media. Social media platforms provide access to a mix of professionally produced content and user generated content, as well as conversations between users. Britain's underlying commitment to freedom of expression means that the degree of regulation considered as acceptable for the former type of content could not necessarily be applied to the latter. A third regulatory problem posed by social media is that platform owners do not create or commission the content that is accessed by users, although they often have a role in determining what users see (e.g. through algorithms that manage the prominence of items in a news feed or in response to a search query). On this basis, social media platforms, most notably Facebook, have long argued that they are 'technology companies', rather than publishers, or 'media companies', and should not therefore be held legally responsible for material distributed via their platforms (Rajan, 2016). Finally, the multi-national nature of social media means that the main platform operators are not based in Britain. They may also provide British users with content uploaded by users based abroad. To be effective, the regulation of content accessed via social media is likely to require close collaboration with regulatory authorities in other countries, which may not always be possible to achieve.

In 2021, the British government published its *Online Safety Bill*, which set out how the government plans to overcome some, if not all, of these issues (House of Commons, 2022b). The legal approach proposed by the Bill is for all 'user to user services' (i.e. social media platforms) with 'links to Britain' to be required to abide by a code/s of conduct set out by Ofcom. Most significantly, Ofcom would require relevant services to operate 'proportionate systems and processes' to minimise the 'presence and dissemination of illegal content' (e.g. terrorist content and activity, child sexual exploitation and abuse), the length of time this content is present online, and to swiftly take down illegal content when alerted to its presence. Services likely to be accessed by children are also to be required to ensure they operate in a way that protects young users from accessing content that is 'harmful' to children (e.g. pornography; content on self-harming). The proposed legislation also obliges the largest user to user services – 'Category 1 services' (e.g. Facebook, Instagram, TikTok, etc.) – to tackle harmful content that is legal, but potentially harmful (e.g. content about eating disorders, self-harm, or suicide) to adults. Under the terms of the Bill, the most popular social media platforms also have a duty to protect 'content of democratic importance', such as election campaign material and/or content critical of government. If services do not comply with Ofcom's code/s of conduct, the regulator will have the power to issue fines of up to £18 million or 10 per cent of annual global turnover (Woodhouse, 2022).

Two features of the British government's proposed legislation have proved particularly controversial. First, the Bill's intention to ensure social media platforms regulate 'legal, but harmful' content has been seen by various critics as a threat to freedom of expression. For example, in early 2022, in its report on the proposed legislation, the House of Commons Culture Select committee raised 'urgent concerns' that the Bill did not adequately protect freedom of expression (House of Commons, 2022b: p.3). Second, some critics have also questioned the Bill's deliberate exemption from regulatory oversight of content from news publisher web sites (e.g. *Mail Online*) (MRC, 2022). For the Media Reform Coalition, a group that campaigns for media pluralism and freedom of expression, this exclusion could lead to a 'two tier' system of journalism, whereby traditional newspaper brands escape regulation, but citizen journalists, bloggers, and activists find themselves subject to regulatory restrictions (MRC, 2022: p.5).

Over the last decade, a broad consensus has formed within Parliament and the wider public over the need to hold social media companies legally accountable for the content available via their sites. At the same time, however, there remains much debate over how to best regulate social media platforms and, in particular, how to do so without undermining freedom of expression. The British government's planned legislation to tackle online harms is therefore likely to mark a milestone in an ongoing debate, rather than its conclusion.

Conclusion

Over the last decade or so, the rise of social media has arguably constituted the biggest single change to the British media landscape. The relationship between the audience and social media is a defining feature of the sector and is manifestly different to that of any of the other media industry sectors considered throughout this book. For social media platforms, the audience is both the principal source of content and also the provider of data that is then utilised by specially designed computer algorithms to facilitate micro targeted content, including advertising. The underlying economic characteristics of social media are also significantly different to other sectors within the media industries. A second defining feature of social media discussed in this chapter is that they operate as platforms in multi-sided markets (e.g. advertisers, individual users, business users, etc.), rather than the dual-sided markets that characterise other sectors, such as magazines, the press, radio, and television. Inherently linked to these two distinctive features of social media, a third important characteristic of the social media industry is the vital importance of network effects. Network effects are not unique to social media as they are also found in other traditional media sectors, such as radio and television, but they are particularly acute in relation to social media and go a long way to explain the dominance of the sector by a handful of media organisations, namely Meta (Facebook, Instagram, and WhatsApp) and Alphabet (YouTube). Concentration of ownership is one of the common features identified throughout this book, but even here the case of social media is a little different. In other sectors, British-based media organisations have commonly been significant players at one time or another and then either been acquired by US investors (e.g. newspapers, videogames, music) or usurped by new entrants from the US (e.g. pay television). There has never been a significant distinctively British presence within the social media industry and it seems unlikely that there ever will be. With British government attempts to regulate both competition and content within the social media industry gathering pace in recent years, it remains to be seen to what extent, if any, the domination of the sector by US-based media organisations represents an obstacle to effective regulation. How these efforts play out will go a long way in indicating whether it will become ever more appropriate to talk about the media industries in Britain rather than about the British media industries, a superficially subtle but actually quite substantial shift in the politics, economics, and organisation of the media.

Bibliography

Adams, L. (2021) 'The *Life of Brian* controversy explained: Blasphemy, bans, and looking on the bright side', *SlashFilm*, 14 December. Available at: www.slashfilm.com/706912/the-life-of-brian-con troversy-explained-blasphemy-bans-and-looking-on-the-bright-side/ (Accessed January 2022).

Adorno, T. and Horkheimer, M. (1947) *Dialectic of Enlightenment*. London: Verso Books.

Advertising Association (2015) *Advertising Pays 3: The value of advertising to the UK's culture, media and sport*. London: Advertising Association.

Ahmed, R. and Pisiou, D. (2019) 'The far right online: An overview of recent studies', *Vox-Pol*, 13 November. Available at: www.voxpol.eu/the-far-right-online-an-overview-of-recent-studies/ (Accessed August 2022).

Alberge, D. (2022) 'Rising costs post threat to independent film-making in UK, says BFI', *The Guardian*, 20 July. Available at: www.theguardian.com/film/2022/jul/20/rising-costs-pose-threa t-to-independent-film-making-in-uk-says-bfi (Accessed February 2023).

Annan, Lord (Chairman) (1977) *Committee on the future of broadcasting*, Cmnd, 6753, London: HMSO.

Antal, D., Fletcher, A. and Ormosi, P.L. (2021) 'Music streaming: Is it a level playing field?', *Competition Policy International*, 23 February. Available at: www.competitionpolicyinterna tional.com/music-streaming-is-it-a-level-playing-field/ (Accessed August 2022).

APA (2005) 'Proving and benchmarking the effectiveness of customer magazines', *APA*. London: Millward Brown. Available at: www.the-cma.com/uploads/apa_documents/advantage_exsum-mar-05.pdf (Accessed May 2022).

Arrese, Á. (2016) 'From gratis to paywalls', *Journalism Studies*, 17 (8): 1051–1067.

Arthur, C. (2012) 'Text messages turns 20 – but are their best years behind them?', *The Guardian*, 3 December. Available at: www.theguardian.com/technology/2012/dec/02/text-messaging-turns-20 (Accessed June 2021).

Baird, D. (2015) 'Mail Online soars past 200m monthly browsers as newspaper sites bounce back', *The Guardian*, 20 February. Available at: www.theguardian.com/media/2015/feb/20/ma il-online-gains-17m-unique-browsers-as-newspaper-sites-bounce-back (Accessed May 2020).

Bakare, L. (2020) 'Economics of streaming are "threatening future of music", says Elbow's Guy Garvey', *The Guardian*, 24 November. Available at: www.theguardian.com/business/2020/nov/24/streaming-threatens-future-of-uk-music-says-elbows-guy-garvey?CMP=Share_iOSApp_Other (Accessed August 2022).

Bakker, G. (2005) 'America's master: The European film industry in the United States, 1907–1920', in Sedgwick, J. and Pokorny, M. (eds.) *An economic history of film*. New York: Routledge, pp. 24–47.

Ballaster, R., Beetham, M., Frazer, E., and Hebron, S. (1991) *Women's worlds: Ideology, femininity and the woman's magazine*. Basingstoke: Macmillan.

BARB (British Audience Research Board) (2022a) *The BARB Panel*. Available at: www.barb.co.uk/the-barb-panel-2/ (Accessed August 2022).

BARB (British Audience Research Board) (2022b) *BARB releases Establishment Survey data for Q1 2022*. Available at: www.barb.co.uk/news/barb-releases-establishment-survey-data-for-q1-2022/ (Accessed July 2022).

Barfe, L. (2004) *Where have all the good times gone: The rise and fall of the record industry*. London: Atlantic Books.

Barnett, S. and Seaton, J. (2010) 'Why the BBC matters: Memo to the new parliament about a unique British institution', *Political Quarterly*, 81 (3): 327–332.

Barnett, S. and Townend, J. (2014) '"And what good came of it at least?" Press-politician relations post-Leveson', *The Political Quarterly*, 85 (2): 159–169.

Barr, C. (2009) 'Before Blackmail: Silent British cinema', in R. Murphy (ed.) *The British cinema book*. London: BFI, pp. 145–154.

Barwise, P. and Watkins, L. (2018) 'The evolution of digital dominance: How and why we got to GAFA' in Moore, M. and Tambini, D. (eds.) *Digital dominance: The power of Google, Amazon, Facebook, and Apple*. Oxford: Oxford University Press, pp. 22–49.

Bauer (2019) *Bauer media confirms lead as UK's biggest magazine publisher*, 14 February, Available at: www.bauermedia.co.uk/news/bauer-media-confirms-lead-as-uks-biggest-magazine-publisher-1 (Accessed February 2020).

BBC (2004) *British Broadcasting Corporation, building public value: Renewing the BBC for a digital world*. London: BBC.

BBC (2012) 'Facebook buys Instagram photo sharing network for $1bn', *BBC News*, 10 April. Available at: www.bbc.co.uk/news/technology-17658264 (Accessed August 2022).

BBC (2013) *'Director-General Tony Hall unveils his vision for the BBC'*, Media Release. 8 October. Available at: www.bbc.co.uk/mediacentre/speeches/2013/tony-hall-vision (Accessed June 2022).

BBC (2016a) 'Trinity Mirror's New Day newspaper to close after poor sales', *BBC News*, 5 May. Available at: www.bbc.co.uk/news/uk-36209318 (Accessed December 2019).

BBC (2016b) *A distinctive BBC*. Available at: https://downloads.bbc.co.uk/aboutthebbc/insidethebbc/reports/pdf/bbc_distinctiveness_april2016.pdf (Accessed June 2019).

BBC (2017) 'Premier League: Third of fans say they watch illegal streams of matches – survey', *BBC Sport*, 4 July. Available at: www.bbc.co.uk/sport/football/40483486> (Accessed August 2022).

BBC (2018a) *Speech by James Purnell, Director of Radio & Education, to the EBU's Truth and Power Conference on Tuesday*, 19 June. Available at: www.bbc.co.uk/mediacentre/speeches/2018/james-purnell-ebu (Accessed June 2019).

BBC (2018b) *BBC Sounds to transform what you hear with exclusive music mixes, radio and new podcasts*, News Release, 31 October. Available at: www.bbc.co.uk/mediacentre/mediapacks/bbcsounds (Accessed July 2019).

BBC (2019) 'UK could ban social media over suicide images, minister warns', *BBC News*, 27 January. Available at: www.bbc.co.uk/news/uk-47019912 (Accessed January 2019).

BBC (2020) *BBC iPlayer sets new record for biggest month ever with 570m programmes requested*, Media Release, 30 June. Available at: www.bbc.co.uk/mediacentre/latestnews/2020/iplayer-new-record (Accessed June 2022).

BBC (2021) *BBC Group annual report and accounts*. Available at: https://downloads.bbc.co.uk/aboutthebbc/reports/annualreport/2020-21.pdf (Accessed June 2022).

Beaumont-Thomas, B. (2021) 'Paul McCartney and Kate Bush lead call for change to music streaming payments', *The Guardian*, 20 April. Available at: www.theguardian.com/music/2021/apr/20/paul-mccartney-kate-bush-law-change-music-streaming-payment?CMP=Share_iOSApp_Other (Accessed July 2022).

Beaumont-Thomas, B. (2022) 'David Bowie: publishing rights to song catalogue sold for $250m', *The Guardian*, 3 January. Available at: www.theguardian.com/music/2022/jan/03/david-bowie-publishing-rights-to-song-catalogue-sold-for-250m (Accessed July 2022).

Benton, J. (2021) 'Brexit's done, but anti-Brexit paper The New European is just getting started', *Nieman Lab*, 1 February. Available at: www.niemanlab.org/2021/02/brexits-done-but-anti-brexit-paper-the-new-european-is-just-getting-started/ (Accessed February 2021).

Beveridge, Lord (Chairman) (1951) *Report of the broadcasting committee*, Cmd, 8116, London: HMSO.

BFI (British Film Institute) (2018a) *Statistical Yearbook 2018*. Available at: www.bfi.org.uk/sites/bfi.org.uk/files/downloads/bfi-statistical-yearbook-2018.pdf (Accessed April 2019).

BFI (British Film Institute) (2018b) *Screen Business: How screen sector tax relief powers economic growth across the UK*. Available at: www.bfi.org.uk/sites/bfi.org.uk/files/downloads/screen-business-full-report-2018-10-08.pdf> (Accessed April 2019).

BFI (British Film Institute) (2021) *BFI statistical yearbook*. London: BFI.

Bijker, W.E., Hughes, T.P., and Pinch, T. (1987) *The social construction of technological systems: New directions in the sociology and history of technology*. London: MIT Press.

Black, B. (2013) 'International videogame distribution – handling content-based regulations in the United States and Europe', *Transnational Law & Contemporary Problems*, 22 (2): 539–563.

Bolter, J.D., and Grusin, R. (2000) *Remediation: Understanding new media*. Cambridge, Massachusetts: MIT Press.

Boon, T. (2008) *Films of fact: A history of science in documentary films and television*. London: Wallflower Press.

Booth, P. (ed.) (2016) *The case for privatising the BBC*. London: IEA.

Bossom, A. and Dunning, B. (2016) *Videogames: An introduction to the industry*. London: Bloomsbury.

Bostoen, F. (2021) 'Epic v Apple: Antitrust's latest big tech battle royale', *European Competition and Regulatory Law Review*, 5 (1): 79–85.

Boston, R. (1999) 'The first of the tabloids', *British Journalism Review*, 10 (2): 63–68.

BPG (Broadcasting Policy Group) (2004) *Beyond the Charter: The BBC after 2006*. London: Premium Publishing.

BPI (British Phonographic Industry) (2020) *Submission to the DCMS Select Committee: Inquiry into the economics of music streaming*. Available at: https://committees.parliament.uk/publications/6501/documents/70659/default/ (Accessed July 2022).

Braithwaite, B. (2002) 'Magazines: The bulging bookstalls', in Brigg, A. and Cobley, P. (eds.) *The media: An introduction*. London: Pearson Longmann, pp. 104–120.

Braithwaite, B. (2009) *The press book*. London: Peter Owen.

Briggs, A. (1961) *The history of broadcasting in the United Kingdom: Volume I: The birth of broadcasting*. London: Oxford University Press.

Briggs, A. (1965) *The history of broadcasting in the United Kingdom: Volume II: The golden age of wireless*. London: Oxford University Press.

Briggs, A. (1979) *The history of broadcasting in the United Kingdom: Volume IV: Sound and Vision*. London: Oxford University Press.

Briggs, A. (1995) *The history of broadcasting in the United Kingdom: Volume V: Competition*. London: Oxford University Press.

Broadcasting Act (1981) London: HMSO. Available at: www.legislation.gov.uk/ukpga/1981/68/contents (Accessed February 2023).

Broadcasting Act (1996) London: HMSO. Available at: www.legislation.gov.uk/ukpga/1996/55/contents (Accessed February 2023).

Brooks, T. (2015) 'The Birth of a Nation: The most racist movie ever made?', *BBC Culture*, 6 February. Available at: www.bbc.com/culture/story/20150206-the-most-racist-movie-ever-made (Accessed March 2022).

Brotherton, H. (2018) 'On holiday with: Andy Morris, editor, BA High Life', *Magculture*, 13 August. Available at: https://magculture.com/andy-morris-editor-ba-high-life/ (Accessed June 2020).

Browning, J. and Lanxon, N. (2022) 'UK probes Microsoft's $69 billion purchase of Activision', *Bloomberg UK*, 6 July. Available at: www.bloomberg.com/news/articles/2022-07-06/uk-probes-microsoft-s-69-billion-purchase-of-activision (Accessed July 2022).

Butterfield, D. (2017) 'The death of the album has been exaggerated', *The Spectator*, 7 March. Available at: https://life.spectator.co.uk/2017/03/death-album-exaggerated/ (Accessed May 2020).

Cabras, I., Goumagias, N.D., Fernandes, K., Cowling, P., Li, F., Kudenko, D., Devlin, S., and Nucciarellli, A. (2017) 'Exploring survival rates of companies in the UK video-games industry: An empirical study', *Technological Forecasting & Social Change*, 117: 305–314.

Cacciottolo, M. (2016) 'Fleet Street: Last journalists leave former home of national newspapers', *BBC News*, 5 August. Available at: www.bbc.co.uk/news/uk-36882573 (Accessed December 2019).

Calcutt, A. (2014) 'What is a magazine?', in Stam, D. and Scott, A. (eds.) *Inside magazine publishing*. London: Routledge, pp: 131–136.

Campbell, V. (2004) *Information age journalism: Journalism in international context*. London: Arnold.

Campbell, V. (2013) 'Playing with controversial images in videogames: The terrorist mission controversy in Call of Duty: Modern Warfare 2', in Atwood, F., Campbell, V., Hunter, I.Q., and Lockyer, S. (eds.) *Controversial images*. Basingstoke: Palgrave Macmillan, pp. 254–268.

Castells, M. (2009) *The rise of the network society*. Oxford: Wiley-Blackwell.

Caston, E. (2021) 'Gatekeepers of culture in the music video supply chain' in McDonald, P. (ed.) *The Routledge companion to media industries*. London: Routledge, pp. 382–391.

Cathcart, B. (2016) 'A better press: A response to John Lloyd's "Regulate yourself"', *The Political Quarterly*, 87 (1): 6–11.

Chang, L. (2016) 'Watch out for your wearable – New report expresses concerns about big data', *Digital Trends*, 17 December. Available at: www.digitaltrends.com/wearables/wearable-big-data -advertisers/ (Accessed March 2020).

Chapman, L. (2021) '"They wanted a bigger, more ambitious film": Film finances and the American "Runaways" that ran away', *Journal of British Cinema and Television*, 18 (2): 176–197.

Chibnall, S. (2019) 'Hollywood-on-Thames: The British productions of Warner Bros. – First National, 1931–1945', *Historical Journal of Film, Radio and Television*, 39 (4): 687–724.

Christophers, B. (2008) 'Television power relations in the transition to digital: The case of the United Kingdom', *Television and New Media*, 9 (3): 239–257.

Clement, J. (2022) 'Digital video game revenue in selected European countries in 2022', *Statista*, 14 July. Available at: www.statista.com/forecasts/461229/digital-games-revenue-european-coun tries-digital-market-outlook (Accessed July 2022).

Clementi, D. (2016) *A review of the governance and regulation of the BBC*. London: DCMS. Available at: https://assets.publishing.service.gov.uk/government/uploads/system/uploads/atta chment_data/file/504003/PDF_FINAL_20160224_AM_Clementi_Review.pdf (Accessed April 2019).

CMA (Competition and Markets Authority) (2020) *Online platforms and digital advertising: Market study final report*. Available at: https://assets.publishing.service.gov.uk/media/5fa 557668fa8f5788db46efc/Final_report_Digital_ALT_TEXT.pdf (Accessed August 2022).

CMA (Competition and Markets Authority) (2022) *Music and streaming: Market study update*. Available at: https://assets.publishing.service.gov.uk/government/uploads/system/up loads/attachment_data/file/1093698/220726_Music_and_streaming_-_update_paper.pdf > (Accessed August 2022).

Coase, R. (1950) *British broadcasting: A study in monopoly*. London:Longman.

Cohendet, P., Grandadam, D., Mehouachi, C., and Simon, L. (2018) 'The local, the global and the industry common: The case of the video game industry', *Journal of Economic Geography*, 18: 1045–1068.

Cole, P. (2008) 'Compacts', in Franklin, B. (ed.) *Pulling newspapers apart: Analysing print journalism*. London: Routledge, pp. 183–191.

Coleman, C. (2020) 'Milly Dowler's family "was targeted" by Sunday People', *BBC News*, 27 January. Available at: www.bbc.co.uk/news/uk-51258880 (Accessed February 2020).

Collins, R. (2009) *Three myths of internet governance: Making sense of networks, government and regulation.* Chicago: Intellect.

Collins, R. and Murroni, C. (1996) *New media, new policies.* Cambridge: Polity Press.

Communications Act (2003) London. HMSO. Available at: www.legislation.gov.uk/ukpga/2003/21/contents (Accessed February 2023).

Competition Commission (2009) *A report on the anticipated joint venture between BBC Worldwide Limited, Channel Four Television Corporation and ITV plc relating to the video on demand sector.* Available at: https://webarchive.nationalarchives.gov.uk/ukgwa/20140402233800mp_/http://www.competition-commission.org.uk/assets/competitioncommission/docs/pdf/non-inquiry/rep_pub/rep orts/2009/fulltext/543.pdf (Accessed June 2022).

Consalvo, M. (2006) 'Console video games and global corporations: Creating a hybrid culture', *New Media & Society,* 8 (1): 117–137.

Coughlan, S. (2006) 'Music Downloads', *The Guardian,* 1 April. Available at: www.theguardian.com/money/2006/apr/01/moneysupplement2 (Accessed July 2022).

Cox, H. and Mowatt, S. (2012) 'Vogue in Britain: Authenticity and the creation of competitive advantage in the UK magazine industry', *Business History,* 54 (1): 67–87.

CPS (Crown Prosecution Service) (2022) *The Counter-Terrorism Division of the Crown Prosecution Service (CPS) – Successful prosecutions since 2016.* Available at: www.cps.gov.uk/crime-info/terrorism/counter-terrorism-division-crown-prosecution-service-cps-successful-prosecutions-2016 (Accessed August 2022).

Crawford, Lord (1926) *Report of the broadcasting committee.* Cmd 2599. London:HMSO.

Creasey, S. (2018) 'Magazine sector finds ways to buck the trend', *PrintWeek,* 25 June, Available at: www.printweek.com/print-week/feature/1164839/magazine-sector-finds-ways-to-buck-the-trend (Accessed August 2019).

Cringley, R.X. (1996) *Accidental empires: How the boys of Silicon Valley make their millions, battle foreign competition, and still can't get a date.* London: Penguin.

Crisell, A. (1994) *Understanding radio.* London: Routledge.

Crisell, A. (2002) *An introductory history of British broadcasting.* London: Routledge.

Cunningham, S., Flew, T., and Swift, A. (2015) *Media economics.* London: Palgrave.

Curran, J. and Seaton, J. (2010) *Power without responsibility: Press, broadcasting and the internet in Britain.* 7th edn. London: Routledge.

Curran, J. and Seaton, J. (2018) *Power without responsibility: Press, broadcasting and the internet in Britain.* 8th edn. London: Routledge.

Dams, T. (2020) 'The stage is set for UK studios', *Broadcast,* 21 December. Available at: www.broadcastnow.co.uk/tech/the-stage-is-set-for-uk-studios/5155871.article (Accessed January 2021).

D'Arma, A., Raats, T., and Steemers, J. (2021) 'Public service media in the age of SVoDs: A comparative study of PSM strategic responses in Flanders, Italy and the UK', *Media, Culture and Society,* 43 (4): 682–700.

Davidson, A. (1992) *Under the hammer: The inside story of the 1991 ITV franchise battle.* London: Heinemann.

Davis, N. (2014) 'Phone-hacking trial failed to clear up mystery of Milly Dowler's voicemail', *The Guardian,* 26 June. Available at: www.theguardian.com/uk-news/2014/jun/26/phone-hacking-trial-milly-dowler-voicemail (Accessed September 2020).

Davis, N. (2022) 'Watching less TV could cut heart disease, study finds', *The Guardian,* 24 May. Available at: www.theguardian.com/society/2022/may/24/couch-potatoes-at-higher-risk-of-coronary-heart-disease-study-finds (Accessed May 2022).

DCMS (Department for Culture, Media and Sport) (2003) *Review of the BBC's Royal Charter.* London: DCMS.

DCMS (Department for Digital, Culture, Media and Sport) (2014) *Media ownership and plurality: Consultation report.* Available at: www.parliament.uk/documents/lords-committees/communications/Mediaplurality/Governmentresponse.pdf (Accessed April 2019).

DCMS (Department for Digital, Culture, Media and Sport) (2016) *A BBC for the future: A broadcaster of distinction*. Available at: https://assets.publishing.service.gov.uk/government/up loads/system/uploads/attachment_data/file/524863/DCMS_A_BBC_for_the_future_linked_rev1. pdf (Accessed January 2020).

DCMS (Department for Digital, Culture, Media and Sport) (2018) *Government response to the Internet Safety Strategy Green Paper*. Available at: https://assets.publishing.service.gov.uk/gov ernment/uploads/system/uploads/attachment_data/file/708873/Government_Response_to_the_ Internet_Safety_Strategy_Green_Paper_-_Final.pdf (Accessed January 2019).

DCMS (Department for Digital, Culture, Media and Sport) (2020) *Government response to the Cairncross Review: A sustainable future for journalism*, 27 January. Available at: www.gov.uk/gov ernment/publications/the-cairncross-review-a-sustainable-future-for-journalism/government-resp onse-to-the-cairncross-review-a-sustainable-future-for-journalism (Accessed January 2020).

DCMS (Department for Digital, Culture, Media and Sport) (2022) *Up next: The government's vision for the broadcasting sector*. Available at: https://assets.publishing.service.gov.uk/governm ent/uploads/system/uploads/attachment_data/file/1071939/E02740713_CP_671_Broadcasting_ White_Paper_Accessible__1_.pdf (Accessed June 2022).

DCMS (Department for Digital, Culture, Media and Sport) and DTI (Department of Trade and Industry) (2000) *A new future for communications*, Cm 5010. London: The Stationery Office.

DCMS and Home Office (2020) *Online Harms White Paper: Full government response to the consultation*. Available at: https://assets.publishing.service.gov.uk/government/uploads/system/up loads/attachment_data/file/944310/Online_Harms_White_Paper_Full_Government_Response_ to_the_consultation_CP_354_CCS001_CCS1220695430-001__V2.pdf (Accessed August 2022).

Deloitte (2016) *Media metrics: The state of UK media and entertainment 2016*. Available at: www2.deloitte.com/uk/en/pages/technology-media-and-telecommunications/articles/media-metrics-2016.html# (Accessed April 2017).

Devlin, J. (2018) *From analogue to digital radio: Competition and cooperation in the UK radio industry*. Basingstoke. Palgrave Macmillan.

D'Emilio, I. (2021) 'BBC Who Do You Think You Are: Joe Sugg's life from Strictly star girl-friend he met on the show to famous sister', *My London News*, 23 November. Available at: www.mylondon.news/news/tv/bbc-who-you-think-you-22247197 (Accessed August 2022).

Deuze, M. (2009a) 'Convergence culture and media work', in Holt, J. and Perren, A. (eds.) *Media industries: History, theory, and method*. Chichester: Wiley-Blackwell, pp: 144–156.

Deuze, M. (2009b) 'Media industries, work and life', *European Journal of Communication*, 24 (4): 467–480.

De Zoysa, R. and Newman, O. (2002) 'Globalization, soft power and the challenge of Holly-wood', *Contemporary Politics*, 8 (3): 185–202.

Dickinson, M. and Harvey, S. (2005) 'Film policy in the United Kingdom: New Labour at the movies', *Political Quarterly*, 76 (3): 420–429.

DNH (Department of National Heritage) (1994) *The future of the BBC: Serving the nation, competing world-wide*, Cmnd 2621, London: HMSO.

Dogruel, L. and Joeckel, S. (2013) 'Video game rating systems in the US and Europe: Comparing their outcomes', *International Communication Gazette*, 75 (7): 672–692.

Doyle, G. (2002) *Media ownership: The economics and politics of convergence and concentration in the UK and European media*. London: Sage.

Doyle, G. (2010) 'From television to multi-platform: Less from more, or more for less?', *Convergence*, 16 (4): 431–449.

Doyle, G. (2013a) *Understanding media economics*. London: Sage.

Doyle, G (2013b) 'Re-invention and survival: Newspapers in the era of digital multiplatform delivery', *Journal of Media Business Studies*, 10 (4): 1–20.

Drazin, C. (2017) 'Make-believe and realism in British Film production: From the coming of sound to the abolition of the National Film Finance Corporation', in Hunter, I.Q., Porter, L., and Smith, J. (eds.) *The Routledge companion to British cinema history*. London: Routledge, pp: 121–129.

Dredge, S. (2015) 'Spotify now has 60m users including 15m paying subscribers', *The Guardian*, 12 January. Available at: www.theguardian.com/technology/2015/jan/12/spotify-60m-users-15m-subscribers (Accessed August 2022).

Dredge, S. (2022) 'How many users do Spotify, Apple Music and other streaming services have?', *Musically*, 3 February. Available at: https://musically.com/2022/02/03/spotify-apple-how-many-users-big-music-streaming-services/ (Accessed August 2022).

Dubois, E. and Blank, G. (2018) 'The echo chamber is overstated: The moderating effect of political interest and diverse media', *Information, Communication & Society*, 21 (5): 729–745.

Dwyer, T. (2010) *Media convergence*. New York: McGraw-Hill Education.

Dyke, G. (2005) *Greg Dyke: Inside story*. London: HarperCollins.

Dyson, L. (2007) 'Customer magazines', *Journalism Studies*, 8 (4): 634–641.

Eggerton, J. (2008) 'More than a "toaster with pictures"', *Broadcasting & Cable*, 19 December. Available at: www.broadcastingcable.com/news/news-articles/more-toaster-pictures/109654 (Accessed May 2020).

Ellis, J. (2007) *TV FAQ: Uncommon answers to common questions about TV*. London: IB Tauris.

Engel, M. (1996) *Tickle the public: One hundred years of the popular press*. London: Indigo.

ERA (The Digital Entertainment Retail Association) (2021) *Value of games market quadruples since 2000*, 10 May. Available at: https://eraltd.org/news-events/press-releases/2021/value-of-games-market-quadruples-since-2000/ (Accessed May 2022).

ERA (The Digital Entertainment Retail Association) (2022) *The ERA yearbook 2022*. Available at: https://eraltd.org/news-events/press-releases/2022/innovation-drove-music-and-video-streaming-spending-to-nearly-45bn-in-2021/ (Accessed July 2022).

Europol (2021) *Online Jihadist propaganda – 2020 in review*. Luxembourg: Publications Office of the European Union.

Evens, T., Iosifidis, P., and Smith, P. (2013) *The political economy of television sports rights*. Basingstoke:Palgrave.

Eyles, M. (2016) 'A first-hand account of Quicksilva and its part in the birth of the UK games industry, 1981–1982', *Cogent Arts & Humanities*, 3 (1): 1–19.

Ferguson, M. (1983) *Forever feminine: Women's magazines and the cult of femininity*. London: Heinemann.

Fildes, N. (2021) '5G spectrum auction raises just £1.3bn for UK government', *Financial Times*, 17 March. Available at: www.ft.com/content/41a10fce-4b6a-443d-8c0f-26f62bf2470c (Accessed May 2022).

Flew, T. (2014) *New media*. Oxford: Oxford University Press.

Franklin, B. (2008) 'Introduction: Newspapers: Trends and developments', in Franklin, B. (ed.) *Pulling newspapers apart: Analysing print journalism*. London: Routledge, pp: 1–35.

Fraser, C. (2020) 'Target didn't figure out a teenager was pregnant before her father did, and that one article that said they did was silly and bad', *Medium*, 4 January. Available at: https://medium.com/@colin.fraser/target-didnt-figure-out-a-teen-girl-was-pregnant-before-her-father-did-a6be13b973a5 (Accessed August 2022).

Freedman, D. (2008) *The politics of media policy*. Cambridge: Polity Press.

Frith, S. (1988) *Music for pleasure: Essays in the sociology of pop*. Cambridge: Polity Press.

Frith, S. (2004) 'Music and the media' in Frith, S. and Marshall, L. (eds.) *Music and copyright*. Edinburgh: Edinburgh University Press, pp. 171–188.

Frith, S. and Marshall, L. (2004) 'Making sense of copyright' in Frith, S. and Marshall, L. (eds.) *Music and copyright*. Edinburgh: Edinburgh University Press, pp. 1–18.

Fuchs, C. (2014) *Social media: A critical introduction*. London: Sage.

Furman, J. (chair) (2019) *Unlocking digital competition: Report of the digital competition expert panel*. Available at: https://assets.publishing.service.gov.uk/government/uploads/system/uploads/attachment_data/file/785547/unlocking_digital_competition_furman_review_web.pdf (Accessed August 2022).

Gaber, I. (2012) 'Rupert and the 'three card trope' – What you see ain't necessarily what you get', *Media, Culture and Society*, 34 (5): 637–646.

García-Favaro, L. and Gill, R. (2016) '"Emasculation nation has arrived": Sexism rearticulated in online responses to lose the lads' mags campaign', *Feminist Media Studies*, 16 (3): 379–397.

Garnham, N. (1987) 'Concepts of culture – Public policy and the cultural industries', *Cultural Studies*, 1 (1): 23–37.

Garnham, N. (2005) 'From cultural to creative industries: An analysis of the implications of the "creative industries" approach to arts and media policy making in the United Kingdom', *International Journal of Cultural Policy*, 11 (1): 15–29.

Garnham, N. (2011) 'The political economy of communication revisited' in Wasko, J., Murdock, G., and Sousa, H. (eds.) *The handbook of political economy of communications*. Oxford: Wiley-Blackwell, pp. 41–61.

Gibbons, T. (1998) *Regulating the media*. London: Sweet & Maxwell.

Giles, P. (1993) 'History with holes: Channel Four television films of the 1980s', in Friedman, L. (ed.) *British cinema and Thatcherism*. London: UCL Press, pp. 70–91.

Gillespie, T. (2017) 'Is "platform" the right metaphor for the technology companies that dominate digital media?', *Niemen Lab*, 25 August. Available at: www.niemanlab.org/2017/08/is-platform-the-right-metaphor-for-the-technology-companies-that-dominate-digital-media/ (Accessed May 2020).

Gillespie, T., Boczkowski, P.J., and Foot, K.A. (eds.) (2014) *Media technologies: Essays on communication, materiality, and society*. Cambridge, Massachusetts: MIT Press.

Goddard, P. (2017) 'Distinctiveness' and the BBC: A new battleground for public service television?, *Media, Culture & Society*, 39 (7): 1089–1099.

Goggin, G. (2011) *Global mobile media*. London: Routledge.

Goldie, G. (1977) *Facing the nation: Television and politics 1936–1976*. London: Bodley Head.

Golding, P. and Murdock, G. (2005) 'Culture, communications and political economy' in Curran, J. and Gurevitch, M. (eds.) *Mass media and society*. London: Hodder Education, pp. 60–83.

Goodwin, P. (1998) *Television under the Tories: Broadcasting policy 1979–1997*. London: British Film Institute.

Gough-Yates, A. (2003) *Understanding women's magazines: Publishing, markets and readership*. London: Routledge.

Gough-Yates, A. (2010) 'Magazines' in Albertazzi, D. and Cobley, P. (eds.) *The media: An introduction*. 3rd edition. London: Routledge, pp. 153–164.

Grainge, P. and Johnson, C. (2018) 'From catch-up TV to online TV: Digital broadcasting and the case of BBC iPlayer', *Screen*, 59 (1): 21–40.

Gray, T. (2020) *Written evidence submitted by Tom Gray (#BrokenRecord Campaign) (PEG0181)*. London: House of Commons. Available at: https://committees.parliament.uk/writtenevidence/10156/pdf/ (accessed February 2023).

Greenslade, R. (2003) *Press gang: How newspapers make profits from propaganda*. London: Pan.

Greenslade, R. (2014) 'Telegraph Media Group to cut 55 more jobs in digital restructure', *The Guardian*, 21 October. Available at: www.theguardian.com/media/greenslade/2014/oct/21/telegraphmediagroup-national-newspapers (Accessed December 2019).

GUMG (Glasgow University Media Group) (1976) *Bad news*. London: Routledge & Kegan Paul.

Habermas, J. (1992) *The structural transformation of the public sphere*. Oxford: Polity.

Haeusermann, T. (2013) 'Custom publishing in the UK: Rise of a silent giant', *Publishing Research Quarterly*, 29: 99–109.

Hafner, K. and Lyon, M. (2003) *Where wizards stay up late: The origins of the internet*. London: Simon & Schuster.

Halliday, J. (2011) 'Radioplayer launches with hundreds of stations', *The Guardian*, 31 March. Available at: www.theguardian.com/media/2011/mar/31/radioplayer-launches (Accessed January 2020).

Hardy, J. (2014a) *Critical political economy of the media: An introduction*. London: Routledge.

Hardy, J. (2014b) 'Policies for UK media plurality' in Williams, G. (ed.) *Big media & internet titans*. London: Campaign for Press and Broadcasting Freedom, pp. 160–171.

Havens, T. and Lotz, A. (2012) *Understanding media industries*. Oxford: Oxford University Press.

Hegarty, P., Stewart, A.L., Blockmans, I.G.E., and Horvath, M.A.H. (2018) 'The influence of magazines on men: Normalizing and challenging young men's prejudices with "lads' mages"', *Psychology of Men & Masculinity*, 19 (1): 131–144.

Hendy, D. (2013) *Public service broadcasting*. Basingstoke: Palgrave Macmillan.

Herbert, D., Lotz, A.D., and Punathambekar, A. (2020) *Media industry studies*. Cambridge: Polity Press.

Herman, E. and Chomsky, N. (1988) *Manufacturing consent: The political economy of the mass media*. New York: Pantheon.

Hermes, J. (1995) *Reading women's magazines: An analysis of everyday media use*. Cambridge: Polity Press.

Hern, A. (2016) 'Facebook, YouTube, Twitter and Microsoft sign EU hate speech code', *The Guardian*, 16 May. Available at: www.theguardian.com/technology/2016/may/31/facebook-you tube-twitter-microsoft-eu-hate-speech-code (Accessed January 2019).

Hern, A. and Jolly, J. (2019) 'Google fined €1.49bn by EU for advertising violations', *The Guardian*, 20 March. Available at: www.theguardian.com/technology/2019/mar/20/google-fi ned-149bn-by-eu-for-advertising-violations (Accessed April 2019).

Hesmondhalgh, D. (2009) 'The digitalization of music' in Jeffcut, P. and Pratt, A.C. (eds.) *Creativity and innovation in the cultural economy*. London: Routledge, pp. 57–73.

Hesmondhalgh, D. (2019) *The cultural industries*. London: Sage.

Hesmondhalgh, D. (2021) 'Is music streaming bad for musicians? Problems of evidence and argument', *New Media and Society*, 23 (12): 3593–3615.

Hesmondhalgh, D. and Meier, L.M. (2018) 'What the digitalisation of music tells us about capitalism, culture and the power of the information technology sector', *Information, Communication & Society*, 21 (11): 1555–1570.

Higgins, C. (2014) 'The BBC informs, educates and entertains – but in what order?', *The Guardian*, 1 July. Available at:www.theguardian.com/media/2014/jul/01/bbc-inform-educate-enterta in-order(AccessedFebruary 2023).

Higson, A. (ed.) (2002) *Young and innocent? The cinema in Britain, 1896–1930*. Exeter: Exeter University Press.

Higson, A. (2010) *Film England: Culturally English filmmaking since the 1990s*. London: IB Tauris.

Hill, J. (1996) 'British film policy' in Moran, A. (ed.) *Film policy: International, national and regional perspectives*. London: Routledge, pp. 101–113.

Hill, J. (2004) 'UK film policy, cultural capital and social exclusion', *Cultural Trends*, 13 (2): 29–39.

Hill, J. (2012) 'This is for the Batmans as well as the Vera Drakes: Economics, Culture and UK Government Film Production Policy in the 2000s', *Journal of British Cinema and Television*, 9 (3): 333–356.

Hill, J. (2016) 'Living with Hollywood: British film policy and the definition of "nationality"', *International Journal of Cultural Policy*, 22 (5): 706–723.

Hoggart, R. (1957) *The uses of literacy*. London: Penguin.

Holmes, S. (2005) *British TV and film culture in the 1950s: Coming to a TV near you*. Bristol: Intellect Books.

Holmes, T. and Nice, L. (2012) *Magazine journalism*. London: Sage.

Hope, E. (2007) 'Competition policy and sector-specific economic media regulation: And never the Twain shall meet?' in Seabright, P. and Hagen, J. (eds.) *The economic regulation of broadcasting markets: Evolving technology and challenges for policy*. Cambridge: Cambridge University Press, pp. 310–343.

Horsman, M. (1997) *Sky high: The inside story of BSkyB.* London: Orion Business Books.

Hotho, S. and McGregor, N. (eds.) (2013) *Changing the rules of the game: Economic, management and emerging issues in the computer games industry.* Basingstoke: Palgrave Macmillan.

House of Commons (Digital, Culture, Media and Sport Committee) (2018) *Disinformation and 'fake news': Interim report.* Available at: https://publications.parliament.uk/pa/cm201719/cm select/cmcumeds/363/363.pdf (Accessed August 2020).

House of Commons (Digital, Culture, Media and Sport Committee) (2021a) *The future of public service broadcasting.* Available at: https://committees.parliament.uk/publications/5243/docum ents/52552/default/ (Accessed June 2022).

House of Commons (Digital, Culture, Media and Sport Committee) (2021b) *Economics of Music Streaming: Second Report of Session 2021–22.* Available at: https://committees.parliament.uk/p ublications/6739/documents/72525/default/ (Accessed July 2022).

House of Commons (Digital, Culture, Media and Sport Committee) (2022a) *The Draft Online Safety Bill and the legal but harmful debate.* Available at: https://committees.parliament.uk/p ublications/8609/documents/86961/default/ (Accessed August 2022).

House of Commons (2022b) *Online Safety Bill.* Available at: https://bills.parliament.uk/bills/ 3137/publications (Accessed August 2022).

House of Lords (Select Committee on Communications) (2008) *The ownership of the news.* Available at: https://publications.parliament.uk/pa/ld200708/ldselect/ldcomuni/122/122i.pdf (Accessed August 2022).

Human Rights Act (1998) *London: HMSO.* Available at: www.legislation.gov.uk/ukpga/1998/42/ schedule/1 (Accessed August 2022).

Hume, M. (2013) 'Keep your nose out of the press', *British Journalism Review,* 24 (1): 25–30.

Hutchison, D. (1999) *Media policy: An introduction.* Oxford: Blackwell.

Hutton, Lord (2004) *Report of the inquiry into the circumstances surrounding the death of Dr David Kelly C.M.G.* London: HMSO.

IFPI (International Federation of the Phonographic Industry) (2022) *The Global Music Report.* Available at: www.ifpi.org/wp-content/uploads/2022/04/IFPI_Global_Music_Report_2022-Sta te_of_the_Industry.pdf (Accessed July 2022).

Ingham, T. (2020) 'Loss-making Spotify will continue to put growth before losses ahead of profit "for next few years"', *Music Business Worldwide,* 6 May. Available at: www.musicbusinessworldwide. com/loss-making-spotify-will-continue-to-focus-on-growth-over-profit-for-next-few-years/ (Accessed August 2022).

IPO (Intellectual Property Office) (2019) *Online copyright infringement tracker.* Available at: https://a ssets.publishing.service.gov.uk/government/uploads/system/uploads/attachment_data/file/867708/ oci-tracker-2020.pdf (Accessed August 2022).

IPO (Intellectual Property Office) (2021) *Music creators' earnings in the digital era.* Available at: https://assets.publishing.service.gov.uk/government/uploads/system/uploads/attachment_data/ file/1020133/music-creators-earnings-report.pdf (Accessed August 2022).

Ipsos Mori (2017) *BBC distinctiveness: A report prepared for Ofcom.* Available at: www.ofcom. org.uk/__data/assets/pdf_file/0025/102958/bbc-distinctiveness-ipsos-mori.pdf (Accessed June 2019).

ITV (2021) *ITV plc Annual Report and Accounts for the year ended 31 December 2021: Digital Acceleration.* Available at: www.itvplc.com/~/media/Files/I/ITV-PLC/documents/reports-a nd-results/annual-report-2021.pdf (Accessed June 2022).

Izushi, H. and Aoyama, Y. (2006) 'Industry evolution and cross-sectoral skill transfers: A comparative analysis of the video game industry in Japan, the United States, and the United Kingdom', *Environment and Planning,* 38: 1843–1861.

Jackson, J. (2016) 'Facebook inflated video viewing times for two years', *The Guardian,* 23 September. Available at: www.theguardian.com/media/2016/sep/23/facebook-video-viewing-tim es-ad-agencies-metric (Accessed January 2017).

James, J. (2018) 'Ofcom will now allow networked breakfast shows', *Radio Today*, 26 October. Available at: https://radiotoday.co.uk/2018/10/ofcom-will-now-allow-networked-breakfast-shows/ (Accessed July 2019).

Johnson, C. (2017) 'Beyond catch-up: VoD interfaces, ITV Hub and the repositioning of television online', *Critical Studies in Television*, 12 (2): 121–138.

Johnson, C. (2019) *Online TV.* London: Routledge.

Johnson, C. and Turnock R. (2005) 'From start up to consolidation: Institutions, regions and regulation over the history of ITV' in Johnson, C. and Turnock, R. (eds.) *ITV cultures: Independent television over 50 years.* Maidenhead: Open University Press, pp. 15–35.

Kanter, J. (2013) 'Hall calls for the consultants', *Broadcast*, 19 July, p. 1.

Kelion, L. (2018) 'Facebook Watch video service launches worldwide', *BBC News*, 29 August. Available at: www.bbc.co.uk/news/technology-45333962 (Accessed August 2020).

Kennedy, M. (2017) 'Jack Monroe wins Twitter libel case against Katie Hopkins', *The Guardian*, 10 March. Available at: www.theguardian.com/media/2017/mar/10/jack-monroe-wins-twitter-libel-case-against-katie-hopkins (Accessed November 2018).

Kent, S.L. (2001) *The Ultimate History of Videogames*, Vol 1. New York: Three Rivers Press.

Kent, S.L. (2021) *The Ultimate History of Videogames*, Vol 2. New York: Crown.

Kerr, A. (2013) 'Space wars: The politics of games production in Europe', in Huntemann, N.B. and Aslinger, B. (eds.) *Gaming globally: Production, play and place.* New York: Palgrave, pp. 215–231.

Kerr, A. (2017) *Global games: Production, circulation and policy in the networked era.* New York: Routledge.

King, A. (1998) 'Thatcherism and the emergence of Sky television', *Media, Culture and Society*, 20 (2): 277–293.

King, A. and Plunkett, J. (2005) *Victorian print media: A reader.* Oxford: Oxford University Press.

King, P. (2007) 'Newspaper reporting and attitudes to crime and justice in late eighteenth and early nineteenth century London', *Continuity and Change*, 22 (1): 73–112.

Kleinman, Z. and Russon, M. (2019) 'Apple dissolves iTunes into new apps', *BBC News*, 3 June. Available at: www.bbc.co.uk/news/technology-48501890 (Accessed August 2022).

Knox, S. (2020) 'Bringing the Battle to Britain: *Band of Brothers* and television runaway production in the UK', *Journal of British Cinema and Television*, 17 (3): 313–333.

Kuhn, R. (2007) *Politics and the media in Britain.* Basingstoke: Palgrave.

Larson, C. (2015) 'Shouting "fire" in a theater': The life and times of Constitutional law's most enduring analogy', *William & Mary Bill of Rights Journal*, 24 (1), 181–212. Available at: https://scholarship.law.wm.edu/wmborj/ (Accessed April 2019).

Lean, T. (2012) 'Mediating the microcomputer: The educational character of the 1980s British popular computing boom', *Public Understanding of Science*, 22 (5): 546–558.

Lee, D. (2014) 'Facebook buys Oculus VR: Web reactions', *BBC News*, 26 March. Available at: www.bbc.co.uk/news/technology-26745044 (Accessed August 2022).

Lee, D. (2018) 'Facebook details scale of abuse on its site', *BBC News*, Available at: www.bbc.co.uk/news/technology-44122967 (Accessed January 2019).

Lee, R.S. (2012) 'Home videogame platforms', in Peitz, M. and Waldfogel, J. (eds.) *The Oxford handbook of the digital economy.* Oxford: Oxford University Press, pp.83–107.

Leveson Inquiry(2012) *The Report into the Culture, Practices and Ethics of the Press.* Available at: http://webarchive.nationalarchives.gov.uk/20140122145147/ http://www.levesoninquiry.org.uk/about/thereport/(AccessedFebruary 2023).

Levinson, P. (1997) *The soft edge: Natural history and future of the information revolution.* London: Routledge.

Leyshon, A. and Watson, A. (2021) 'User as asset, music as liability: The moral economy of the "value gap" in a platform musical economy' in McDonald, P. (ed.) *The Routledge companion to media industries.* London: Routledge, pp. 267–280.

Lister, M., Dovey, J., Giddings, S., Grant, I., and Kelly, K. (2009) *New media: A critical introduction*. London: Routledge.

Lloyd, J. (2015) 'Regulate yourself', *The Political Quarterly*, 86 (3): 393–402.

Loiperdinger, M. (2004) 'Lumière's "Arrival of the Train": Cinema's founding myth', *The Moving Image*, 4 (1): 89–118.

Long, P. and Wall, T. (2009) *Media studies: Texts, production and context*. London: Routledge.

Lotz, A. (2017) *Portals: A treatise on internet-distributed television*. Ann Arbor, MI: Maize Books.

Lotz, A. (2018) 'Evolution or revolution? Television in transformation', *Critical Studies in Television: The International Journal of Television Studies*, 13 (4): 491–494.

Lotz, A. (2020) 'The future of televisions: A response', *Media, Culture and Society*, 42 (5): 800–802.

Luckhurst, T. and Phippen, L. (2014) 'Good behaviour can be taught', *British Journalism Review*, 25 (1): 56–61.

Lunt, P. and Livingstone, S. (2012) *Media regulation: Governance and the interests of citizens and consumers*. London: Sage.

MacDonald, K. and Hern, A. (2018) 'Red Dead Redemption 2 gamers queue for midnight release', *The Guardian*, 26 October. Available at: www.theguardian.com/games/2018/oct/26/red-dead-redemption-2-gamers-queue-for-midnight-release (Accessed August 2022).

Mackenzie, D. and Wajcman, J. (eds.) (1999) *The social shaping of technology*. Buckingham: Open University Press.

Macnab, G. (2018) *Stairways to heaven: Rebuilding the British film industry*. London: I.B. Tauris.

Madhumita, M. (2017) 'Netflix expands its vision for European TV', *Financial Times*, 2 March, p. 14.

Magor, M. and Schlesinger, P. (2009) '"For this relief much thanks." Taxation, film policy and the UK government', *Screen*, 50 (3): 299–317.

Mahindru, V. and Gems, J. (2017) *Who killed British cinema?* Birmingham: Quota Films Ltd.

Mair, J., Clark, T., Fowler, N., Snoddy, R., and Tait, R. (eds.) (2018) *Anti-social media? The impact on journalism and society*. Bury St. Edmunds: Abramis.

Majid, A. (2023) 'Top 50 biggest news websites in the world: December a slow month for top ten brands', *Press Gazette*, 17 January. Available at: https://pressgazette.co.uk/media-audience-and-business-data/media_metrics/most-popular-websites-news-world-monthly-2/ (Accessed February 2023).

Manovich, L. (2013) 'Media after software', *Journal of Visual Culture*, 12 (1): 30–37.

Marketforce (2019) *ABC Market Summary Report: July–December 2018*. Marketforce (UK) Ltd.

Martin, R. (2019) 'Global to network Capital, Heart and Smooth breakfast shows', *Radio Today*, 26 February. Available at: https://radiotoday.co.uk/2019/02/global-to-network-capital-heart-and-smooth-breakfast-shows/ (Accessed January 2020).

Martinson, J. (2016) 'Netflix's glittering Crown could leave BBC looking a little dull', *The Guardian*, 31 October. Available at: www.theguardian.com/media/2016/oct/31/netflix-glittering-crown-bbc-dull-launch-tv (Accessed February 2023).

Martinson, J. and Plunkett, J. (2015) 'BBC to take on £750m cost of subsidy for over-75s in licence fee deal', *The Guardian*, 6 July. Available at: www.theguardian.com/media/2015/jul/06/bbc-pay-cost-free-tv-licences-over-75s-fee-deal (Accessed June 2022).

Mayhew, F. (2017) 'Print ABCs: Bulks boost *Times* as *Trinity Mirror* nationals and Scottish dailies record double-digit circulation falls', *Press Gazette*, 18 May. Available at: www.pressgazette.co.uk/print-abcs-bulks-boost-times-as-trinity-mirror-nationals-and-scottish-dailies-record-double-digital-circulation-falls/ (Accessed December 2019).

Mayhew, F. (2019) 'Phone-hacking pot grows by £12.5m at Mirror, Express and Start publisher Reach+ full 2018 accounts', *Press Gazette*, 25 February. Available at: www.pressgazette.co.uk/phone-hacking-pot-grows-by-12-5m-at-mirror-express-and-star-publisher-reach-full-2018-accounts/ (Accessed May 2019).

McDonald, P. (ed.) (2021) *The Routledge companion to media industries.* London: Routledge.

McGuiness, P. (2022) 'Decca Records: A history of "The Supreme Record Company"', *Udiscovermusic.* Available at: www.udiscovermusic.com/in-depth-features/decca-records-label-history/ (Accessed July 2022).

McKay, J. (2019) *The magazines handbook.* London: Routledge.

McLuhan, M. (1964/2001) *Understanding media.* London: Routledge.

McQuail, D. (2010) *McQuail's mass communication theory.* London: Sage.

McRobbie, A. (1991) *Feminism and youth culture: From 'Jackie' to 'Just Seventeen',* Basingstoke: Macmillan.

Meech, P. (2008) 'Advertising', in Franklin, B. (ed.) *Pulling newspapers apart: Analysing print journalism.* London: Routledge, pp. 235–243.

Meert, K., Pandelaere, M., and Patrick, V.M. (2014) 'Taking a shine to it: How the preference for glossy stems from an innate need for water', *Journal of Consumer Psychology,* 24 (2): 195–206.

Merrin, W. (2014) *Media studies 2.0.* London: Routledge.

Mills, T. (2016) *The BBC: Myth of a public service.* London: Verso.

Mills, T.(2019) 'If the BBC wants to know why nearly a million listeners have dropped the Today programme, they might want to look at their political coverage first', *The Independent,* 19 September. Available at:www.independent.co.uk/voices/bbc-radio-4-today-programme-listening-figures-john-humphries-a8474691.html (Accessed February 2023).

Morris, J.W. (2015) *Selling digital music: Formatting culture.* Oakland, California: University of California Press.

MRC (Media Reform Coalition) (2021) *Who owns the UK media?* Available at: www.mediareform.org.uk/wp-content/uploads/2021/03/Who-Owns-the-UK-Media_final2.pdf (Accessed July 2022).

MRC (Media Reform Coalition) (2022) *The Online Safety Bill: A briefing.* Available at: www.mediareform.org.uk/wp-content/uploads/2022/04/Online-Safety-briefing.pdf (Accessed August 2022).

Murphie, A. and Potts, J. (2003) *Culture & technology.* Basingstoke: Palgrave Macmillan.

Murphy, R. (ed.) (2009) *The British cinema book.* London: BFI.

Music Week (2022) 'Ed Sheeran's legal team on what the superstar's High Court copyright victory means for songwriters', *Music Week,* 25 April. Available at: www.musicweek.com/publishing/read/ed-sheeran-s-legal-team-on-what-the-superstar-s-high-court-copyright-victory-means-for-songwriters/085676 (Accessed July 2022).

Nair, R. (2021) 'Premier League clubs renew UK TV deals, skip auction', *Reuters,* 13 May. Available at: www.reuters.com/world/uk/premier-league-clubs-agree-three-year-renewal-uk-tv-deals-2021-05-13/ (Accessed June 2022).

Napoli, P. (2009) 'Media economics and the study of media industries' in Holt, J. and Perren, A. (eds.) *Media industries: History, theory and method.* London: Wiley-Blackwell, pp. 161–170.

Nassetti, C. (2013) 'Laying down the libel law', *The Lawyer,* 16 October. Available at: www.thelawyer.com/issues/online-october-2013/laying-down-the-libel-law/ (Accessed November 2019).

Negrine, R. (1989) *Politics and the mass media in Britain.* London: Routledge.

Newman, J. (2008) *Playing with videogames.* New York: Routledge.

Newsinger, J. (2012) 'British film policy in the age of austerity', *Journal of British Cinema and Television,* 9 (1): 133–144.

Newzoo (2022) 'Top 10 countries/markets by game revenues', *Newzoo.* Available at https://newzoo.com/insights/rankings/top-10-countries-by-game-revenues/ (Accessed August 2022).

Nicholas, S. (2000) 'All the news that's fit to broadcast: The popular press versus the BBC, 1922–45' in Catterall, P., Seymour-Ure, C., and Smith, A. (eds.) *Northcliffe's legacy: Aspects of the British popular press, 1896–1996.* London: MacMillan, pp. 121–147.

NMA (News Media Association) (2015) *UK news provision at the crossroads: The news market in the 21st century and the likely implications for the BBC's role.* Available at: www.newsmediauk.

org/write/MediaUploads/PDF%20Docs/OandO_NMA_-_UK_news_provision_at_the_cross roads.pdf (Accessed April 2017).

Nye, J. (2008) 'Public diplomacy and soft power', *The Annals of the American Academy of Political and Social Science*, 616 (1): 94–109.

O'Connor, T.P. (1889/2005) 'The new journalism', in King, A. and Plunkett, J. (eds.) *Victorian print media: A reader*. Oxford: Oxford University Press, pp. 361–365.

Ofcom (2006) *Provision of technical platform guidelines: Guidelines and explanatory statement*. Available at: www.ofcom.org.uk/__data/assets/pdf_file/0015/51711/statement.pdf (Accessed June 2022).

Ofcom (2010a) *Communications market report 2010*. Available at: www.ofcom.org.uk/__data/assets/pdf_file/0013/25222/cmr_2010_final.pdf (Accessed June 2022).

Ofcom (2010b) *Pay TV statement*. 31 March. Available at: www.ofcom.org.uk/__data/assets/pdf_file/0021/55470/paytv_statement.pdf (Accessed June 2022).

Ofcom (2012) *Communications market report 2012*. Available at: www.ofcom.org.uk/__data/assets/pdf_file/0013/20218/cmr_uk_2012.pdf (Accessed June 2022).

Ofcom (2013) *Communications market report 2013*. Available at: www.ofcom.org.uk/__data/assets/pdf_file/0021/19731/2013_uk_cmr.pdf (Accessed June 2022).

Ofcom (2015a) *Strategic review of digital communications: Discussion document*. Available at: www.ofcom.org.uk/__data/assets/pdf_file/0021/63444/digital-comms-review.pdf (Accessed April 2017).

Ofcom (2015b) *Measurement framework for media plurality*. Available at: www.ofcom.org.uk/__data/assets/pdf_file/0024/84174/measurement_framework_for_media_plurality_statement.pdf (Accessed April 2019).

Ofcom (2016) *Communication market report 2016* Available at: www.ofcom.org.uk/__data/assets/pdf_file/0024/26826/cmr_uk_2016.pdf (Accessed June 2022).

Ofcom (2018a) *Addressing harmful online content: A perspective from broadcasting and on-demand standards regulation*. Available at: www.ofcom.org.uk/__data/assets/pdf_file/0022/120991/Addressing-harmful-online-content.pdf (Accessed January 2019).

Ofcom (2018b) *Media nations UK: 2018*. Available at: www.ofcom.org.uk/__data/assets/pdf_file/0014/116006/media-nations-2018-uk.pdf (Accessed October 2019).

Ofcom (2018c) *Consideration of a request from Wireless Group Media (GB) Limited for Ofcom to launch a BBC Competition Review: BBC radio sports rights acquisition*. Available at: www.ofcom.org.uk/__data/assets/pdf_file/0013/130504/Consideration-Wireless-Group-Media-BBC-Competition-Review.pdf (Accessed December 2019).

Ofcom (2018d) *Public service broadcasting in the digital age: Supporting PSB for the next decade and beyond*. Available at: www.ofcom.org.uk/__data/assets/pdf_file/0026/111896/Public-service-broadcasting-in-the-digital-age.pdf (Accessed August 2021).

Ofcom (2018e) *Internet users' experience of harm online: summary of survey research*. Available at: www.ofcom.org.uk/__data/assets/pdf_file/0018/120852/Internet-harm-research-2018-report.pdf (Accessed January 2019)

Ofcom (2019a) *Media nations UK: 2019*. Available at: www.ofcom.org.uk/__data/assets/pdf_file/0019/160714/media-nations-2019-uk-report.pdf (Accessed January 2020).

Ofcom (2019b) *Online nation: 2019 report*. Available at: www.ofcom.org.uk/__data/assets/pdf_file/0025/149146/online-nation-report.pdf (Accessed August 2022).

Ofcom (2019c) *Review of prominence for public service broadcasting: Recommendations to Government for a new framework to keep PSB TV prominent in an online world*. Available at: www.ofcom.org.uk/__data/assets/pdf_file/0021/154461/recommendations-for-new-legislative-framework-for-psb-prominence.pdf (Accessed February 2023).

Ofcom (2020a) *The Ofcom Broadcasting Code (with the Cross Promotion Code and the On Demand Programme Services Rules)*. Available at: www.ofcom.org.uk/tv-radio-and-on-demand/broadcast-codes/broadcast-code (Accessed August 2022).

Ofcom (2020b) *Small screen: Big debate consultation: The future of public service media*. Available at: www.smallscreenbigdebate.co.uk/__data/assets/pdf_file/0032/208769/consultation-future-of-public-service-media.pdf (Accessed May 2022).

Ofcom (2020c) *Online nation 2020.* Available at: www.ofcom.org.uk/__data/assets/pdf_file/0027/196407/online-nation-2020-report.pdf (Accessed August 2022).

Ofcom (2021a) *Adults' media use and attitudes report 2020/21.* Available at: www.ofcom.org.uk/__data/assets/pdf_file/0025/217834/adults-media-use-and-attitudes-report-2020-21.pdf (accessed July 2022).

Ofcom (2021b) *Media nations 2021.* Available at: www.ofcom.org.uk/__data/assets/pdf_file/0023/222890/media-nations-report-2021.pdf (Accessed May 2022).

Ofcom (2021c) *Media nations 2021: Interactive report.* Available at: www.ofcom.org.uk/research-and-data/tv-radio-and-on-demand/media-nations-reports/media-nations-2021/interactive-report (Accessed June 2022).

Ofcom (2021d) *Online nation 2021 report.* Available at: www.ofcom.org.uk/__data/assets/pdf_file/0013/220414/online-nation-2021-report.pdf (Accessed June 2022).

Ofcom (2022a) *News consumption in the UK: 2022.* Available at: www.ofcom.org.uk/__data/assets/pdf_file/0027/241947/News-Consumption-in-the-UK-2022-report.pdf (Accessed August 2022).

Ofcom (2022b) *Online nation: 2022 report.* Available at: www.ofcom.org.uk/__data/assets/pdf_file/0023/238361/online-nation-2022-report.pdf (Accessed August 2022).

Ofcom (2022c) *Media nations: 2022.* Available at: www.ofcom.org.uk/__data/assets/pdf_file/0016/242701/media-nations-report-2022.pdf (Accessed August 2022).

O'Malley, T. (1994) *Closedown? The BBC and government broadcasting policy 1979–92.* London: Pluto Press.

O'Malley, T. (2013) 'Seventy years and counting: the unsolved problem of press regulation', *History & Policy*, 29 March. Available at: www.historyandpolicy.org/policy-papers/papers/seventy-years-and-counting-the-unsolved-problem-of-press-regulation (Accessed August 2019).

O'Reilly, L. and Edwards, J. (2014) 'These are the UK newspapers failing to tackle the switch to digital', *Business Insider UK*, 16 December. Available at: http://uk.businessinsider.com/the-state-of-the-uk-national-newspaper-industry-2014-12?r=US&IR=T (Accessed September 2019).

PACT (Producers Alliance for Cinema and Television) (2021) *UK television exports report 2020–2021.* Available at: www.pact.co.uk/members-hub/resourcelibrary.html?q=UK+TV+Exports+Report+2020-2021(Accessed August 2022).

Page, W. (2021) 'The music industry makes more money but has more mouths to feed', *Financial Times*, 19 February. Available at: www.ft.com/content/77768846-a751-45ec-9a12-20fff27ddefb (Accessed August 2022).

Pariser, E. (2011) *The Filter Bubble: what the internet is hiding from you.* London: Penguin.

Parker, R.(2018) 'Ofcom calls for end to "standards lottery"', *Broadcast*, 18 September. Available at: www.broadcastnow.co.uk/broadcasters/ofcom-calls-for-end-to-standards-lottery/5132738.article(AccessedFebruary 2023).

Peacock, Professor Alan (Chairman) (1986) *Report of the committee on financing the BBC*, Cmnd, 9824, London: HMSO.

Persily, N. and Tucker, J.A. (eds.) (2020) *Social media and democracy: The state of the field and prospects for reform.* Cambridge: Cambridge University Press.

Petley, J. (1999) 'The regulation of media content' in Stokes, J. and Reading, A. (eds.) *The media in Britain: Current debates and developments.* Basingstoke: Palgrave, pp. 143–157.

Picard, R. (1989) *Media economics: Concepts and issues.* London: Sage.

Pilkington, Sir Harry (Chairman) (1962) *Report of the committee on broadcasting.* Cmnd 1753, London:HMSO.

Plunkett, J. (2004) 'Catalogues in vogue', *The Guardian*, 13 September. Available at: www.theguardian.com/media/2004/sep/13/condenast.mondaymediasection (Accessed June 2020).

Plunkett, J. (2010a) 'Is Radio 1 too similar to commercial stations?', *The Guardian*, Available at: www.theguardian.com/media/organgrinder/2010/oct/26/radio-1-commercial-playlist (Accessed April 2017).

Plunkett, J. (2010b) 'Global Radio to roll out Capital brand across the country', *The Guardian*, 14 September. Available at: www.theguardian.com/media/2010/sep/14/global-radio-capital-rebrand (Accessed January 2020).

Plunkett, J. (2012) 'Global Radio chief, Stephen Miron, says BBC is aping station's output', *The Guardian*, 13 November. Available at: www.theguardian.com/media/2012/nov/13/global-radio-stephen-miron-bbc-one-direction (Accessed June 2019).

Ponsford, D. (2016) '"Heartbroken" reporter Gareth Davies says Croydon Advertiser print edition now "thrown together collection of clickbait", *Press Gazette*, 31 July. Available at: www.pressgazette.co.uk/heartbroken-reporter-gareth-davies-says-croydon-advertser-print-edition-now-thrown-together-collection-of-clickbait/ (Accessed April 2017).

Ponsford, D. (2017a) 'Who says millennials don't read newspapers? Editor Ted Young on the rise and rise of Metro', *Press Gazette*, 24 March. Available at: www.pressgazette.co.uk/who-says-millennials-dont-read-newspapers-editor-ted-young-on-the-rise-and-rise-of-metro/ (Accessed October 2019).

Ponsford, D. (2017b) 'UK magazine ABCs: Winner, losers and full breakdown as circulation declines average 6 per cent', *Press Gazette*, 9 February. Available at: https://pressgazette.co.uk/uk-magazine-abcs-winners-losers-and-full-breakdown-as-circulation-declines-average-6-per-cent/ (Accessed October 2019).

Porter, V. (2009) 'Methodism versus the marketplace: the Rank Organisation and British cinema', in Murphy, R. (ed.) *The British Cinema Book*, 3rd edition. London: BFI, pp: 267–275.

Powell, C. (2013) 'Magalogues v catalogues 2.0', *Marketing*, 30 July. Available at: http://marketingmag.ca/news/media-news/magalogues-vs-catalogues-2-0-84797 (Accessed June 2020).

Purchese, R. (2011) 'Used market cost *Heavy Rain* 1m sales', *Eurogamer*, 12 September, Available at: www.eurogamer.net/used-market-cost-heavy-rain-1m-sales (Accessed August 2022).

RadioCentre (2015) *Response to DCMS Green Paper on BBC Charter Review*. Available at: www.radiocentre.org/wp-content/uploads/2018/07/Radiocentre-response-to-DCMS-Green-Paper-on-BBC-Charter.pdf (Accessed June 2019).

RadioCentre (2018) *RadioCentre response to Ofcom further consultation on localness on commercial radio (Scotland and Wales)*. Available at: www.radiocentre.org/wp-content/uploads/2018/12/RC-response-to-Ofcom-localness-on-comm-radio-Scotland-Wales-FINAL.pdf (Accessed January 2020).

Rajan, A. (2016) 'Facebook: Social network, media company – or both?' *BBC News*, 15 December. Available at: www.bbc.co.uk/news/entertainment-arts-38333249 (Accessed January 2019)

RAJAR (Radio Joint Audience Research) (2022a) *Data release, quarter 1 2022*. Available at: www.rajar.co.uk/docs/news/RAJAR_DataRelease_InfographicQ12022.pdf (Accessed August 2022).

RAJAR (Radio Joint Audience Research) (2022b) *Quarterly summary of radio listening*. Available at: www.rajar.co.uk/docs/2022_06/2022_Q2_Quarterly_Summary_Figures.pdf (Accessed August 2022).

Reed, D. (1998) '"Rise and shine!": The birth of the glossy magazine', *The British Library Journal*, 24 (2): 256–268.

Reeves, N. (1997) 'Cinema, spectatorship and propaganda: "Battle of the Somme" (1916) and its contemporary audience', *Historical Journal of Film, Radio and Television*, 17 (1): 5–28.

van Reijmersdal, E.A., Neijens, P.C., and Smit, E.G. (2010) 'Customer magazines: Effects of commerciality on readers' reactions', *Journal of Current Issues & Research in Advertising*, 32 (1): 59–67.

Reith, J.(1924) *Broadcast over Britain*. London:Hodder & Stoughton.

Reynolds, R. (2015) 'Play Britannia: The development of UK video game policy', in Conway, S. and deWinter, J. (eds.) *Video game policy: Production, distribution and consumption*. London: Routledge, pp: 113–125.

Richards, J. and Robertson, J.C. (2009) 'British film censorship', in Murphy, R. (ed.) *The British cinema book*. London: BFI, pp. 67–77.

Robertson, G. and Nicol, A. (2007) *Robertson & Nicol on media law*. London: Smith & Maxwell.

Rodger, B. and MacCulloch, A. (2009) *Competition law and policy in the EC and UK*. London: Routledge.

Rowbottom, J. (2018) *Media law*. Oxford: Hart Publishing.

Rozenburg, J. (2011) 'Mr Justice Eady on balancing acts', *Index on Censorship*, 12 June. Available at: www.indexoncensorship.org/2011/06/mr-justice-eady-on-balancing-acts/ (Accessed May 2019).

Ruddick, G. (2017) 'Inside Housing: Trade magazine that warned of high-rise fire risks', *The Guardian*, 16 June. Available at: www.theguardian.com/media/2017/jun/16/inside-housing-tra de-magazine-that-warned-of-high-rise-fire-risks (Accessed June 2019).

Rudin R. (2006) 'The development of DAB digital radio in the UK: The battle for control of a new technology in an old medium' *Convergence*, 12 (2): 163–178.

Rudin, R. (2011) *Broadcasting in the 21st century*. Basingstoke: Palgrave Macmillan.

Rushe, D. (2011) 'Myspace sold for $35m in spectacular fall from $12bn heyday', *The Guardian*, 30 June. Available at: www.theguardian.com/technology/2011/jun/30/myspace-sold-35-million-news (Accessed August 2022).

Russell, J. (2017) 'Hollywood blockbusters and UK production today' in Hunter, I.Q., Porter, L., and Smith, J. (eds.) *The Routledge companion to British cinema history*. London: Routledge, pp. 377–386.

Saltzis, K. and Dickinson, R. (2008) 'Inside the changing newsroom: Journalists' responses to media convergence', *Aslib Proceedings*, 60 (3): 216–228.

Savage, M. (2020) 'Collaborations continue to take over pop radio', *BBC News*, 22 June. Available at: www.bbc.co.uk/news/entertainment-arts-53107686 (Accessed August 2022).

Scannell, P. (1990) 'Public service broadcasting: The history of a concept' in Goodwin, A. and Whannel, G. (eds.), *Understanding television*. London: Routledge, pp. 11–26.

Scannell, P.and Cardiff, D.(1982) 'Serving the nation: Public service broadcasting before the war' in Bennett, T., Martin, G., and Waites, B.(eds.), *Popular culture*. London:Routledge, pp. 161–188.

Schlesinger, P. (1987) *Putting 'reality' together*. London: Methuen.

Scorsese, M. (2021) 'Il Maestro: Federico Fellini and the lost magic of the cinema', *Harper's Magazine*, March. Available at: https://harpers.org/archive/2021/03/il-maestro-federico-fellini-ma rtin-scorsese/ (Accessed May 2021).

Sedgwick, J. (1997) 'The British film industry's production sector difficulties in the late 1930s', *Historical Journal of Film, Radio and Television*, 17 (1): 49–66.

Self, W. (2013) 'The skeuomorphs are taking over. Soon our personalities will be purely ornamental', *New Statesman*, 4 October, p. 54.

Selsdon, A. (1994) 'Conservative century' in Selsdon, A. and Ball, S. (eds.) *Conservative century: The escalator to prosperity: The Conservative Party since 1900*. Oxford: Oxford University Press, pp. 17–65.

Sendall, B.(1982) *Independent television in Britain: Volume 1: Origin and foundation 1946–62*. London:Macmillan.

Seymour-Ure, C. (1987) 'Media policy in Britain: Now you see it, now you don't', *European Journal of Communication*, 2 (3): 269–288.

Seymour-Ure, C. (1991) *The British press and broadcasting since 1945*. Oxford: Blackwell.

Shuker, R. (2008) *Understanding popular music culture*. London: Routledge.

Shuker, R. (2010) 'Popular music' in Albertazzi, D. and Cobley, P. (eds.) *The media: An introduction*. Harlow: Pearson, pp. 206–219.

Silverman, R. (2013) 'Almost two thirds of BBC programmes are repeats', *Daily Telegraph*, 26 June. Available at: www.telegraph.co.uk/culture/tvandradio/bbc/10143663/Almost-two-third s-of-BBC-programmes-are-repeats.html (Accessed April 2017).

Simon, J.P.(2019) 'New players in the music industry: lifeboats or killer whales? The role of streaming platforms', *Digital Policy, Regulation and Governance*, 21(6):525–549.

Simonelli, D. (2013) *Working class heroes: Rock music and British society in the 1960s and 1970s.* Lanham, Maryland: Lexington Books.

Smith, A. (ed.) (1974) *British broadcasting.* Newton Abbot: David and Childs.

Smith, A. (1999) *The wealth of nations: Books I–III.* London. Penguin Books.

Smith, A. (2020) 'Instagram reels: What is the new TikTok-style feature that is launching today?', *The Independent*, 5 August. Available at: www.independent.co.uk/tech/instagram-reels-new-up date-latest-tiktok-video-a9655036.html (Accessed August 2022).

Smith, L. (2014) 'Facebook buys WhatsApp in $19bn deal', *The Independent*, 20 February. Available at: www.independent.co.uk/news/business/news/facebook-likes-whatsapp-and-buys-i t-in-19bn-deal-9139846.html (Accessed August 2022).

Smith, P. (2006) 'The politics of UK television policy: The making of Ofcom', *Media, Culture and Society*, 28 (6): 929–940.

Smith, P. (2007) *The politics of UK television policy: The introduction of digital television.* New York: Edwin Mellen.

Smith, P. (2008) 'BBC Charter renewal and the "crisis" of public service broadcasting' in Ross, K. and Price, S. (eds.) *Popular media and communication: Essays on publics, practices and processes.* Cambridge: Cambridge Scholars Publishing, pp. 130–151.

Smith, P. (2013) 'Too much or not enough? Competition law and television broadcasting regulation in the United Kingdom', *Westminster Papers in Communication and Culture*, 9 (3): 143–164.

Smith, P., Evens, T., and Iosifidis, P. (2016) 'The next big match: Convergence, competition and sports media rights', *European Journal of Communication*, 31 (5): 536–550.

Sparks, C. (1999) 'The press' in Stokes, J. and Reading, A. (eds.) *The media in Britain: Current debates and developments.* Basingstoke: Macmillan, pp. 41–60.

Spicer, A. (2017) 'Producers and moguls in the British film industry, 1930–1980', in Hunter, I.Q., Porter, L., and Smith, J. (eds.) *The Routledge companion to British cinema history.* London: Routledge, pp. 139–150.

Stahl, M. (2013) *Unfree masters: Recording artists and the politics of work.* Durham, NC: Duke University Press.

Stam, D. (2014a) 'A short history of British magazine publishing', in Stam, D. and Scott, A. (eds.) *Inside magazine publishing.* London: Routledge, pp. 9–38.

Stam, D. (2014b) 'Changing business models in the magazine world' in Stam, D. and Scott, A. (eds.) *Inside magazine publishing.* London: Routledge, pp. 75–104.

Stam, D. and Scott, A. (eds.) (2014) *Inside magazine publishing*, London: Routledge.

Standage, T. (1998) *The Victorian internet.* London: Phoenix.

Starkey, G. (2015) *Local radio, going global.* Basingstoke: Palgrave Macmillan.

Starkey, G. (2017) 'Radio: The resilient medium in today's increasingly diverse multiplatform media environment', *Convergence*, 23 (6): 660–670.

Starkey, G. and Crisell, A. (2009) *Radio journalism.* London: Sage.

Stelter, B. and Lyall, S. (2008) 'Prince Harry and the secret kept by Fleet Street', *New York Times*, 1 March. Available at: www.nytimes.com/2008/03/01/business/media/01harry.html (Accessed March 2019).

Stokes, J. (1999) 'Publishing' in Stokes, J. and Reading, A. (eds.) *The media in Britain.* Basing-stoke: Palgrave Macmillan, pp. 19–23.

Stoller, T. (2010) *Sounds of your life: A history of independent radio in the UK.* New Barnett: John Libbey Publishing.

Stourton, E.(2017) *Auntie's war: The BBC during the second world war.* London:Penguin.

Street, S. (1997) *British national cinema.* London: Routledge.

Street, S. (2002) *A concise history of British radio: 1922–2002.* Tiverton: Kelly Productions.

Street, S. (2009) 'British film and the national interest, 1927–39' in Murphy, R. (ed.) *The British cinema book.* 3rd edn, London: BFI, pp. 185–192.

Stubbs, J. (2008) '"Blocked" currency, runaway production in Britain and Captain Horatio Hornblower', *Historical Journal of Film, Radio and Television*, 28 (3): 335–351.

Stubbs, J. (2009) 'The Eady Levy: A runaway bribe? Hollywood production and British subsidy in the early 1960s', *Journal of British Cinema and Television*, 6 (1): 1–20.

Sweney, M. (2016) 'Rupert Murdoch's News Corp buys TalkSport owner in £220m deal', *The Guardian*, 30 June. Available at: www.theguardian.com/media/2016/jun/30/rupert-murdochs-news-corp-buys-talksport-owner-in-220m-deal (Accessed June 2019).

Sweney, M. (2017) 'Shaken it off! Taylor Swift ends Spotify spat', *The Guardian*, 9 June. Available at: www.theguardian.com/music/2017/jun/09/shaken-it-off-taylor-swift-ends-spotify-spat (Accessed August 2022).

Sweney, M. (2019) 'Apple 30% app store commission unfair, Spotify claims', *The Guardian*, 13 March. Available at: www.theguardian.com/technology/2019/mar/13/spotify-claim-apple-30-percent-app-store-commission-unfair-european-commission-complaint (Accessed February 2023).

Sweney, M. (2020a) 'Covid pandemic fuelling growth of film and TV studios in UK', *The Guardian*, 7 November. Available at: www.theguardian.com/business/2020/nov/07/covid-pandemic-fuelling-growth-of-film-and-tv-studios-in-uk (Accessed Jan 2021).

Sweney, M. (2020b) 'Sky to make Amazon Prime Video available to subscribers in Europe', *The Guardian*, 14 December. Available at: www.theguardian.com/media/2020/dec/14/sky-to-make-amazon-prime-video-available-to-subscribers-in-europe (Accessed June 2022).

Sweney, M. (2020c) 'Netflix to spend $1bn in UK in 2020 on TV shows and films', *The Guardian*, 25 November. Available at: www.theguardian.com/media/2020/nov/25/netflix-to-spend-1bn-in-uk-in-2020-on-tv-shows-and-films (Accessed June 2022).

Sweney, M. (2020d) 'Tech giants may face billions of pounds in fines from new UK watchdog', *The Guardian*, 8 December. Available at: www.theguardian.com/business/2020/dec/08/tech-giants-may-face-billions-of-pounds-in-fines-from-new-uk-watchdog (Accessed August 2022).

Tambini, D. (2018) 'Social media, power and election legitimacy' in Tambinni, D. and Moore, M. (eds.) *Digital dominance: The power of Google, Amazon, Facebook and Apple*. Oxford: Oxford University Press, pp. 265–293.

Tavinor, G. (2009) *The art of videogames*. Chichester: Wiley-Blackwell.

Temple, M. (2008) *The British press*. Berkshire: Open University Press.

Terrorism Act (2006) London: HMSO. Available at: www.legislation.gov.uk/ukpga/2006/11/contents (Accessed February 2023).

The Economist (2016) 'How to make a hit Hollywood film', *The Economist*, 26 February. Available at: www.economist.com/blogs/graphicdetail/2016/02/daily-chart-19 (Accessed April 2017).

Thomas, R.J. and Finneman, T. (2013) 'Who watches the watchdogs?', *Journalism Studies*, 15 (2): 172–186.

Thompson, M. (2010) *James Mac Taggart Memorial Lecture – Speech at the Media Guardian Edinburgh International Television Festival*, 27 August: Available at: www.bbc.co.uk/pressoffice/speeches/stories/thompson_mactaggart.shtml (Accessed April 2017).

Thomson, O. (2013) 'The history of Radio Times', *Radio Times*, 17 August. Available at: www.radiotimes.com/news/2013-07-17/the-history-of-radio-times/ (Accessed March 2020).

Thurman, N. (2014) 'Newspaper consumption in the digital age', *Digital Journalism*, 2 (2): 156–178.

Thurman, N., Hensmann, T., and Fletcher, R. (2021) 'Large, loyal, lingering? An analysis of online overseas audiences for UK news brands', *Journalism*, 22 (8): 1892–1911.

Tobitt, C. (2018) 'National newspaper ABCs: Metro climbs above The Sun's total circulation as Mirror and Telegraph titles post double-digit drops', *Press Gazette*, 15 March. Available at: www.pressgazette.co.uk/national-newspaper-abcs-metro-climbs-above-the-suns-total-circulation-as-mirror-and-telegraph-titles-post-double-digit-drops/ (Accessed June 2019).

Tobitt, C. (2022) 'Guardian reports cash surplus for first time in a generation', *Press Gazette*, 20 July. Available at: https://pressgazette.co.uk/guardian-media-group-cash-surplus/ (Accessed July 2022).

Tobitt, C. and Majid, A. (2022) 'National press ABCs: FT, Metro, City AM and Sunday Mail report growth in May', *Press Gazette*, 22 June. Available at: https://pressgazette.co.uk/most-popular-newspapers-uk-abc-monthly-circulation-figures/ (Accessed June 2022).

Towse, R. (2020) 'Dealing with digital: The economic organisation of streamed music', *Media, Culture and Society*, 42 (7–8): 1461–1478.

Tracey, M. (2000) 'The BBC and the general strike: May 1926' in Buscombe, E. (ed.) *British television: A reader*. Oxford: Clarendon Press, pp. 25–44.

Tran, K. (2017) 'Viewers find objectionable content on YouTube Kids', *Business Insider*, 7 November. Available at: www.businessinsider.com/viewers-find-objectionable-content-on-you tube-kids-2017-11?r=UK (Accessed January 2019).

Tsang, D. (2021) 'Innovation in the British Video Game Industry since 1978', *Business History Review*, 95: 543–567.

Tulloch, J. (2000) 'The eternal recurrence of new journalism' in Sparks, C. and Tulloch, J. (eds.) *Tabloid tales: Global debates over media standards*. Oxford: Rowman and Littlefield, pp. 131–146.

Tunstall, J. (1996) *Newspaper power: The new national press in Britain*. Oxford: Oxford University Press.

Ukie (2020) *2020 UK consumer games market valuation*. Available at: https://ukiepedia.ukie.org. uk/index.php/2020_UK_Consumer_Games_Market_Valuation (Accessed June 2022).

UK Music (2021) *This is music 2021*. Available at: www.ukmusic.org/wp-content/uploads/2021/ 10/This-is-Music-2021-v2.pdf (Accessed July 2022).

Verdegem, P. (2021) 'Social media industries and the rise of the platform' in McDonald, P. (ed.) *The Routledge companion to media industries*. London: Routledge, pp. 301–311.

Vonderau, P.(2019) 'The Spotify effect: Digital distribution and financial growth', *Television & New Media*, 20(1):3–19.

Wade-Morris, J.(2015) *Selling digital music, formatting culture*. Oakland, California:University of California Press.

Wakefield, J.(2021) 'Apple charged over "anti-competitive" app policies', *BBC News*, 30 April. Available at:www.bbc.co.uk/news/technology-56941173(AccessedFebruary 2023).

Walker, A. (1974) *Hollywood, England: The British film industry in the sixties*. London: Michael Joseph.

Walker, H. (2014) 'The album is dead, long live playlists', *The Guardian*, 30 July. Available at: www.theguardian.com/commentisfree/2014/jul/30/album-is-dead-long-live-playlists (Accessed December 2019).

Walker, J. (2022) *Rewind, replay: Britain and the video boom, 1978–92*. Edinburgh: Edinburgh University Press.

Warner, C. (2016) 'Zuckerberg: "Facebook is not a traditional media company"', *Forbes.com*, 23 December. Available at: www.forbes.com/sites/charleswarner/2016/12/23/zuckerberg-faceboo k-is-not-a-traditional-media-company/#766274d17df4 (Accessed October 2019).

Waterson, J. (2018) 'Ofcom to push for regulation of social networks', *The Guardian*, 17 September. Available at: www.theguardian.com/media/2018/sep/17/ofcom-to-push-for-regulatio n-of-social-media-platforms?CMP=share_btn_tw (Accessed February 2019).

Waterson, J. (2019a) 'Scores of UK radio stations to lose local programmes', *The Guardian*, 26 February. Available at: www.theguardian.com/tv-and-radio/2019/feb/26/scores-of-uk-radio-sta tions-to-lose-local-programmes (Accessed April 2019).

Waterson, J. (2019b) 'Chris Evans' Virgin Radio breakfast show hits 1m listeners a week', *The Guardian*, Available at: www.theguardian.com/media/2019/may/16/chris-evans-virgin-radio-breakfast-show-hits-1m-listeners-a-week (Accessed June 2019).

Waterson, J. (2020) 'Times to launch talk radio station to challenge BBC Radio 4', *The Guardian*, 28 January. Available at: www.theguardian.com/media/2020/jan/28/the-times-to-launch-ta lk-radio-station-to-challenge-bbc-radio-4-times-radio-rupert-murdoch (Accessed August 2022).

Waterson, J. (2022a) 'BBC announces raft of closures with CBBC and BBC Four to be online only', *The Guardian*, 26 May. Available at: www.theguardian.com/media/2022/may/26/bbc-a nnounces-raft-of-closures-cbbc-four-online-only (Accessed June 2022).

Waterson, J. (2022b) 'BBC licence fee to be abolished in 2027 and funding frozen', *The Guardian*, 16 January. Available at: www.theguardian.com/media/2022/jan/16/bbc-licence-fee-to-be-abolish ed-in-2027-and-funding-frozen (Accessed June 2022).

Wayne, M. (2018) 'Netflix, Amazon and branded TV content in subscription video on-demand portals', *Media, Culture and Society*, 40 (5): 725–741.

Webber, N. (2020) 'The Britishness of "British Video Games"', *International Journal of Cultural Policy*, 26 (2): 135–149.

Wheeler, M. (1997) *Politics and the mass media*. Oxford:Blackwell.

White, P. (2016) 'Netflix: diving into the data', *Broadcast*, 26 August, pp. 24–25.

White, P. (2017) 'Sky extends HBO co-pro deal', *Broadcast*, 20 April. Available at: www.broadca stnow.co.uk/news/sky-extends-hbo-co-pro-deal/5116942.article (Accessed April 2017).

Wilson, H. (1961) *Pressure group: The campaign for commercial television*. London:Seeker & Warburg.

Wikström, P. (2020) *The music industry: Music in the cloud*. Cambridge: Polity Press.

Williams, K. (2003) *Understanding media theory*. London: Arnold.

Williams, K. (2009) *Get me a murder a day! A history of media and communication in Britain*. London: Bloomsbury.

Williams, K. (2010) *Read all about it! A history of the British newspaper*. London: Routledge.

Williams, R. (1974/2003) *Television, technology and cultural form*. London: Routledge.

Winner, L. (1980) 'Do artefacts have politics?', *Daedalus*, 109 (1): 121–136.

Winship, J. (1987) *Inside women's magazines*. London: Pandora.

Winston, B. (1998) *Media, technology and society: A history from the Telegraph to the Internet*. London: Routledge.

Woodhouse, J. (2022) *Regulating online harms*. Available at: https://researchbriefings.files.parliam ent.uk/documents/CBP-8743/CBP-8743.pdf (Accessed August 2022).

Wring, D. (2006) 'The news media and the public relations state' in Dunleavy, P., Heffernan, R., Cowley, P., and Hay, C. (eds.) *Developments in British Politics* 8. Palgrave: Basingstoke, pp. 231–250.

Zackariasson, P. and Wilson, T.L. (2010) 'Paradigm shifts in the video game industry', *Competitiveness Review: An international Business Journal*, 20 (2): 139–151.

Zendle, D., Wardle, H., Reith, G., and Bowden-Jones, H. (2019) 'A new public body is necessary to effectively regulate the UK video game industry', *The BMJ*, 9 October. Available at: https:// blogs.bmj.com/bmj/2019/10/09/a-new-public-body-is-necessary-to-effectively-regulate-the-uk-vi deo-game-industry/ (Accessed June 2022).

Zhao, Y. and Lin, Z. (2021) 'Umbrella platform of Tencent eSports industry in China', *Journal of Cultural Economy*, 14 (1): 9–25.

Index

Bold page numbers indicate tables, *italic* numbers indicate figures.